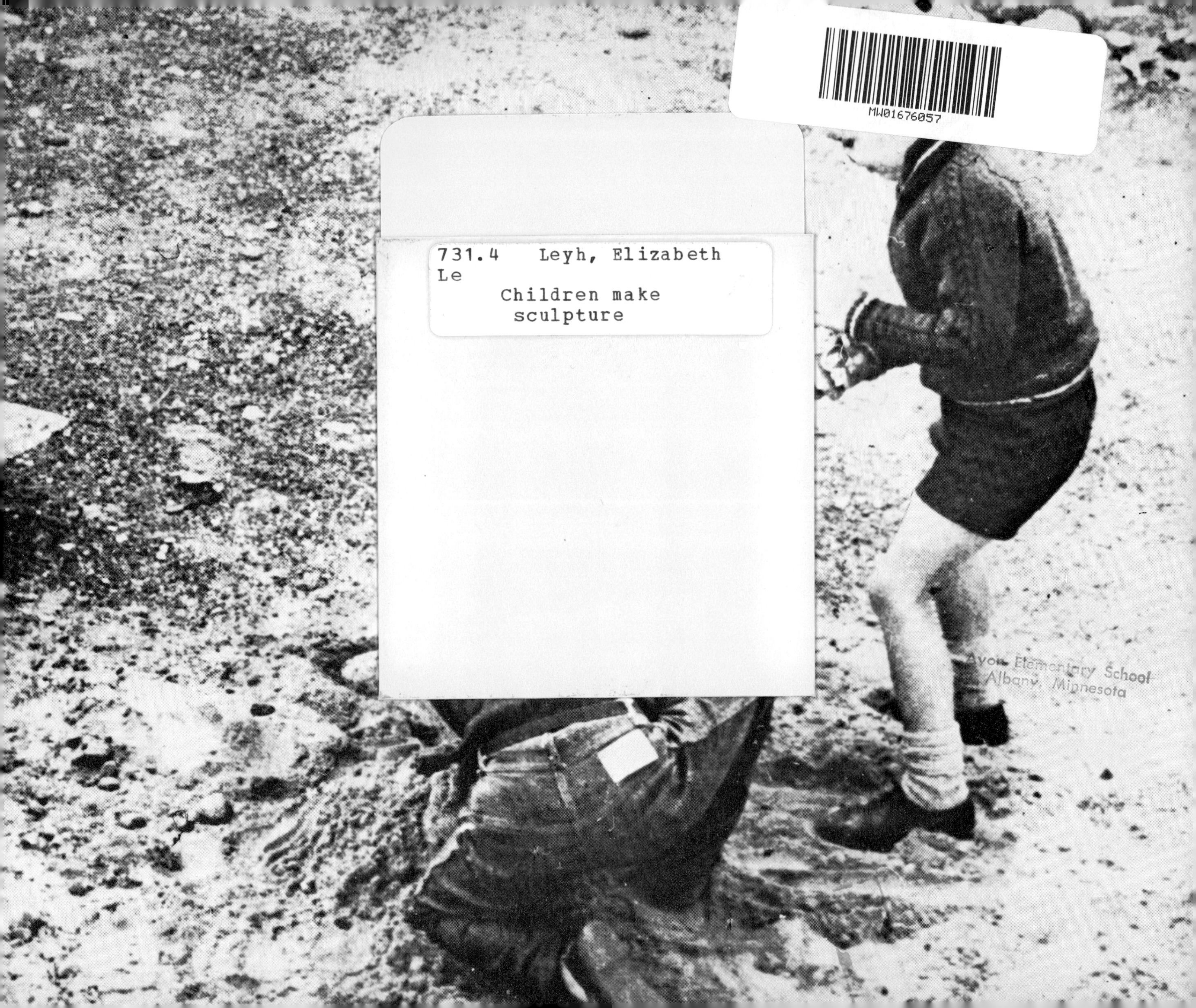

CHILDREN MAKE SCULPTURE

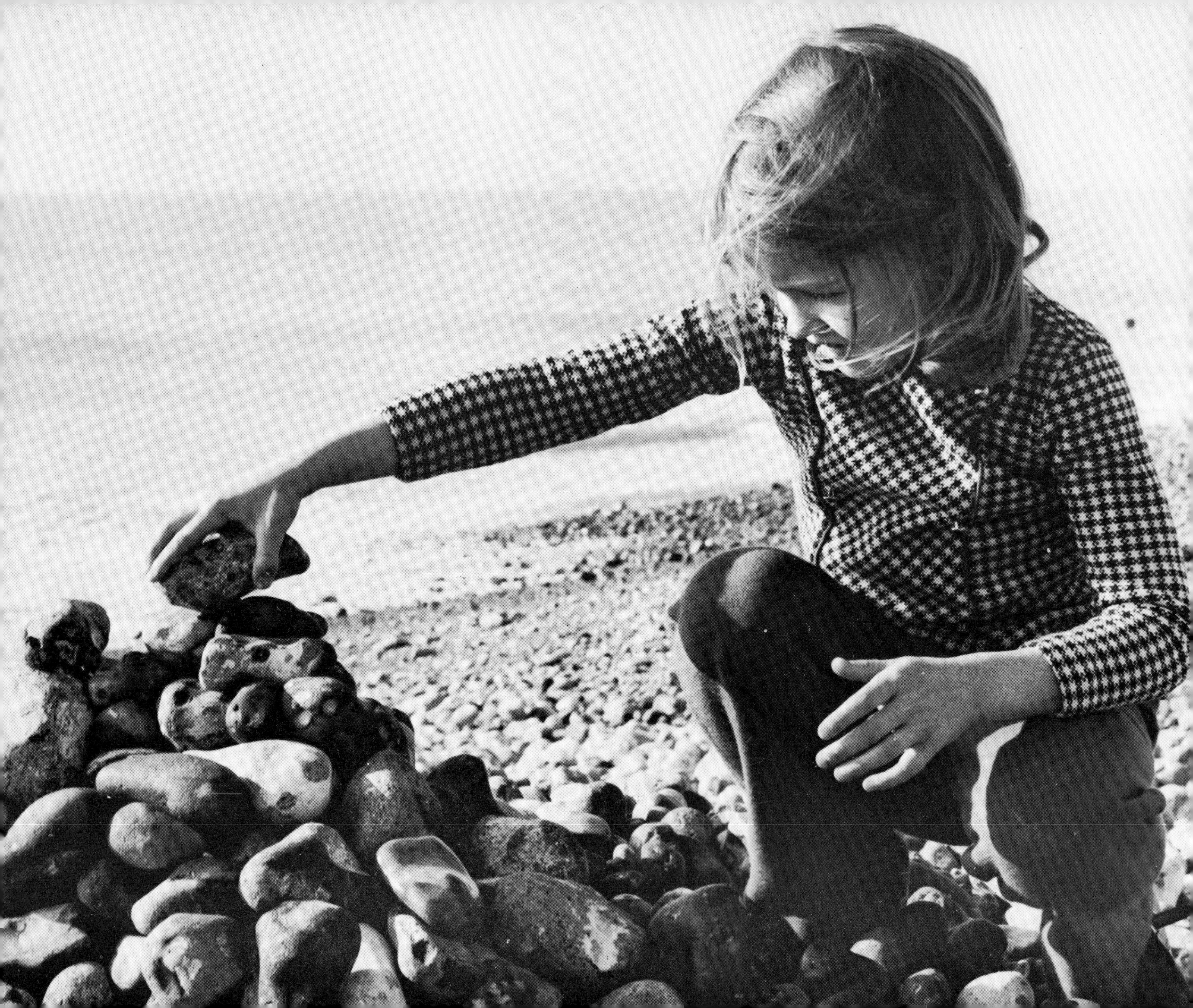

Elizabeth Leyh

CHILDREN MAKE SCULPTURE

VNR VAN NOSTRAND REINHOLD COMPANY
New York · Cincinnati · Toronto · London · Melbourne

Contents

Library of Congress Catalog Card Number 70–155438
ISBN 0 442 04771 1

Designed by Rod Josey
Photography–Alexandra Blanshard
Stuart Barton
Hendryk Szterbin
This book is set in Optima and is printed in Great Britain by Jolly & Barber Limited, Rugby, and bound by Webb Son & Company Limited, at Ferndale, South Wales
Published by Van Nostrand Reinhold Company Limited, Windsor House, 46 Victoria Street, London S.W.1 and Van Nostrand Reinhold Company, Inc 450 West 33rd Street, New York, N.Y. 10001
Published simultaneously in Canada by Van Nostrand Reinhold Company Limited

16 15 14 13 12 11 10 9 8 7 6 5 4 3 2 1

Introduction

The art of children is a form of language. Art is a way in which a child can express, as well as communicate, his experience of the world around him.

Three-dimensional art is a generally unexplored area of the arts in our present educational system and yet the main ideas of sculpture–form, space and materials–are met every day by everyone whatever they are doing.

I hope, however, that this book will provide for children a vocabulary of concepts and materials which will enable them to use form spontaneously and to explore materials which they can use as an aid to expression through the medium of sculpture. I have attempted to show children involved in the activity of creating, and also to illustrate the properties and ideas of the materials they are using. I hope that any child who looks at this book will be encouraged to explore new ideas and develop new avenues of enjoyment.

1 PUTTING THINGS TOGETHER

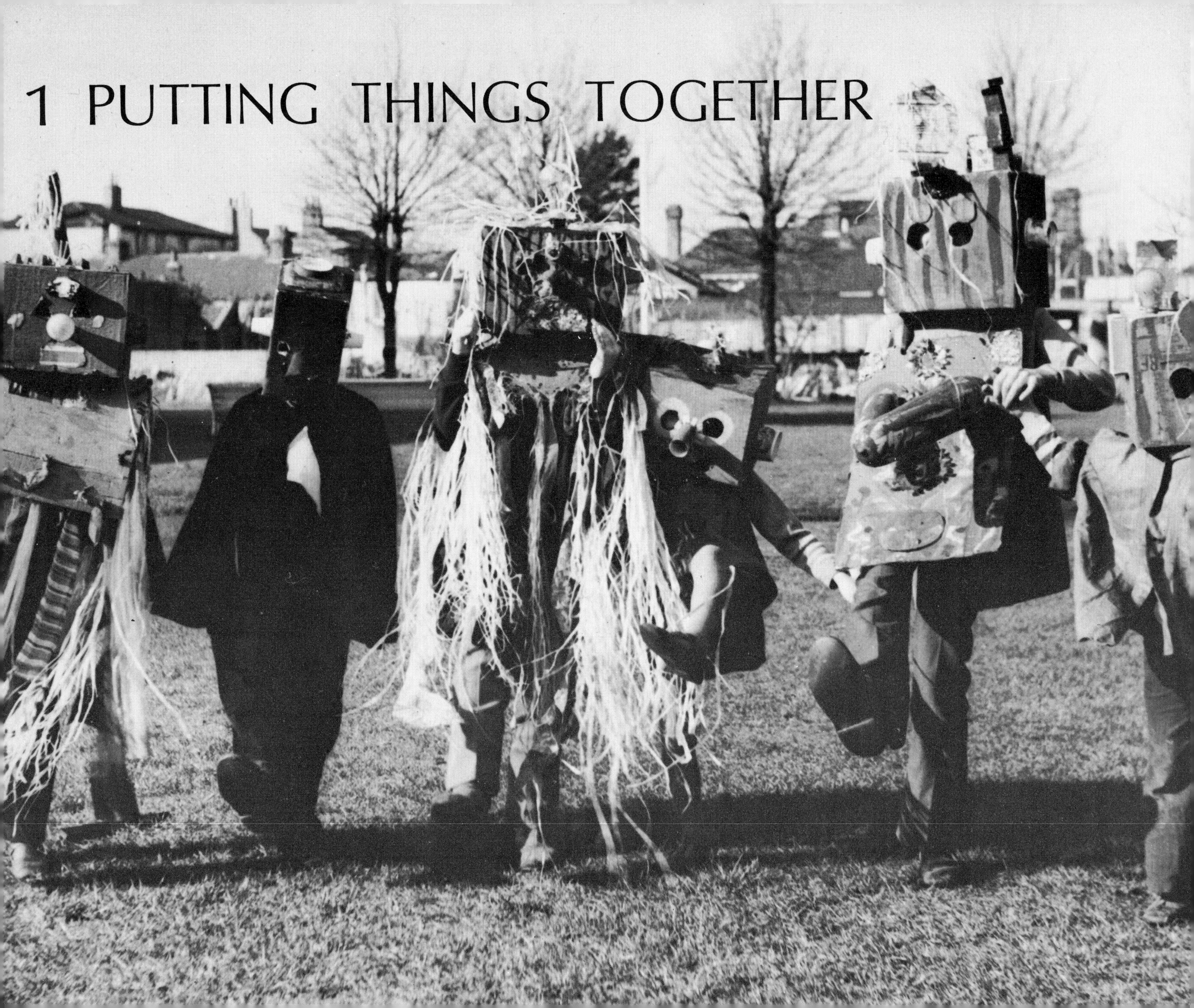

There are many ways to make sculpture. One way is to put things together.

Matchboxes, a paper cup, a cardboard roll and an egg box are all being glued together.

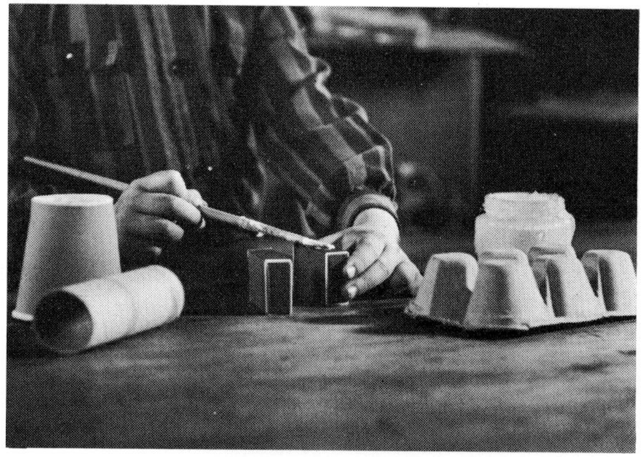

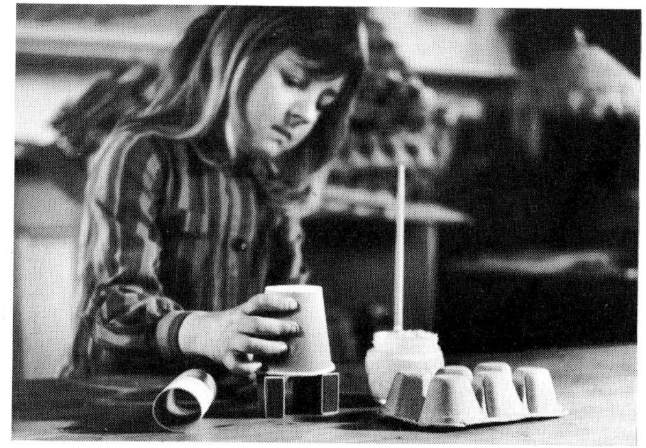

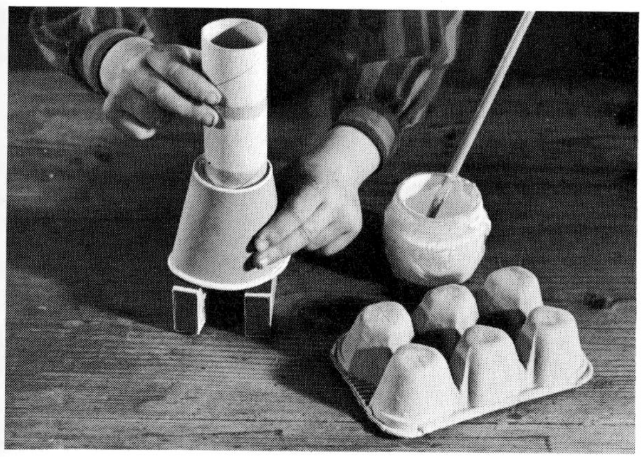

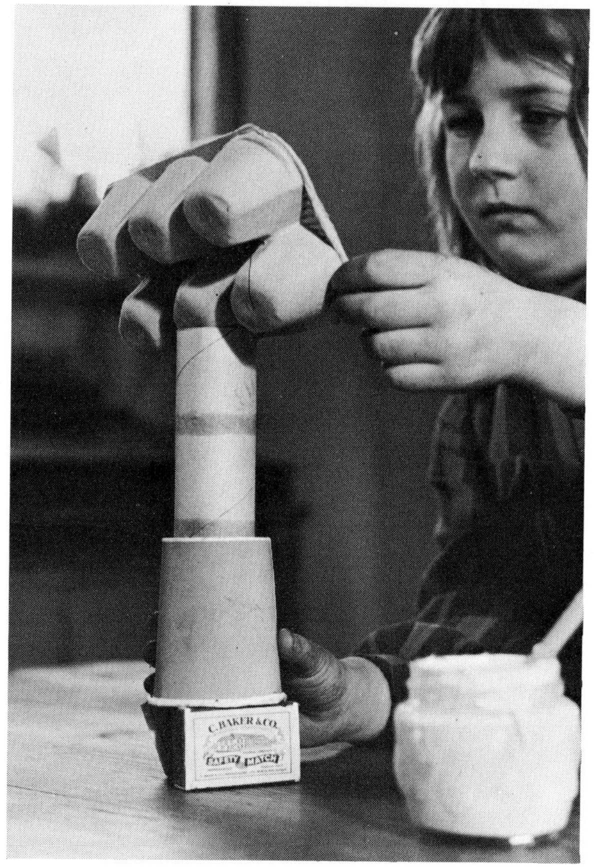

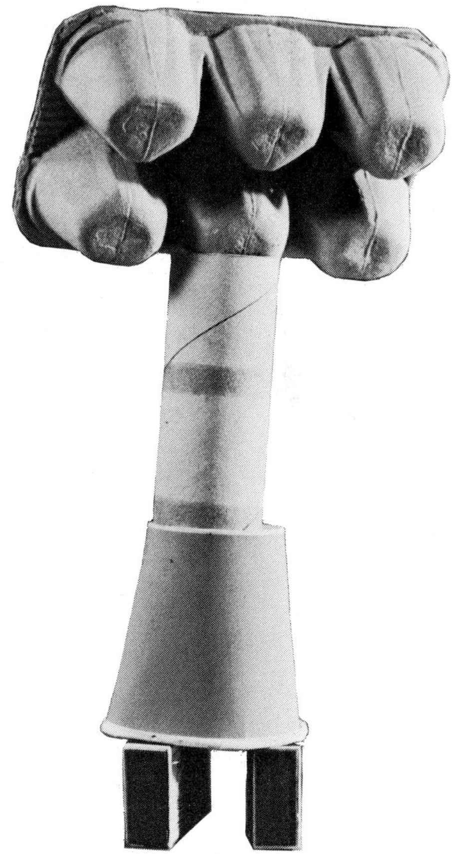

Opposite A parade of robots made from cardboard boxes, rolls, string and other junk materials.

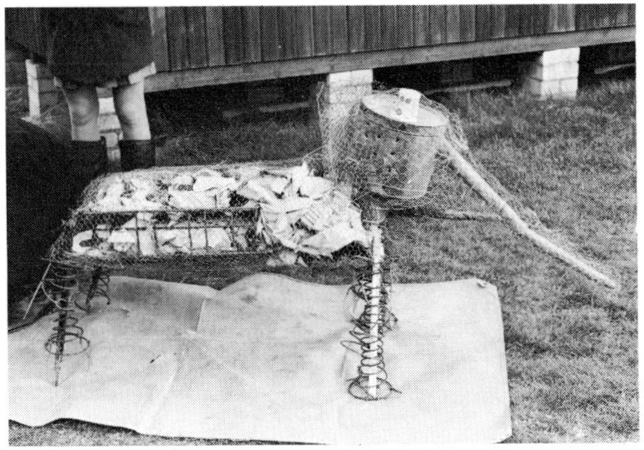

Another way to make sculpture is to build up a form, using materials you can shape yourself.

Here an elephant is made with bed springs, a watering-can, an old metal table and chicken wire. They are put together to make the elephant. Newspapers are stuffed under the chicken wire to keep the cement from falling through the wire. The shape is then built up.

You can make many objects like this elephant from old pieces of junk.

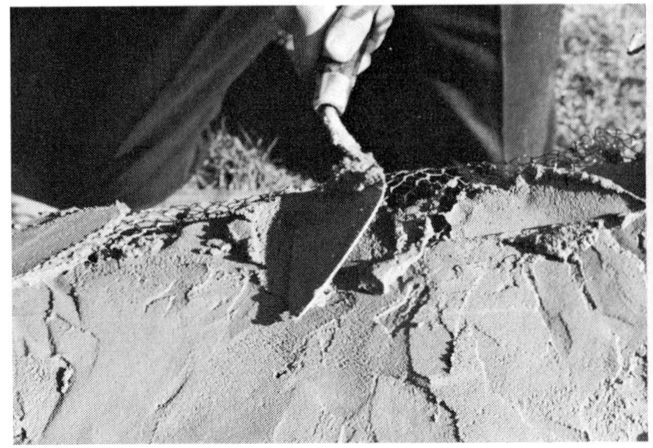

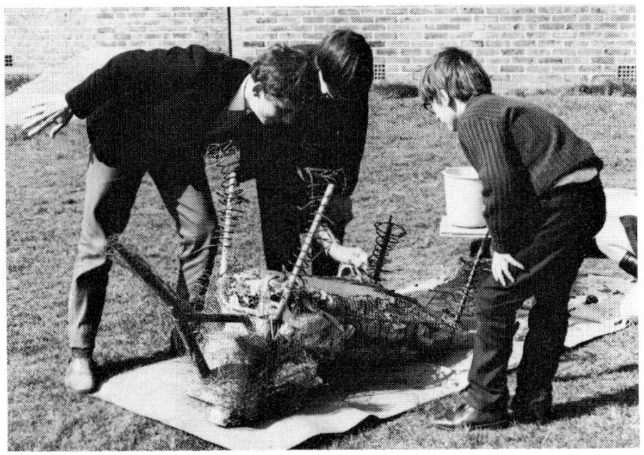

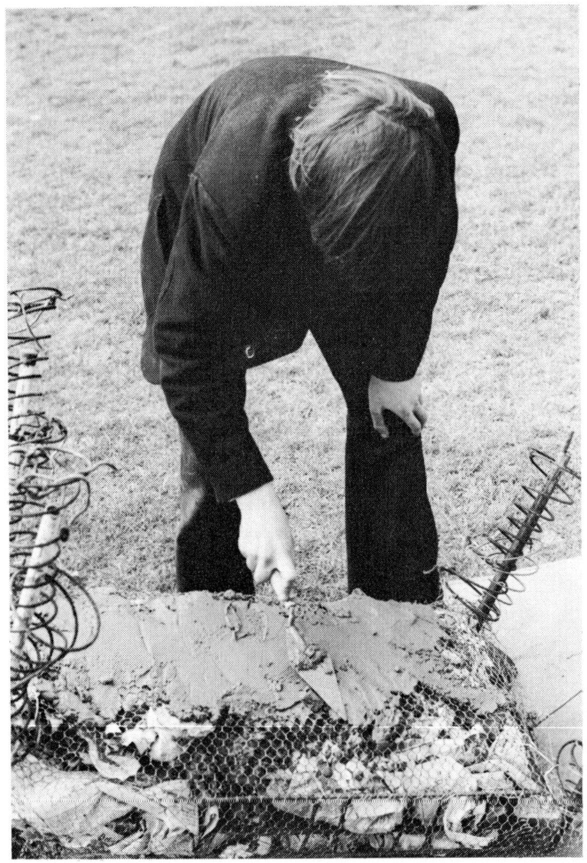

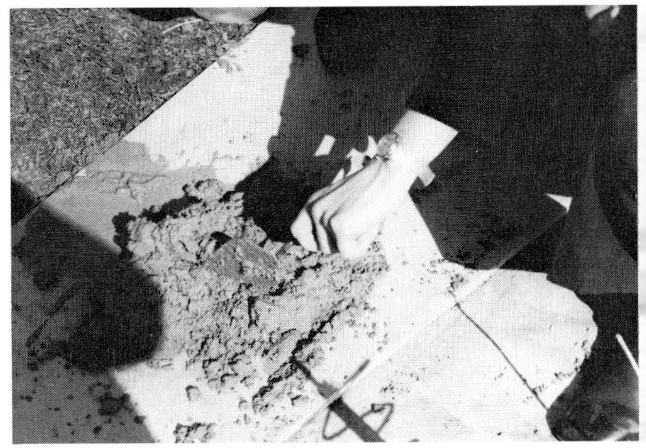

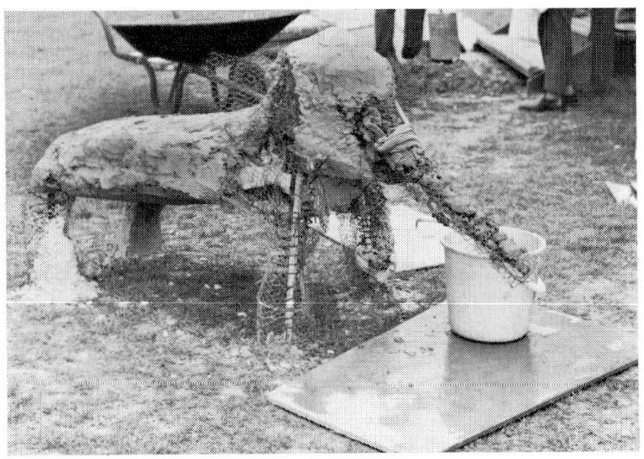

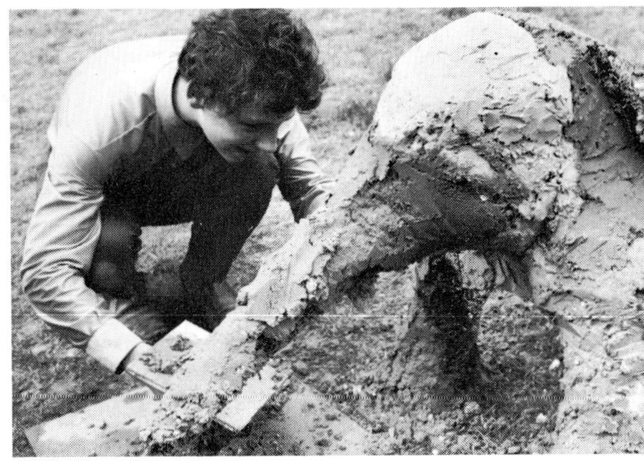

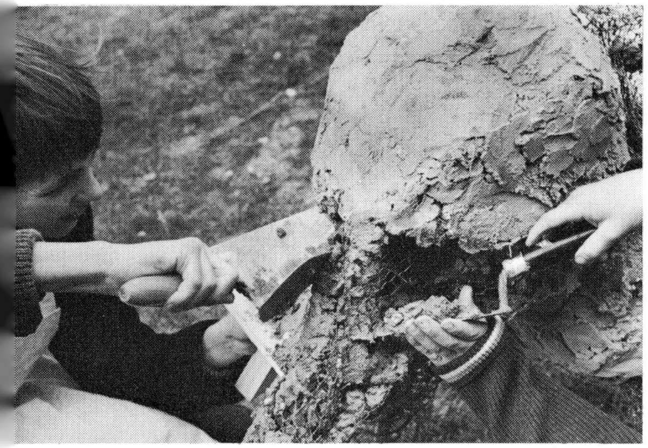
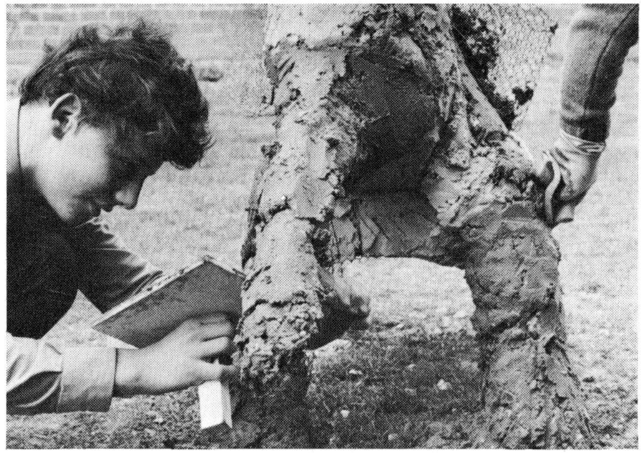
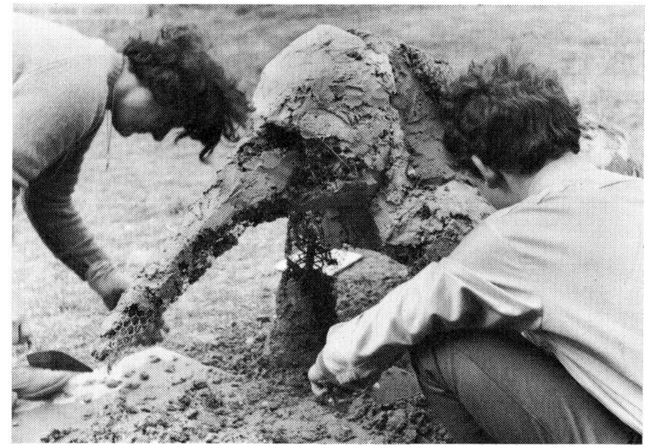
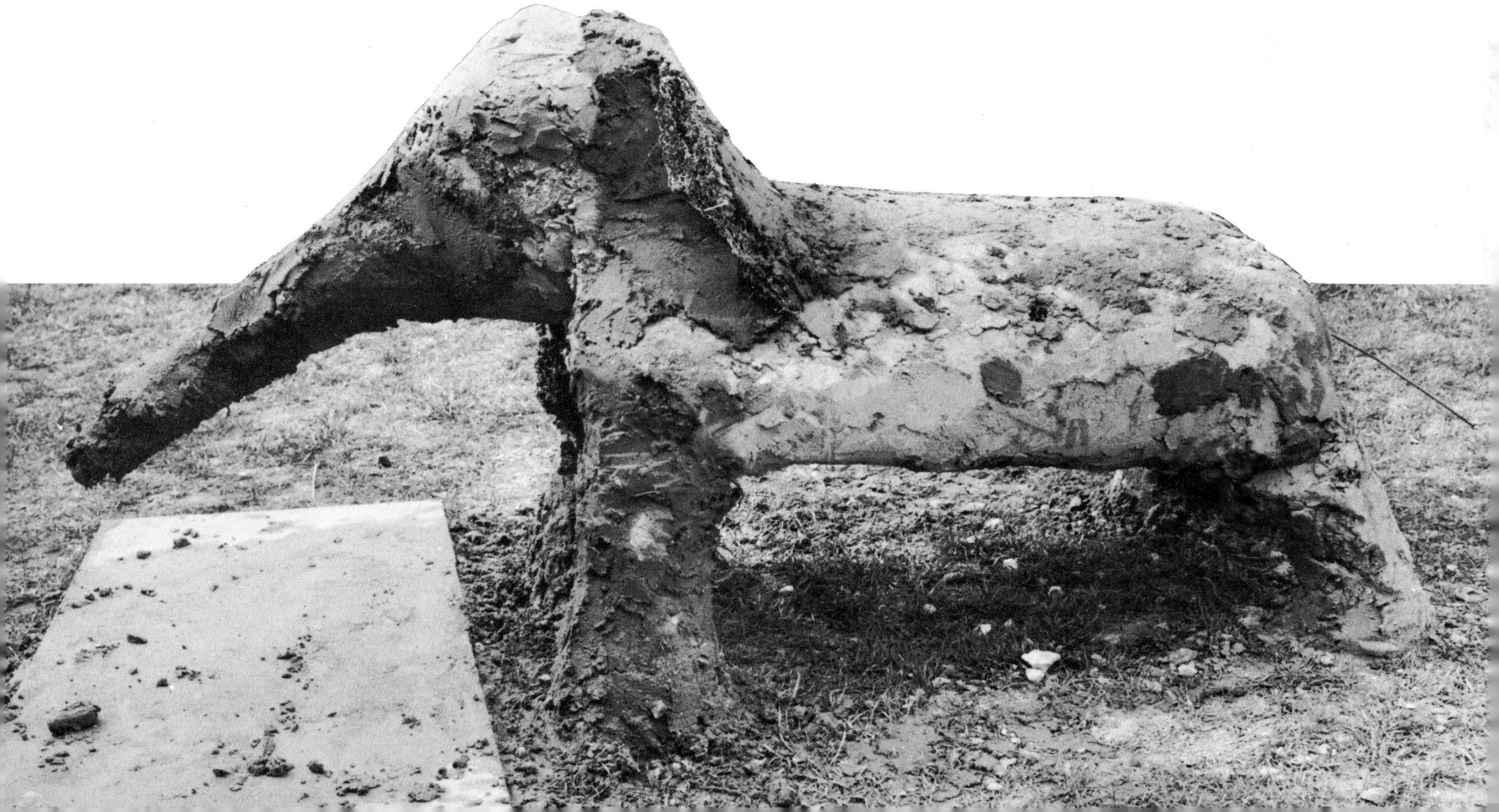

Cardboard

Cardboard is a good material to use for sculpture because it can be found anywhere. It is easy to work with and all you need are scissors and glue to cut and stick the cardboard shapes together. You can bend, twist, fold, cut or glue shapes to make cardboard sculpture.

Here cardboard shapes are being glued together, and the sculpture gets bigger and bigger.

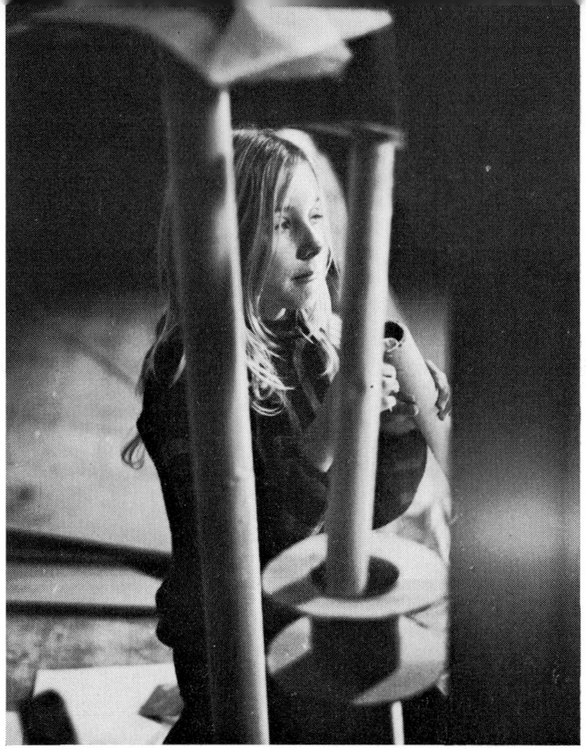

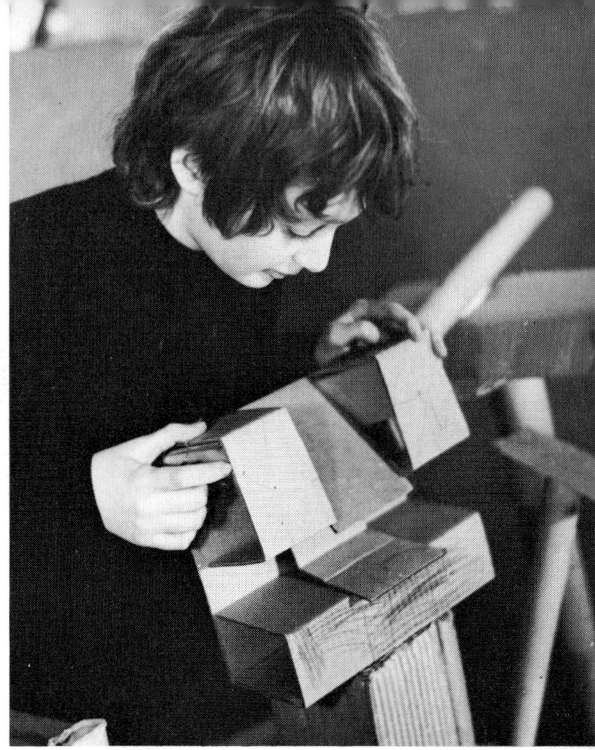

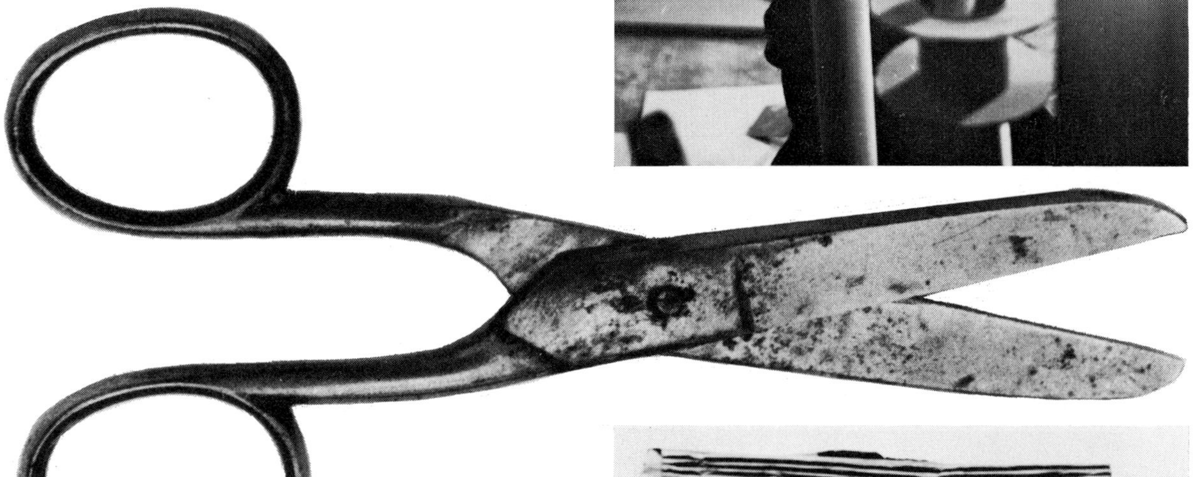

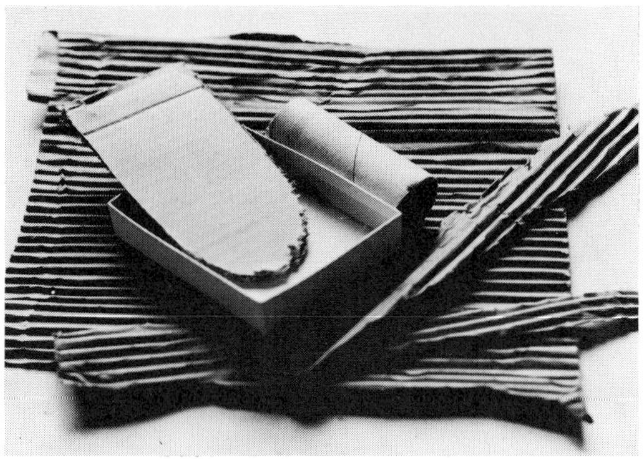

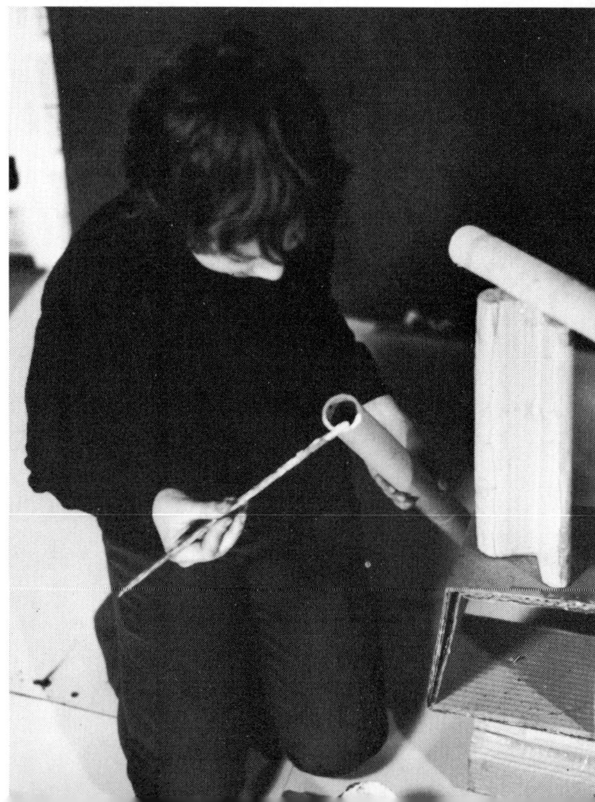

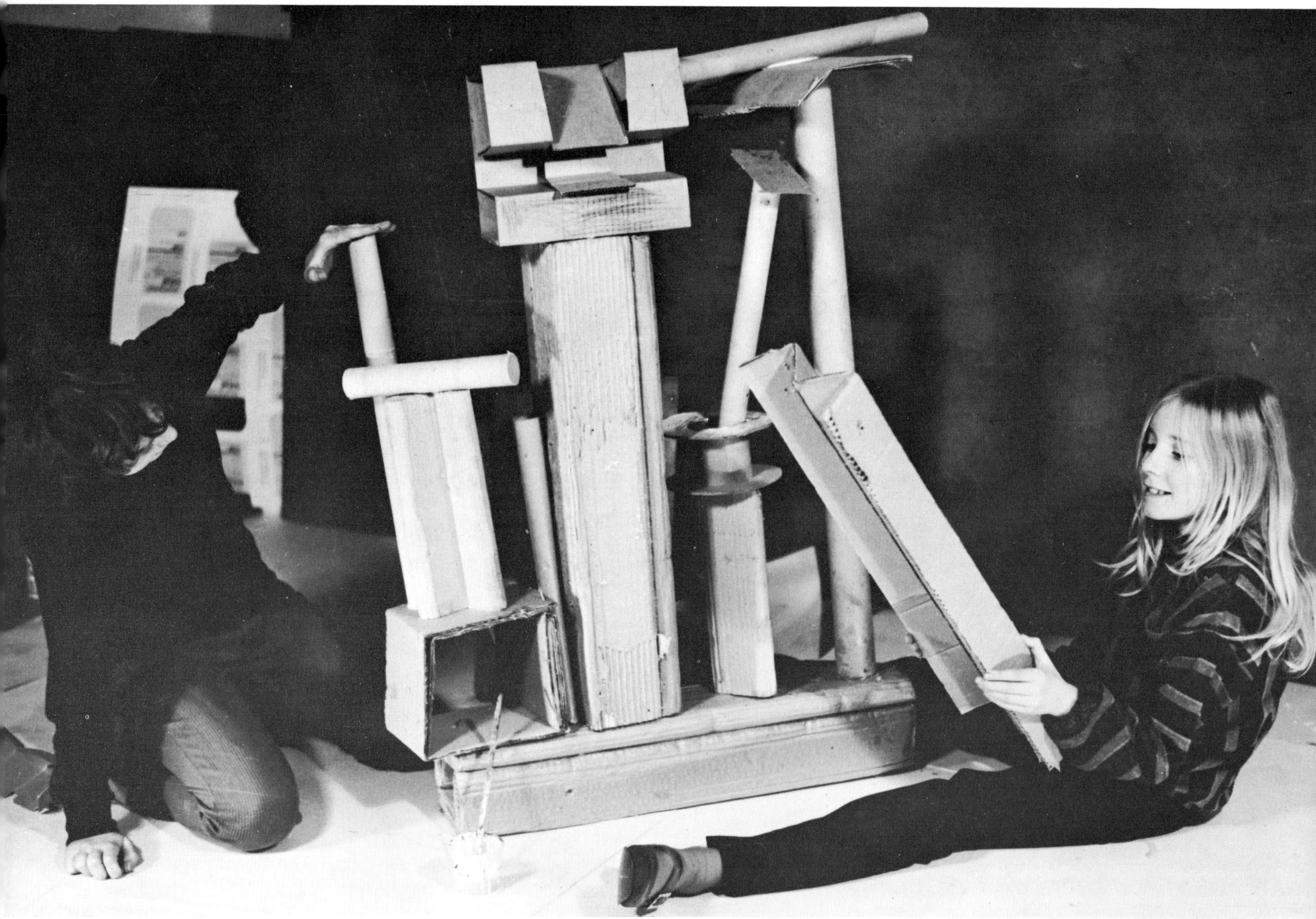

Below A finished sculpture piece made by glueing different cardboard objects and shapes together.

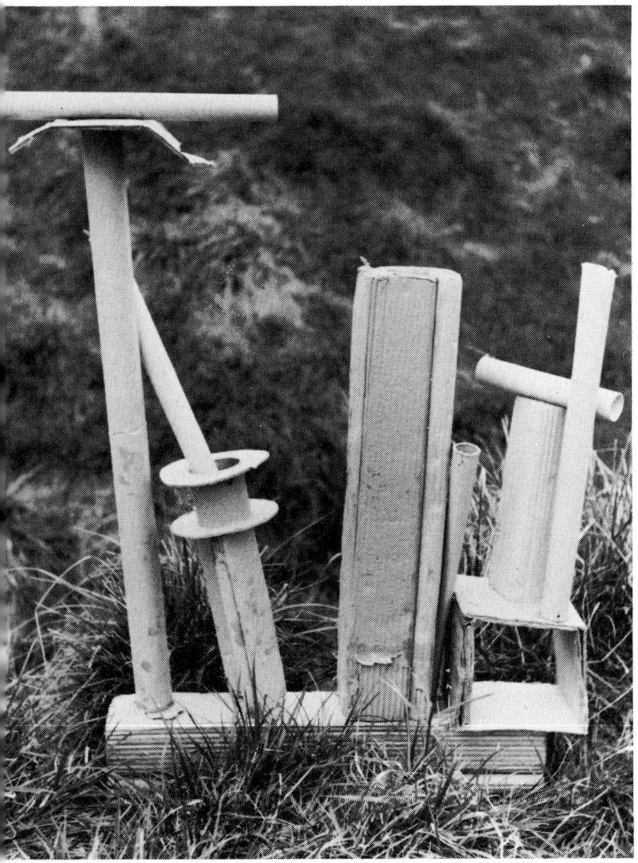

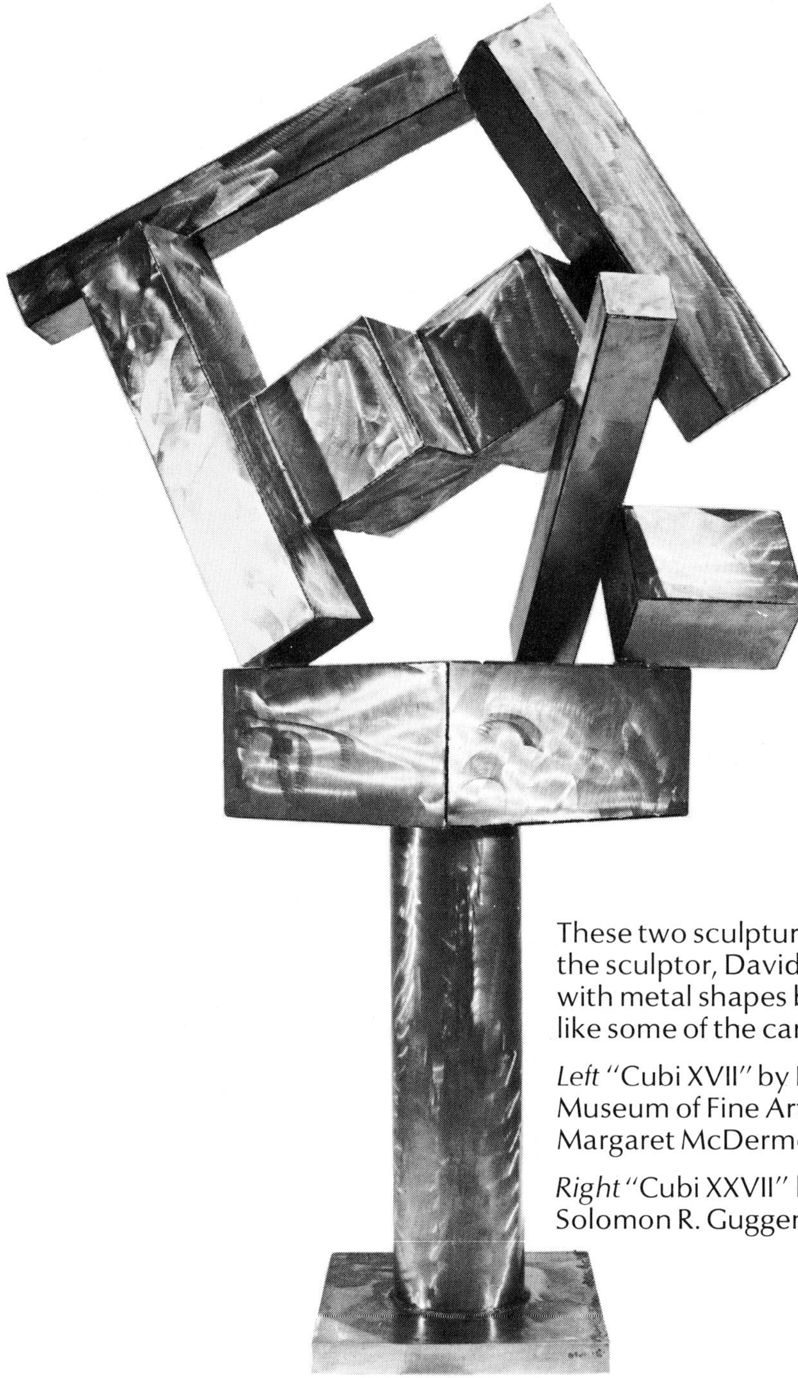

These two sculpture pieces were made by the sculptor, David Smith. They were made with metal shapes but they are very much like some of the cardboard shapes.

Left "Cubi XVII" by David Smith. Dallas Museum of Fine Arts, The Eugene and Margaret McDermott Fund.

Right "Cubi XXVII" by David Smith. Solomon R. Guggenheim Museum.

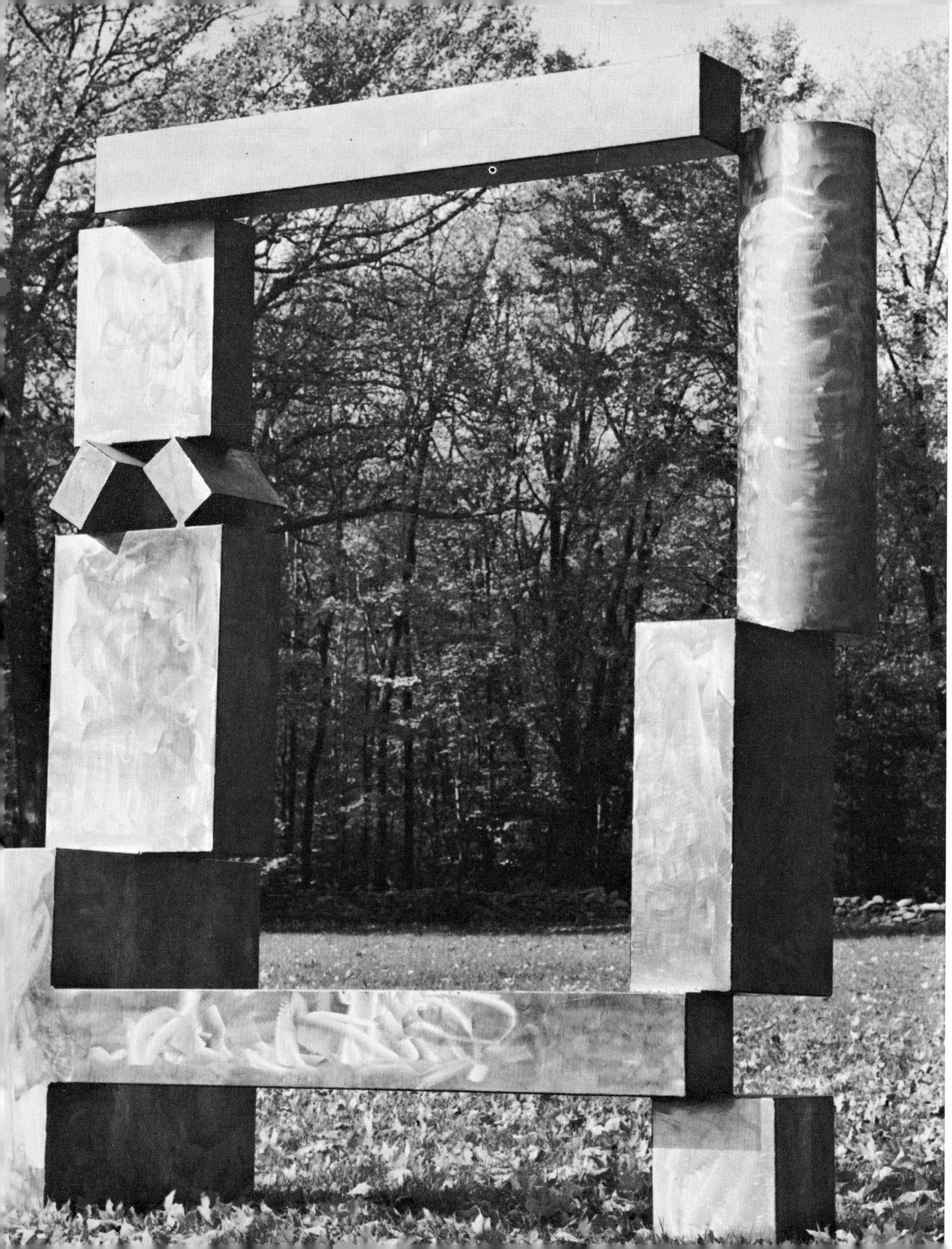

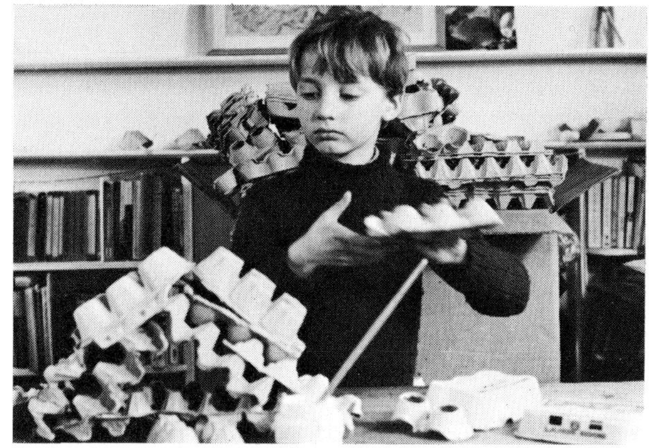

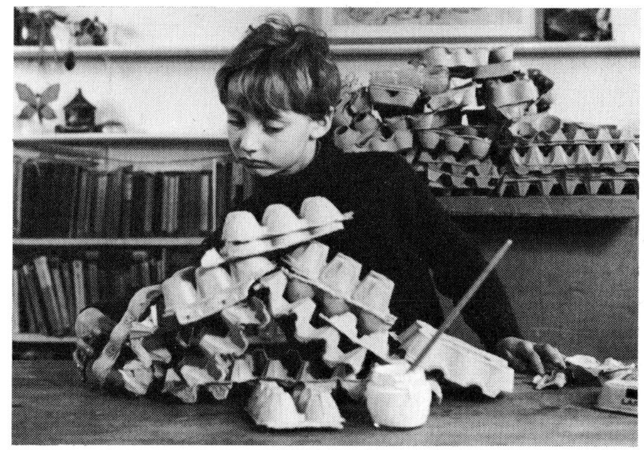

Egg boxes are glued together to make cardboard patterns.

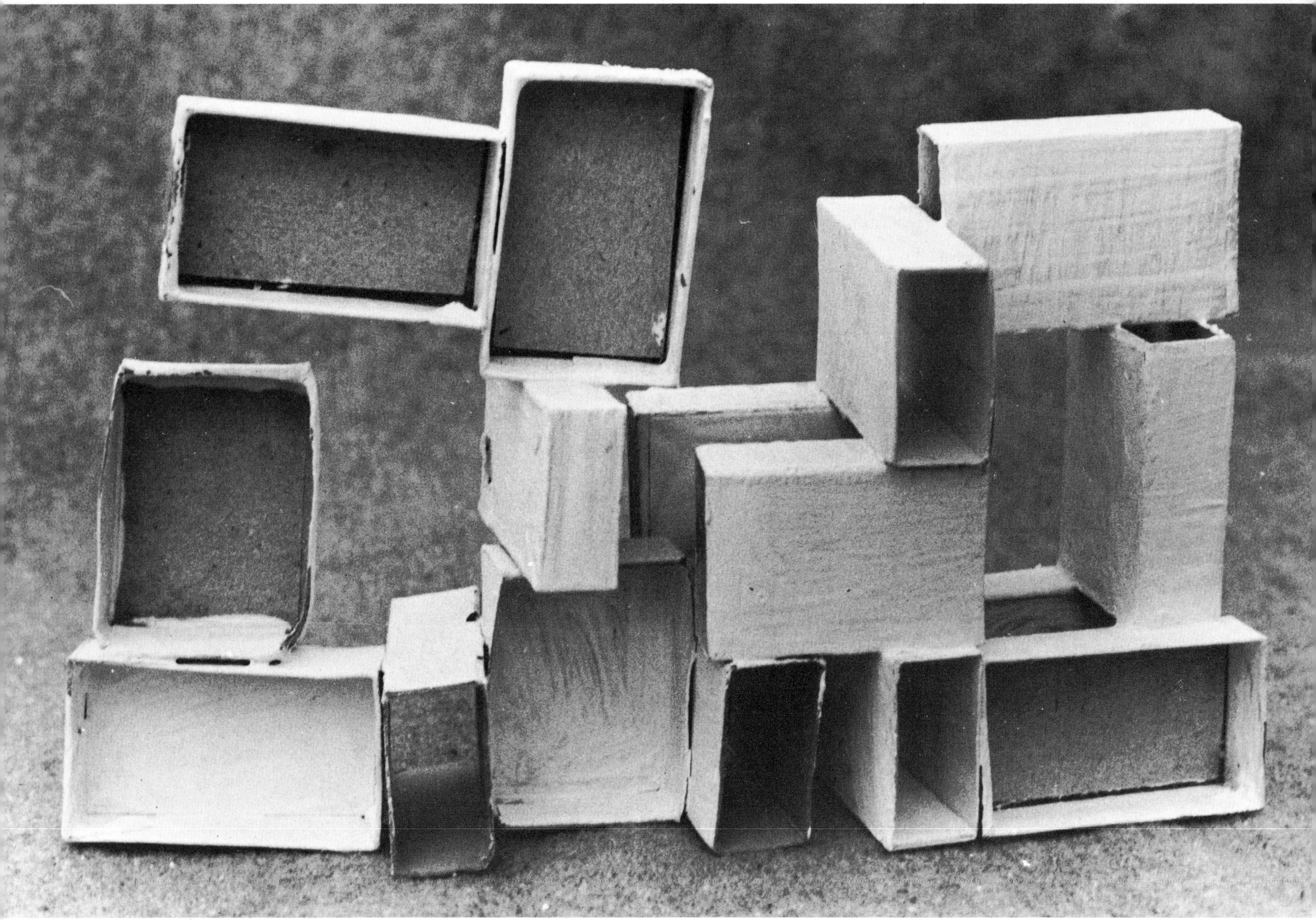

Matchboxes can make very good sculpture when glued together.

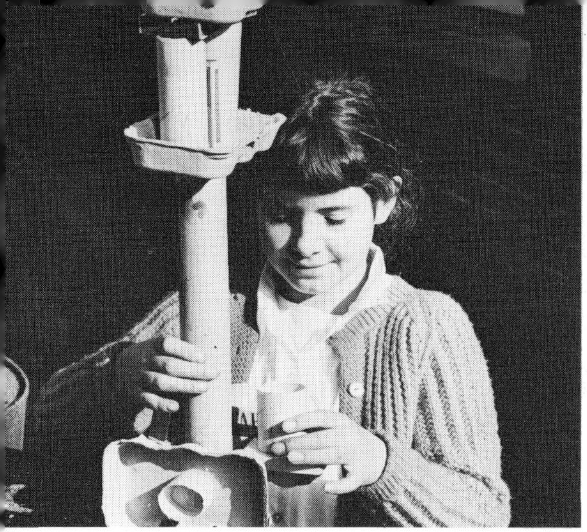

These sculpture pieces on the left and below were made by glueing cardboard shapes together.

Top left Cardboard rolls and egg boxes are glued together.

Bottom left A cardboard sculpture which has been painted.

Below Another painted sculpture piece made with boxes and egg cartons which were glued together and painted by children (ages 3-5 years) in a play centre.

Right Boxes are cut and torn into flat shapes and slotted together.

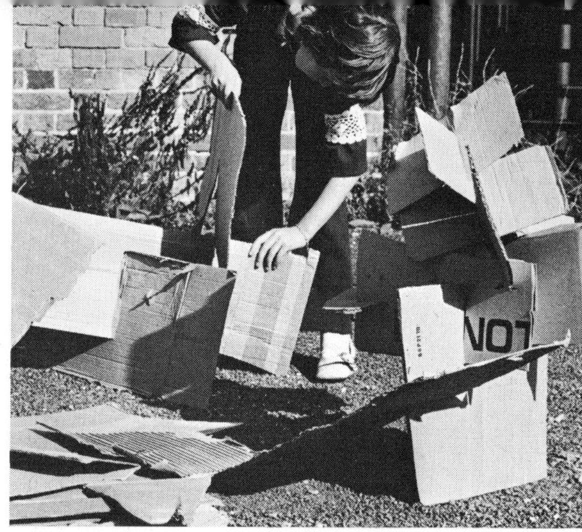

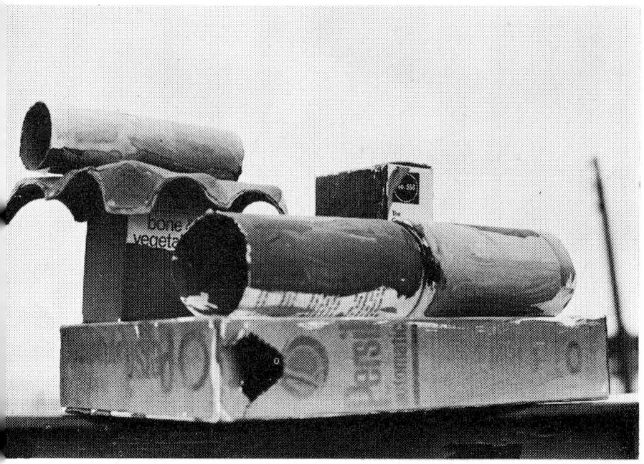

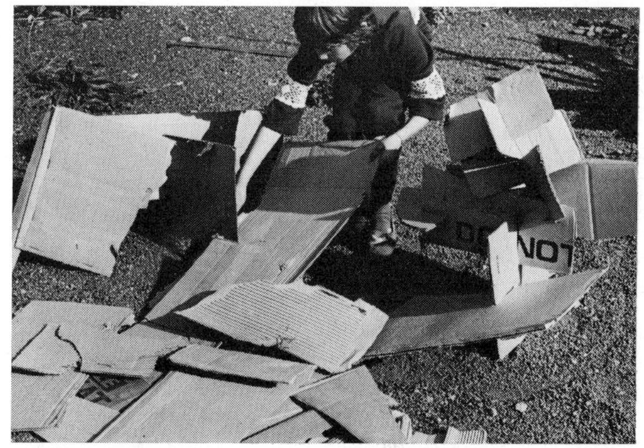

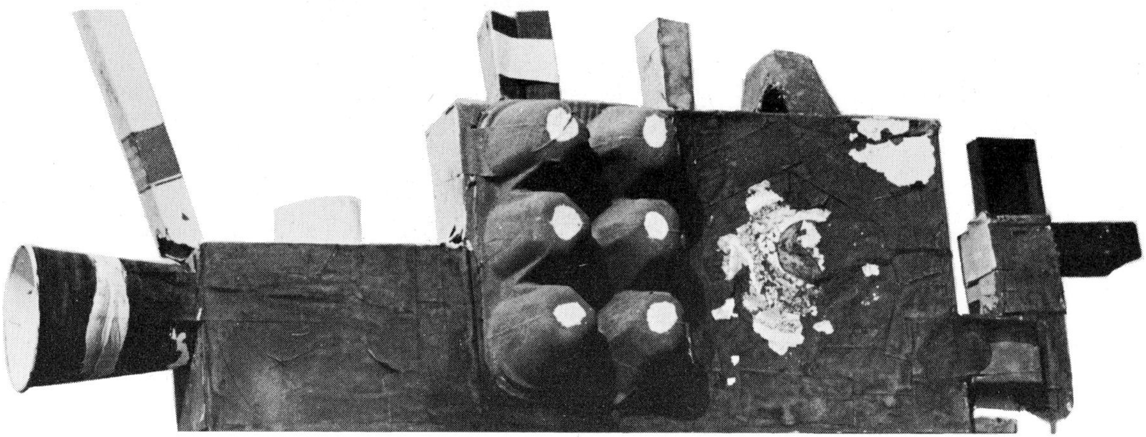

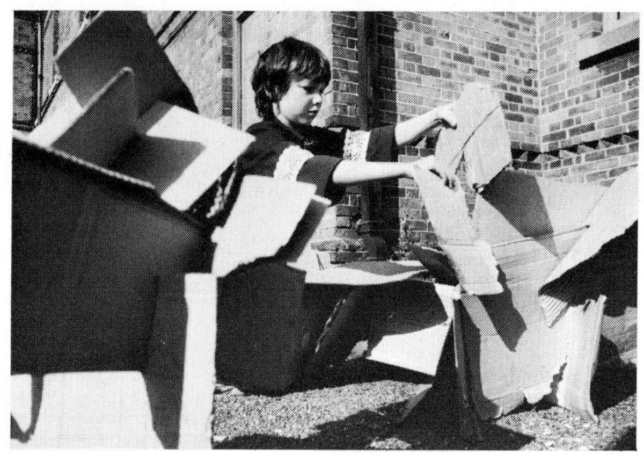

Cardboard sculpture can be made by cutting flat shapes and slitting the ends so that they can be slotted together. Glue can be added to make it stronger.

Below A duck shape in cardboard.

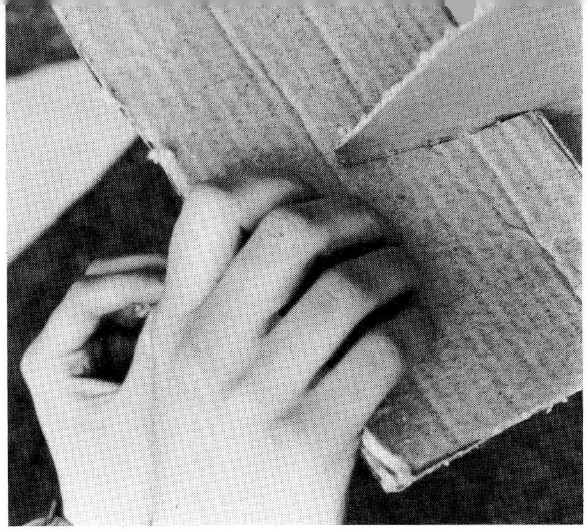

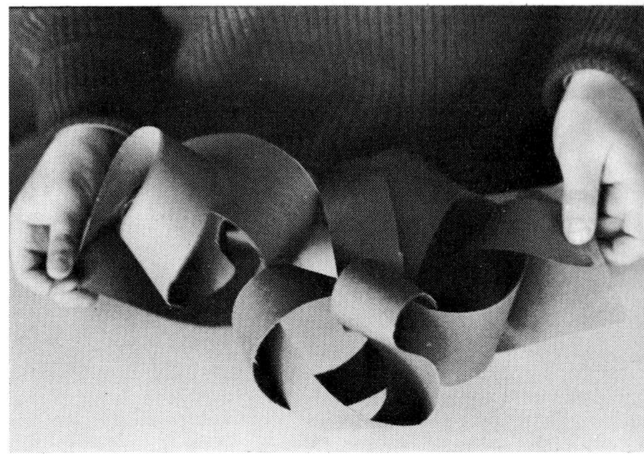

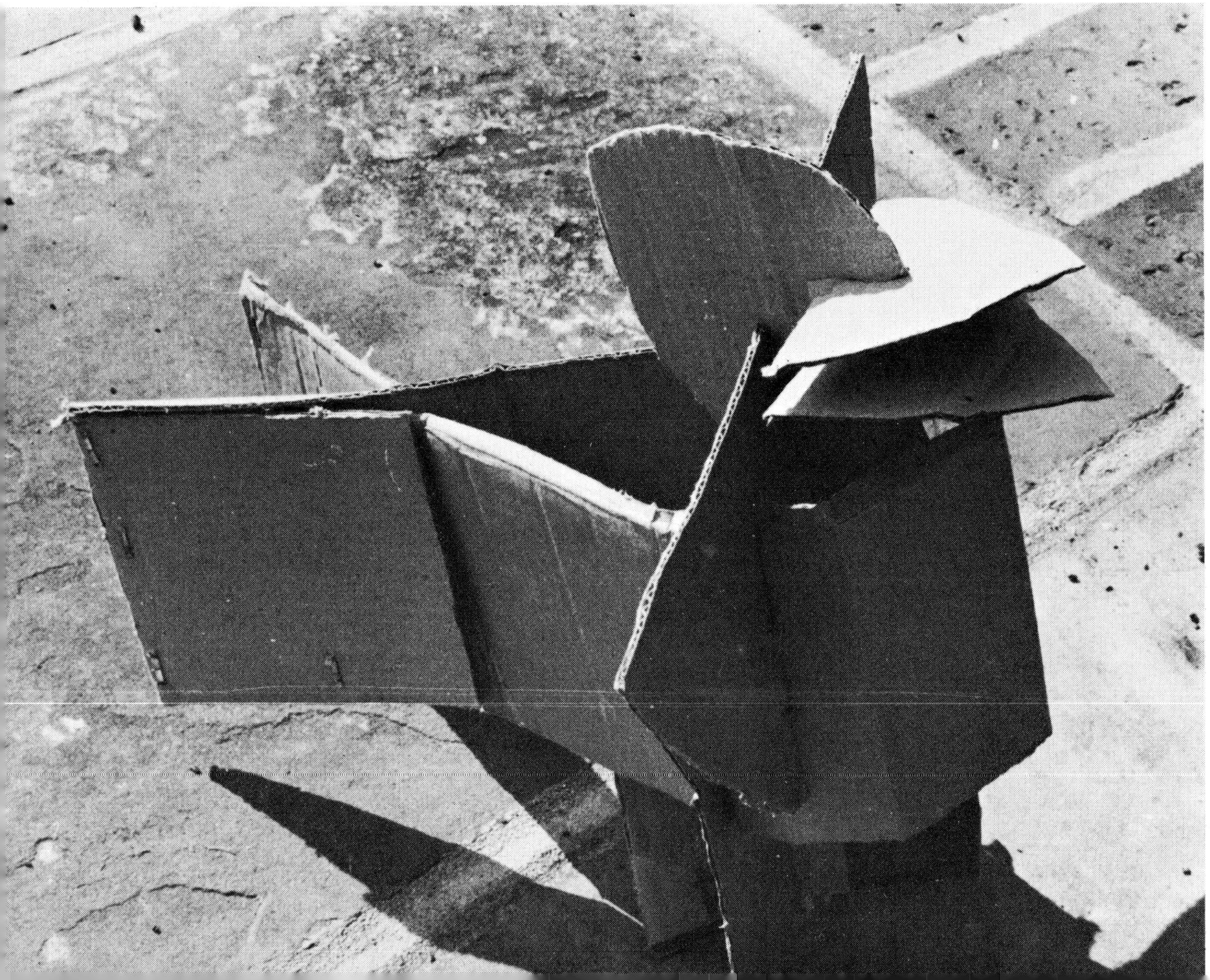

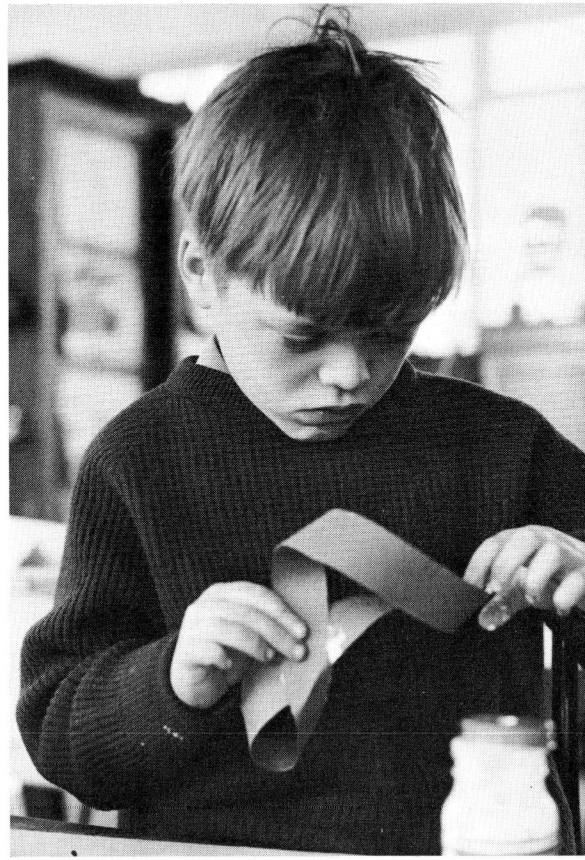

Left Thin cardboard can be twisted into shape and the pieces can be joined together with glue or tape.

Below A twisted cardboard flower shape.

Right Thicker cardboard is twisted into a shape.

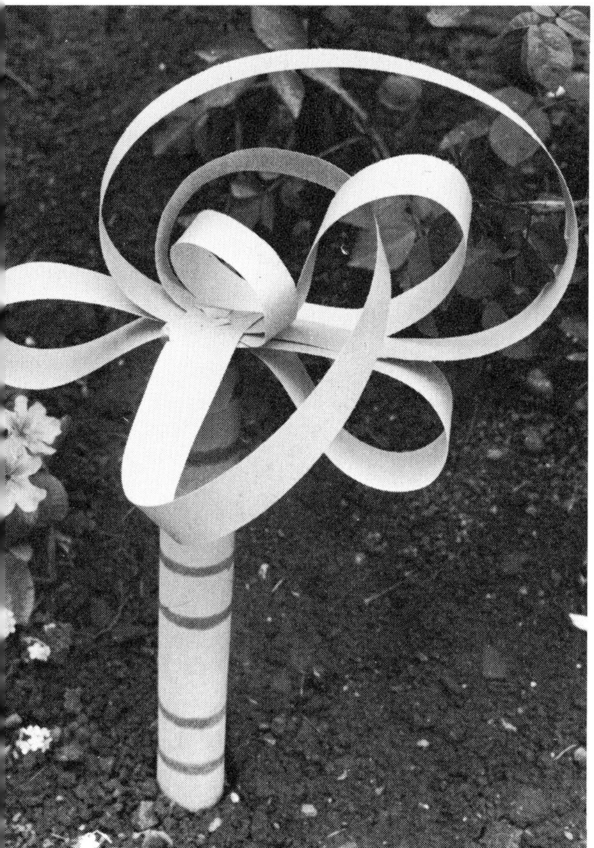

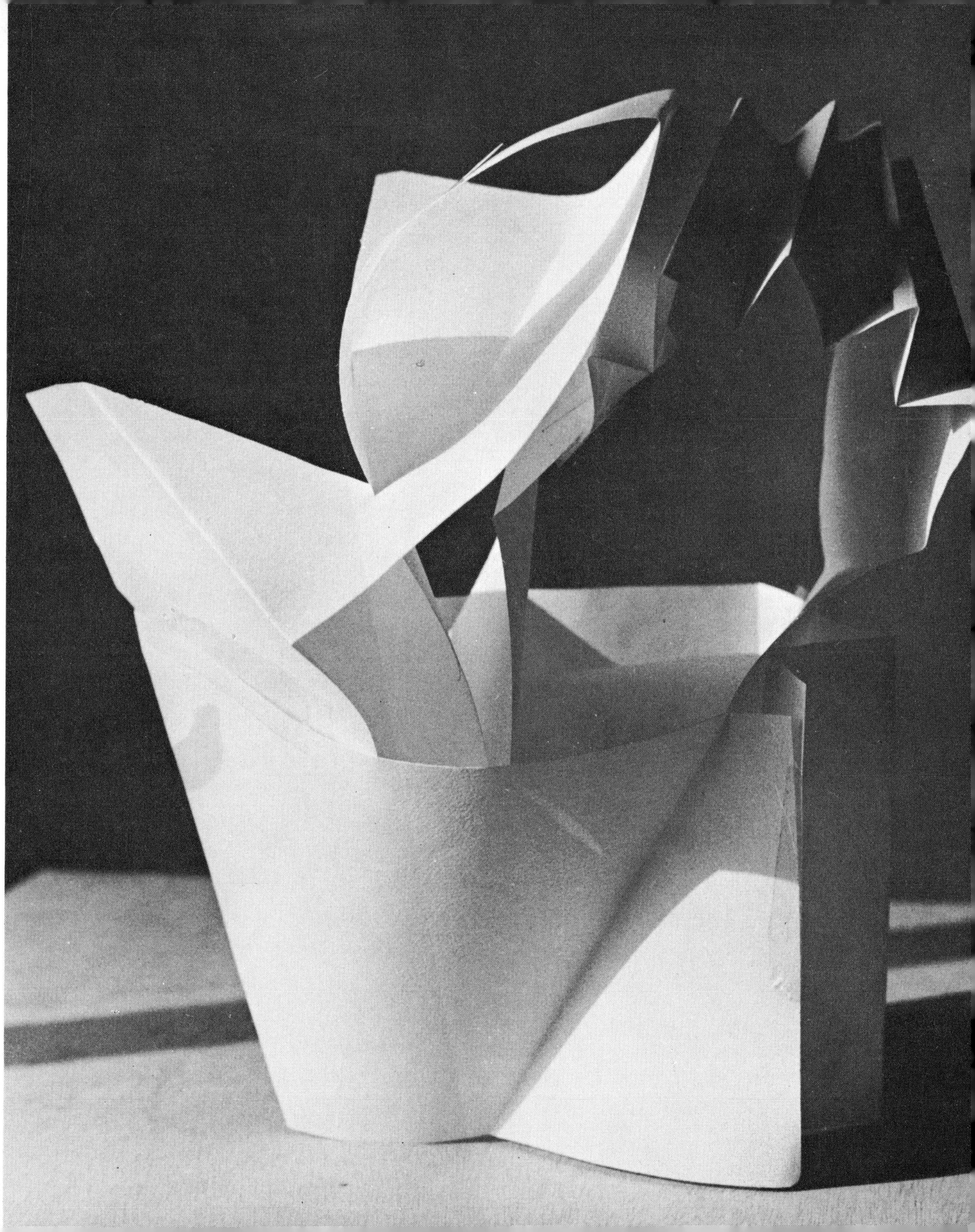

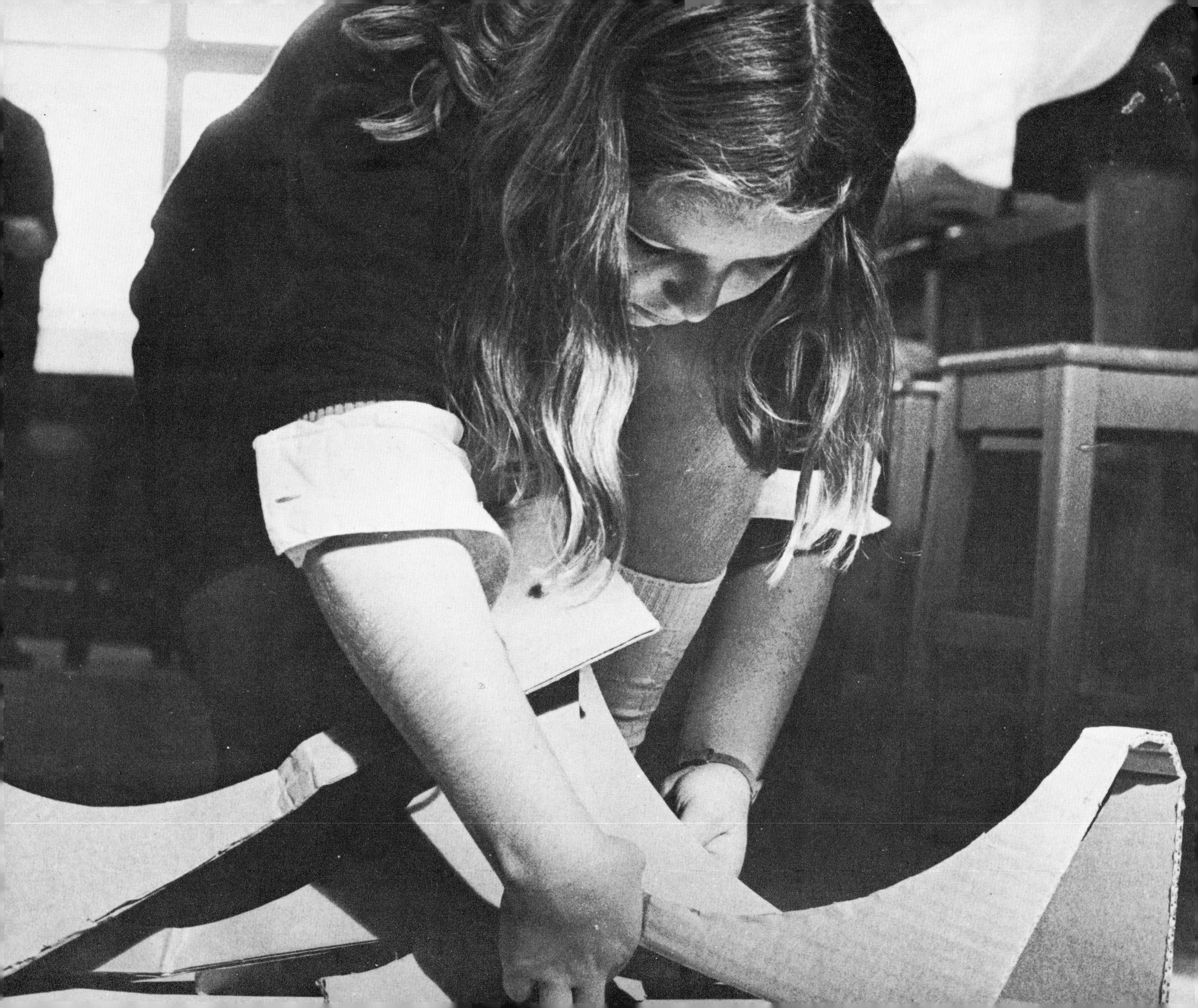

Left A sculpture being made by folding and twisting cardboard.

Here a robot head is being made from a cardboard box. A fringe is cut into a toilet roll. It is flattened and glued on to the box for a nose. Eyes are cut into the box and it is painted.

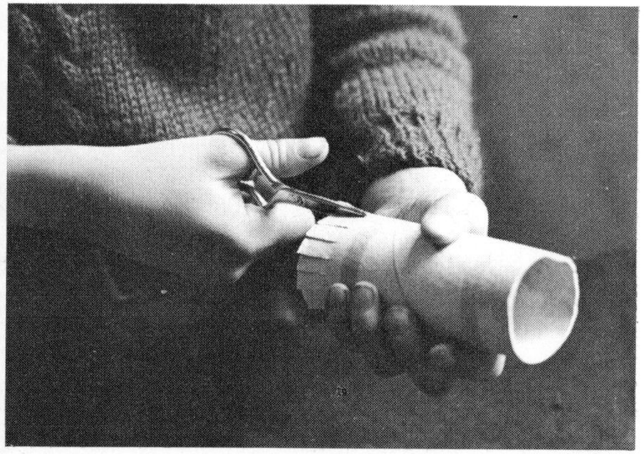

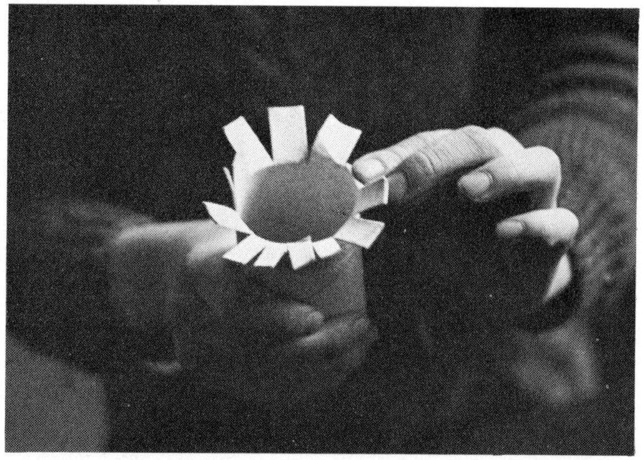

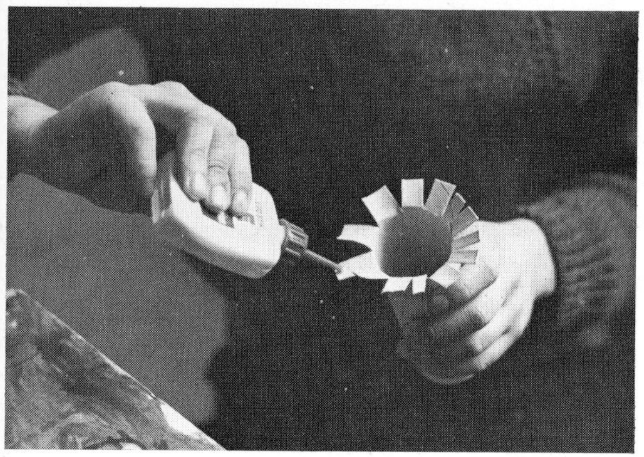

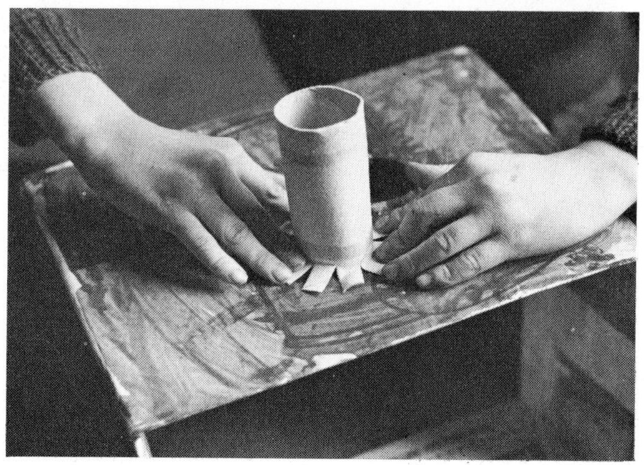

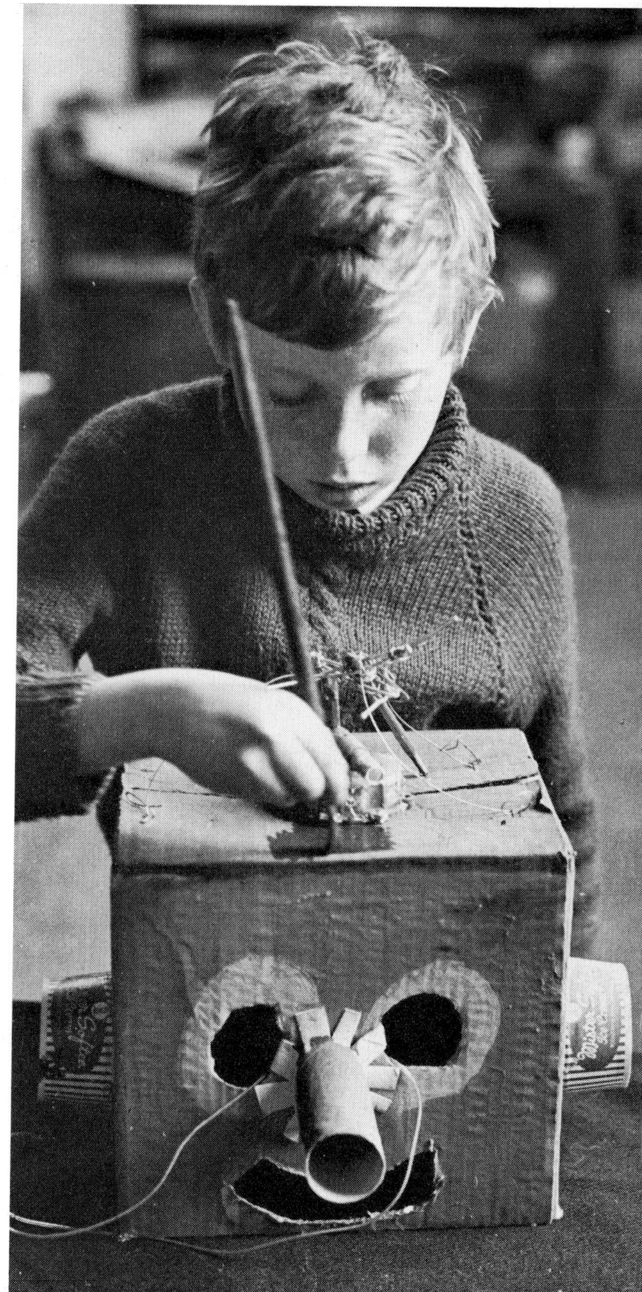

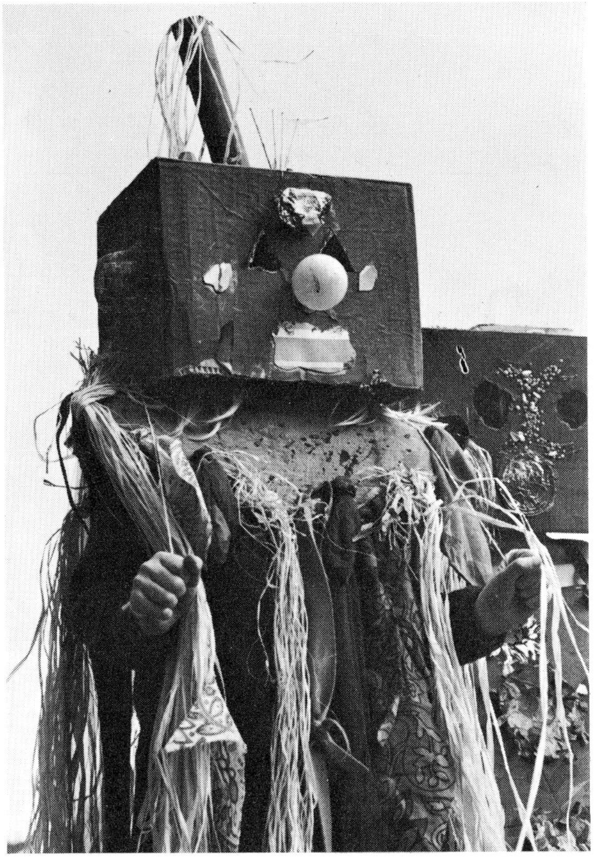

Robots made with cardboard boxes, rolls, string, used light bulbs, glue, paint, and odd bits of junk material.

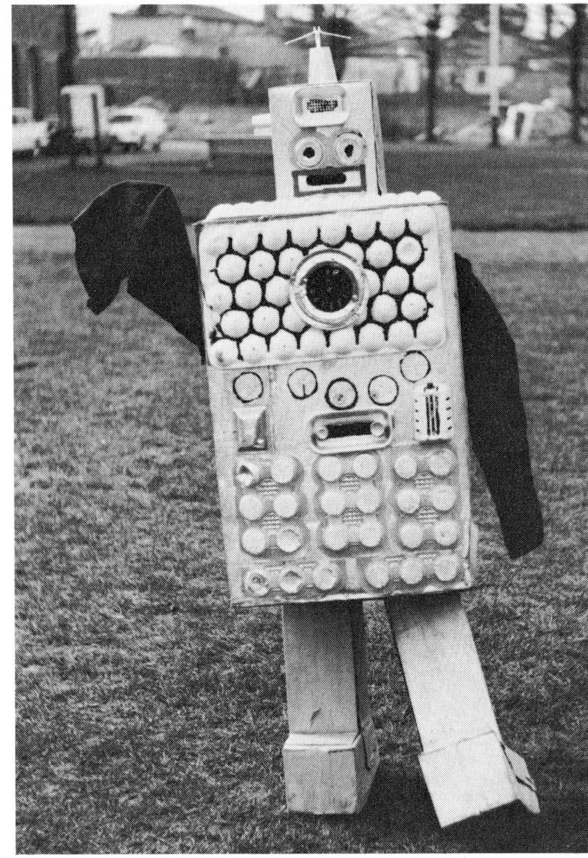

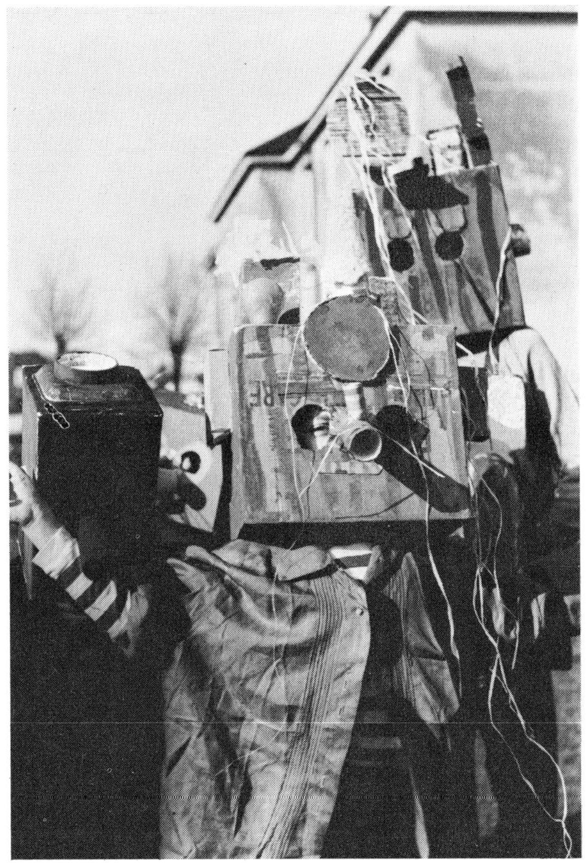

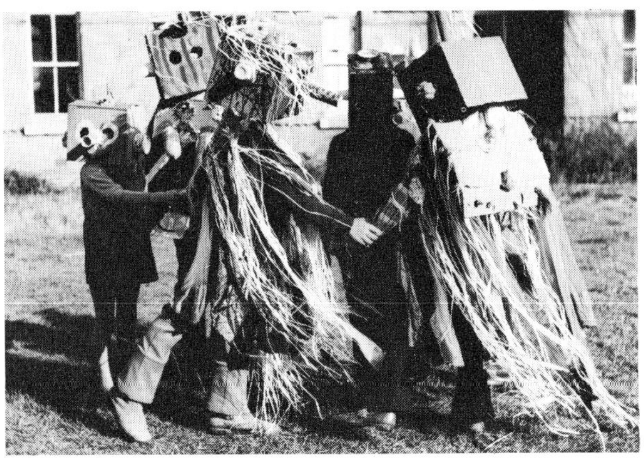

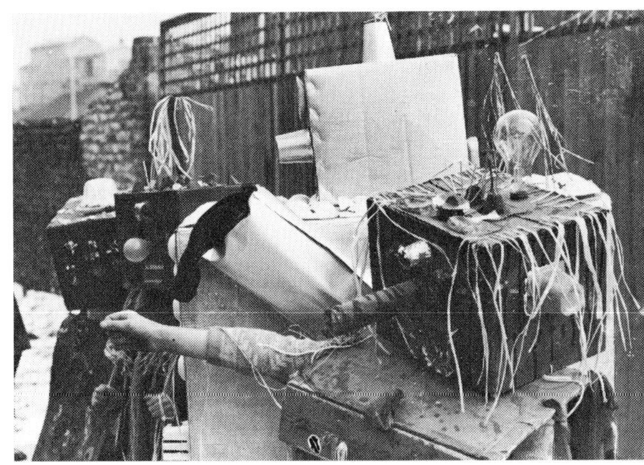

Twigs

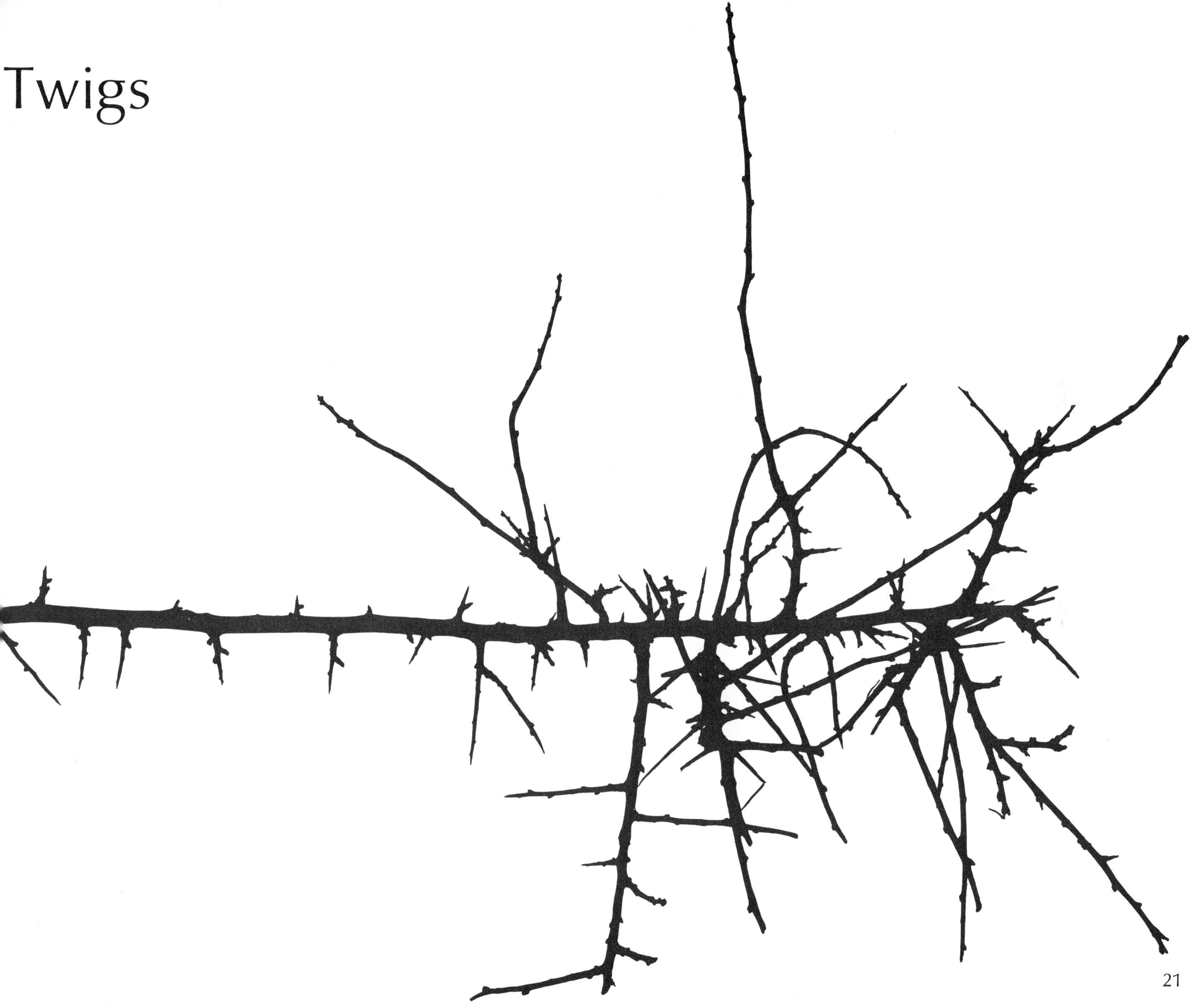

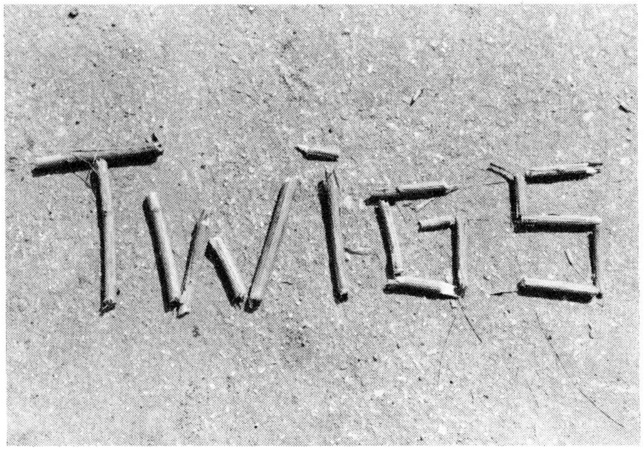

There are many shapes we can see all around us that can be made into sculpture.

Below An animal shape made with twigs and glue.

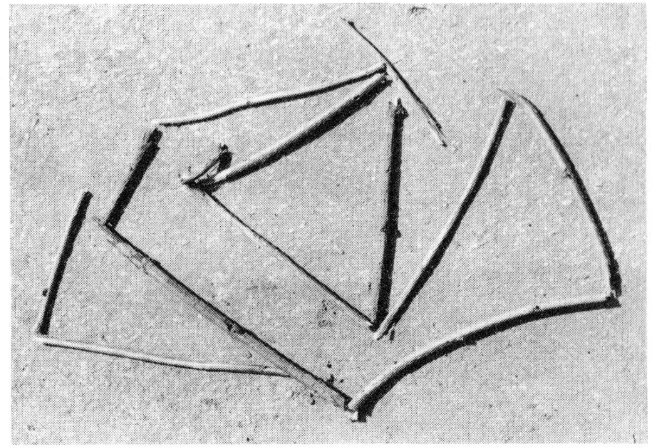

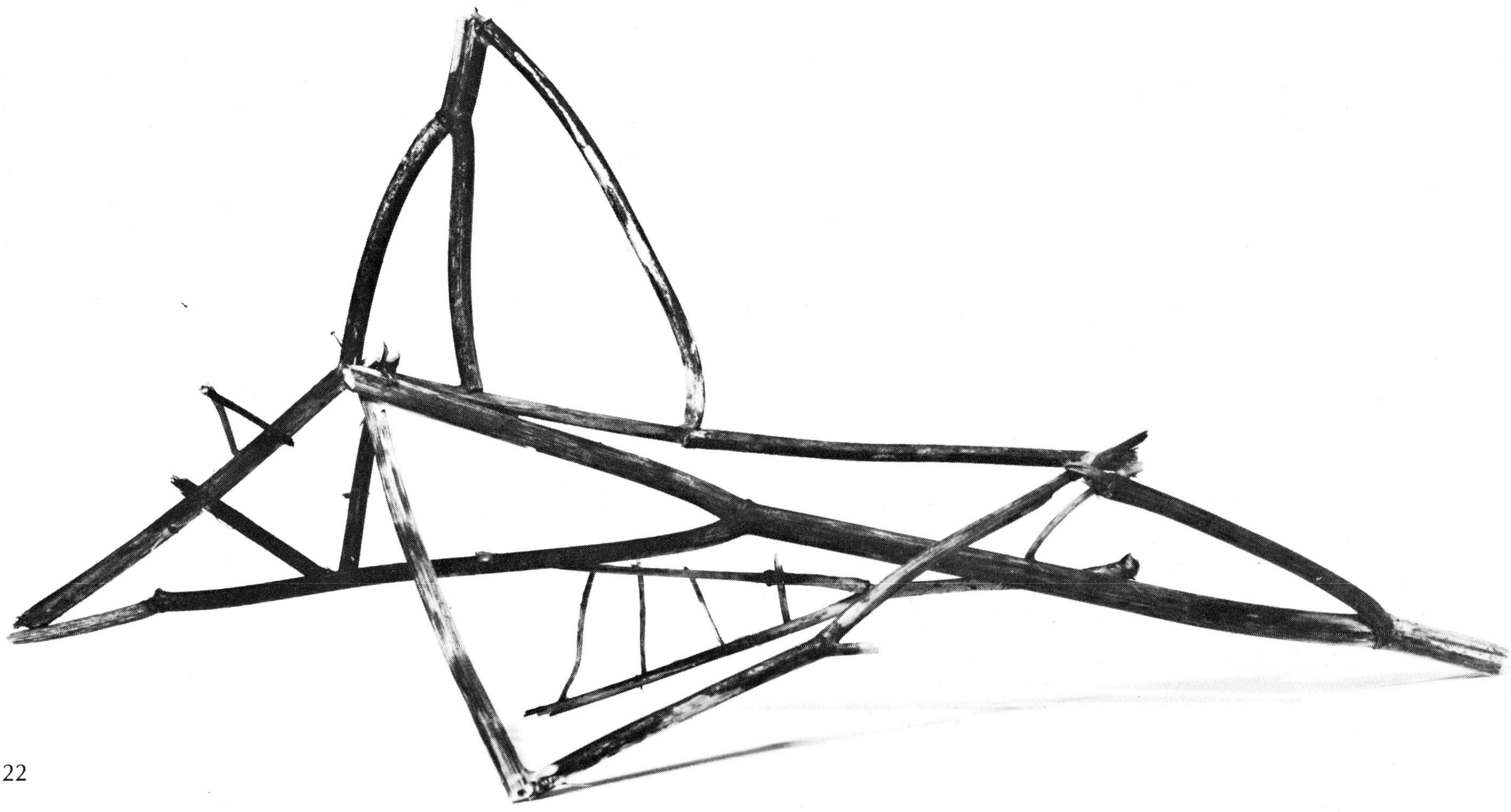

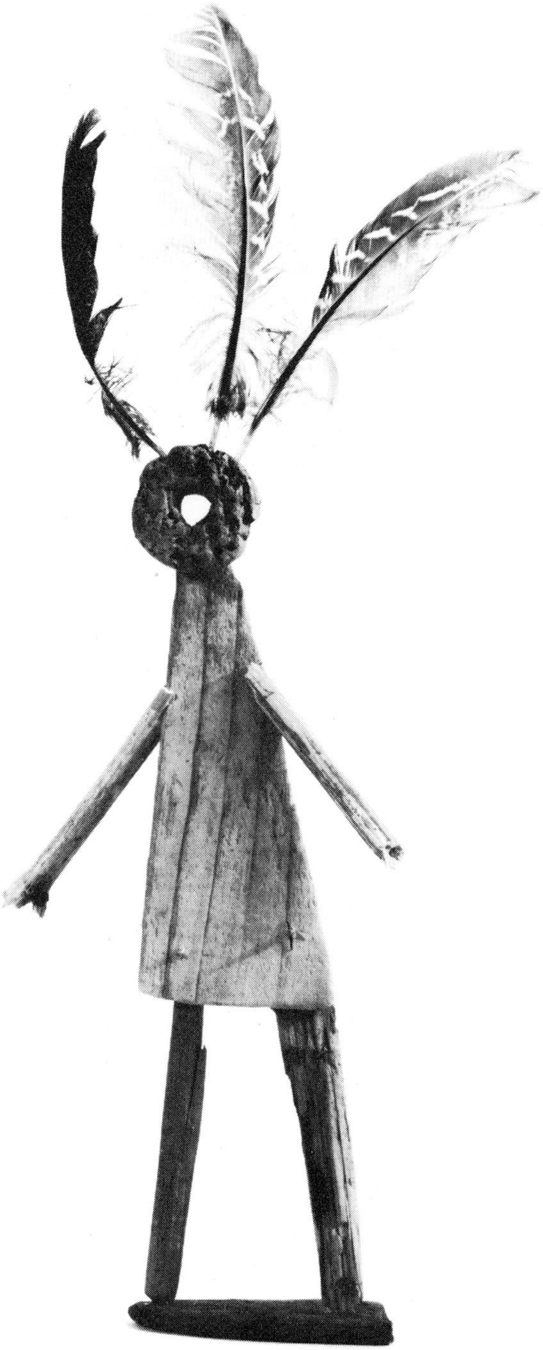

Twigs can be glued together. Pins hold the twigs in place while the glue dries.

A finished twig sculpture.

Left An Indian made with twigs, feathers, scrapwood and glue.

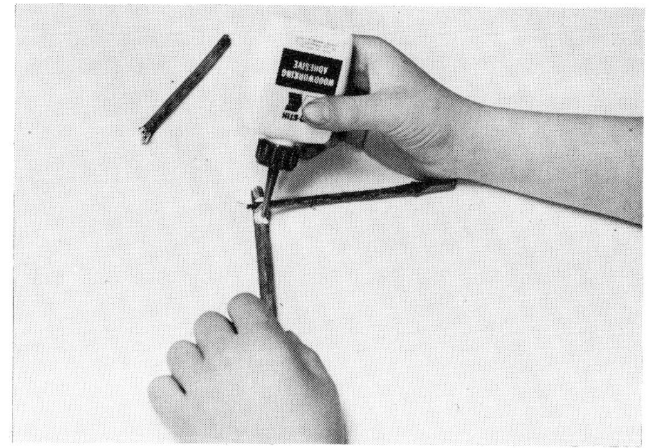

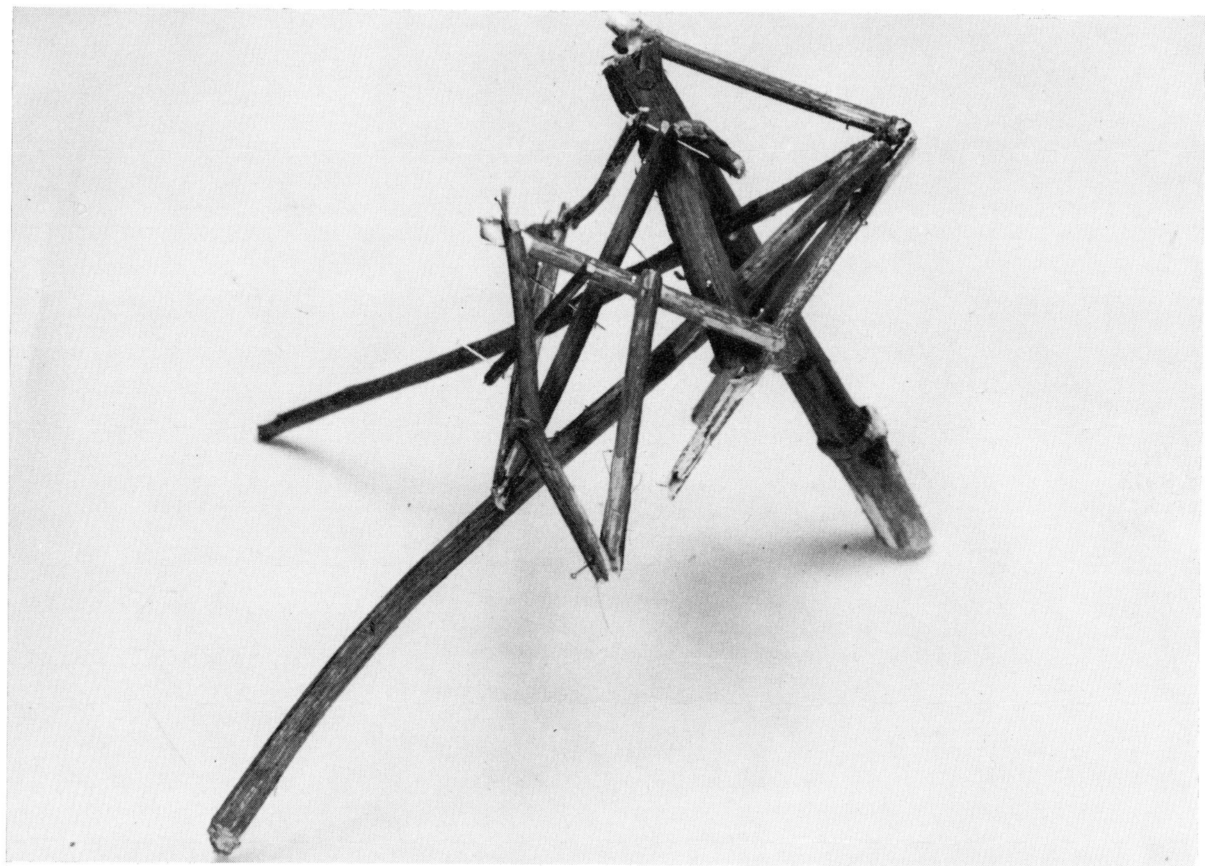

Below A sculpture piece made with twigs and driftwood and glue.

Right Twigs make beautiful patterns. Tying string to the branches makes the pattern much more interesting.

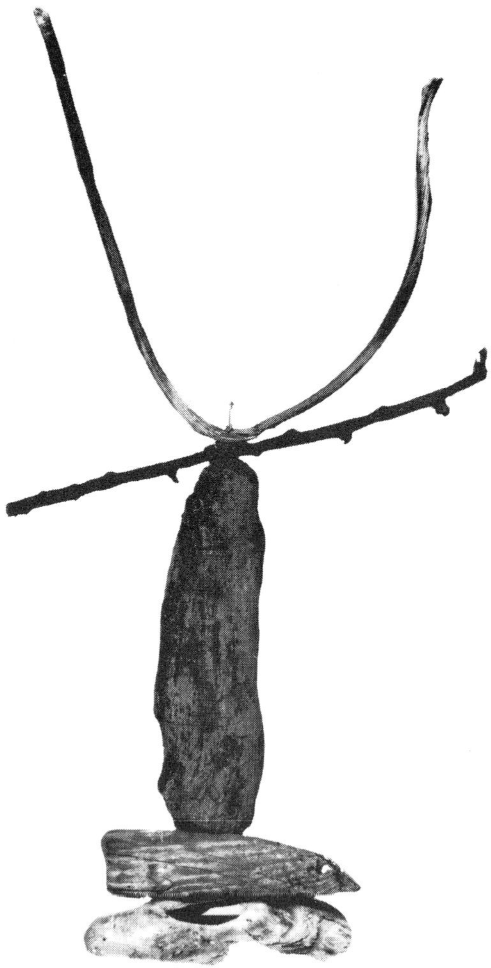

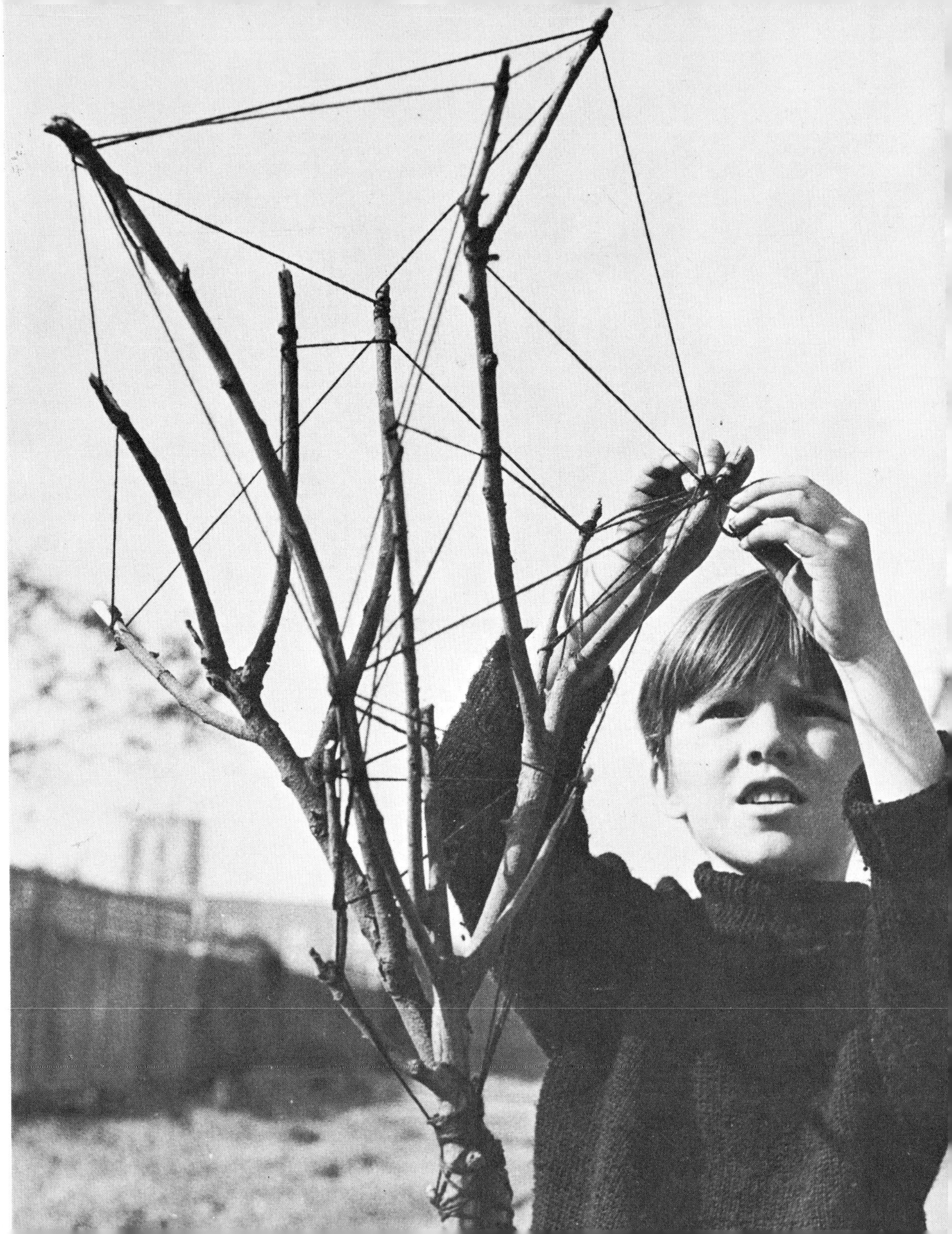

Pebbles

Wind and water have carved these pebbles into interesting shapes.
Can you see animals or birds in these pebbles?
What other shapes can you see?

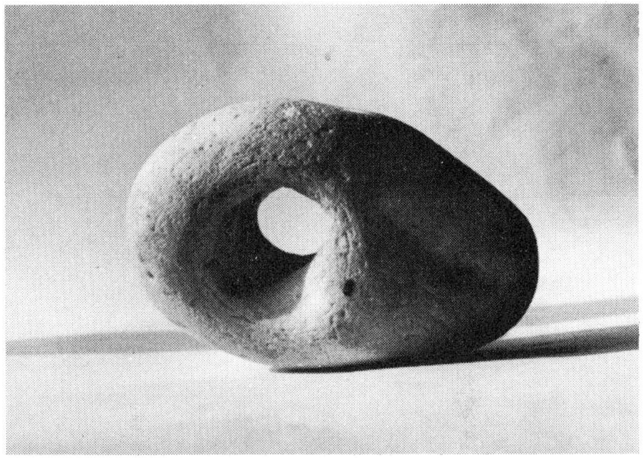

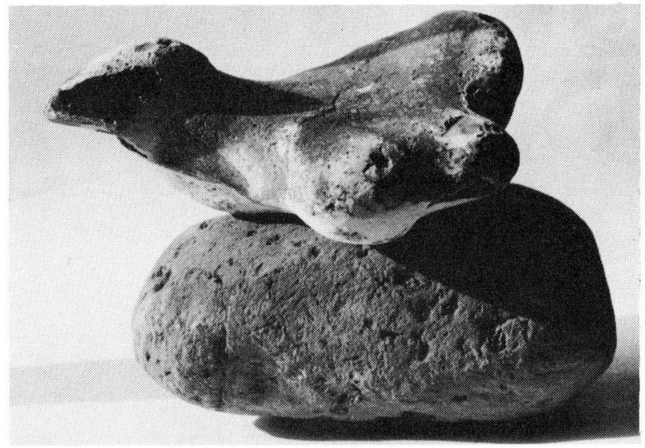

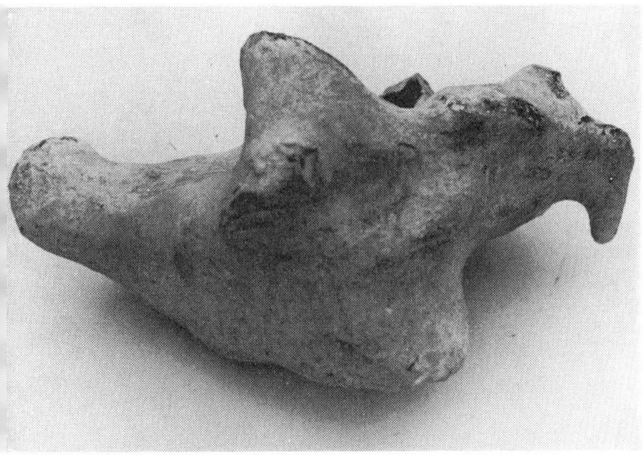

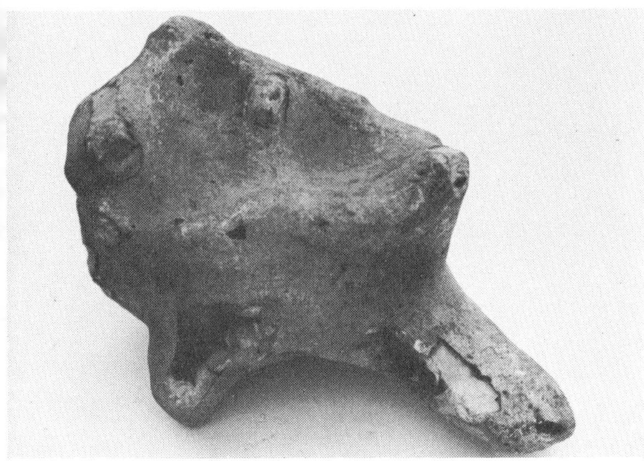

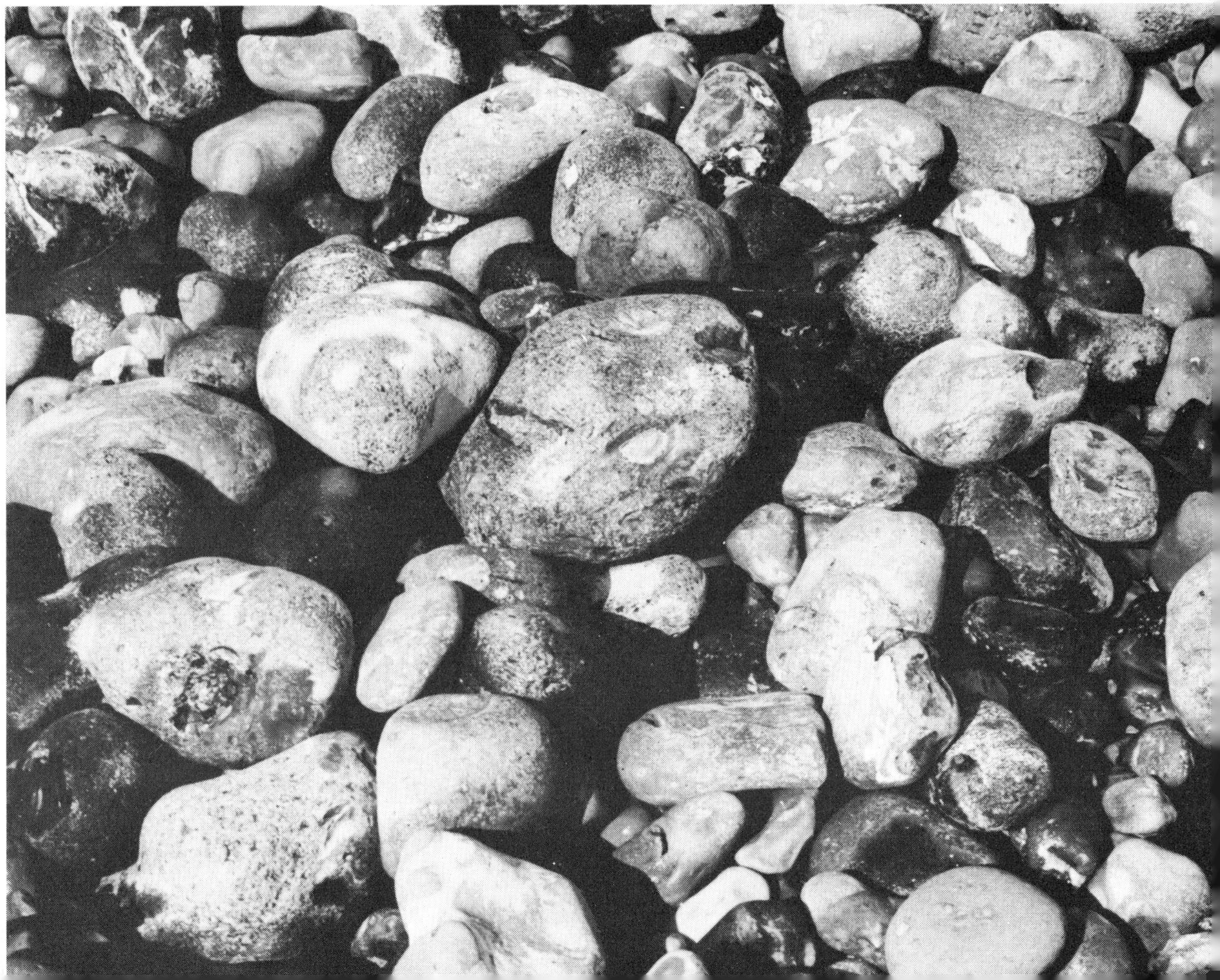

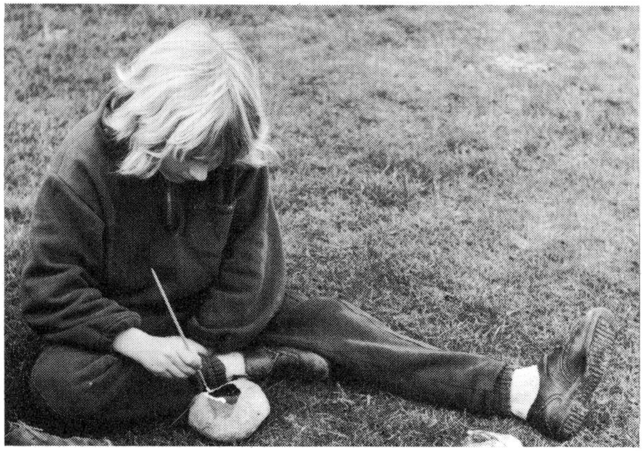

These stones are being painted in a pattern which follows the shape of the stone. This stone has a gentle curve and the painted line is curved along its shape.

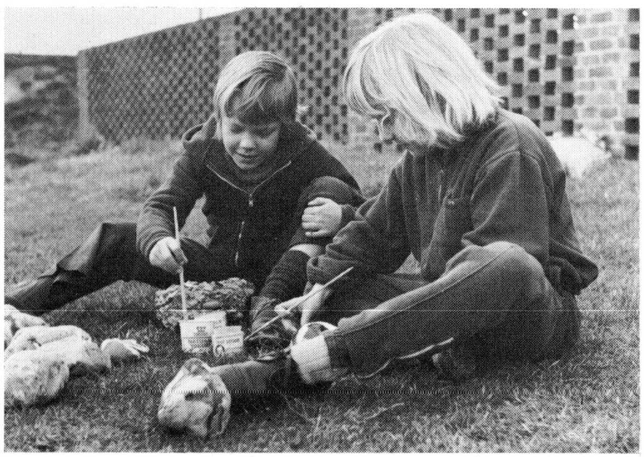

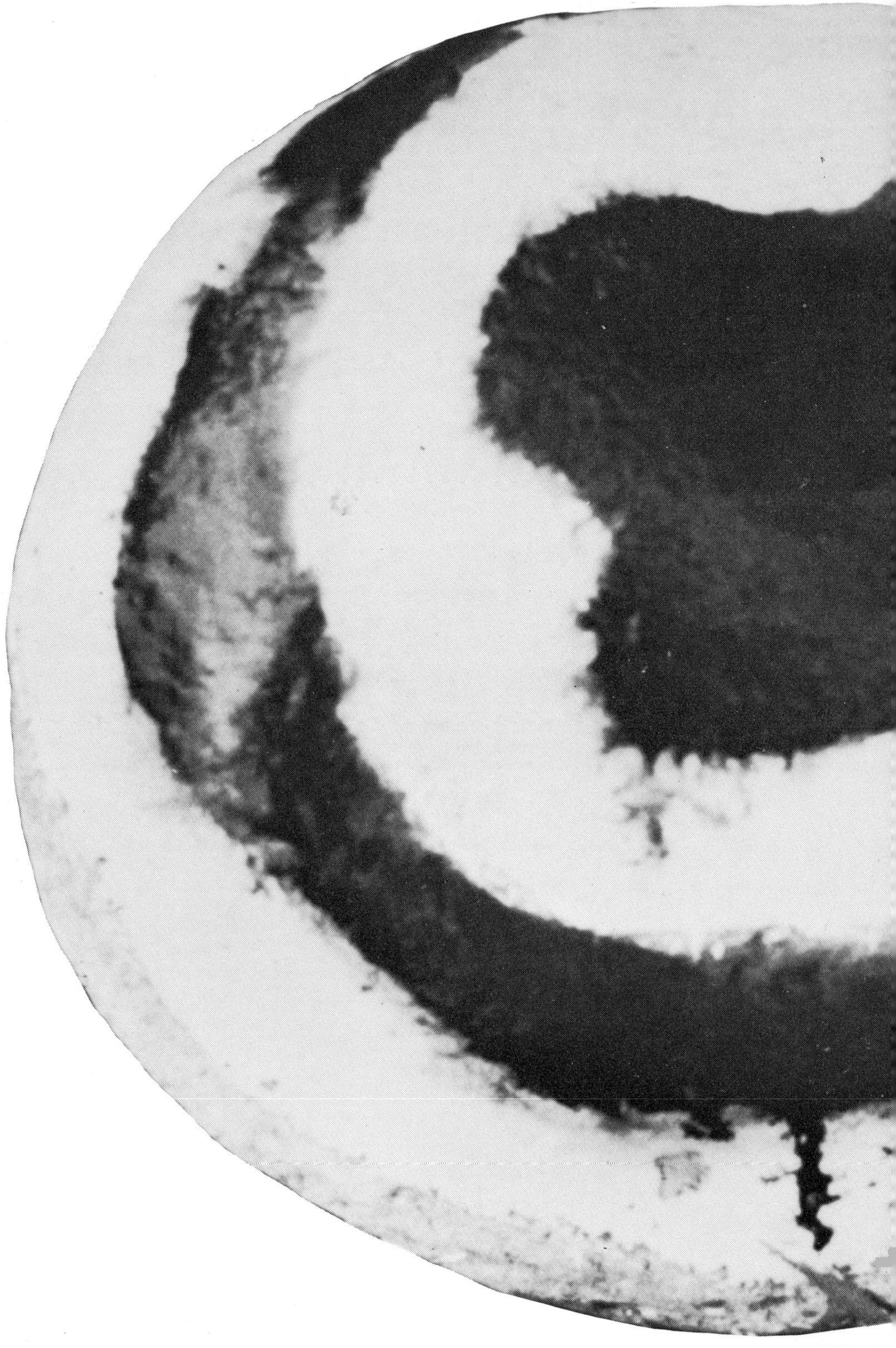

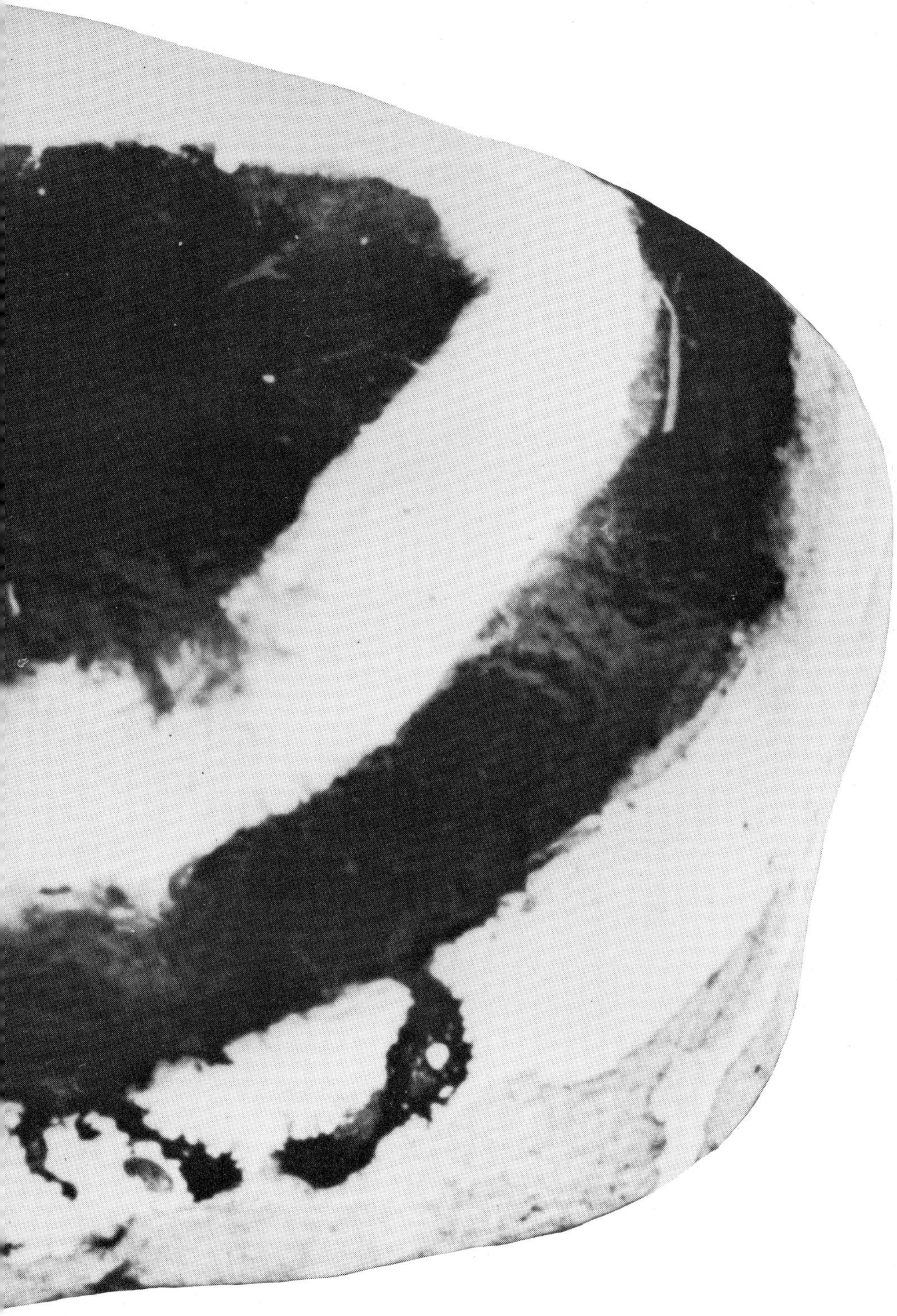

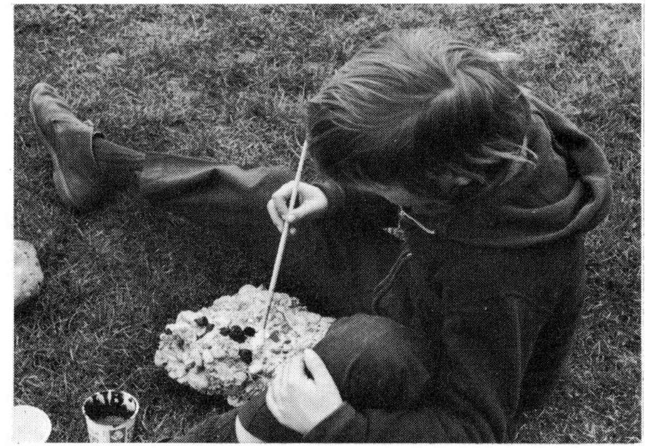

This stone is really a piece of concrete. The small pebbles are painted different colours.

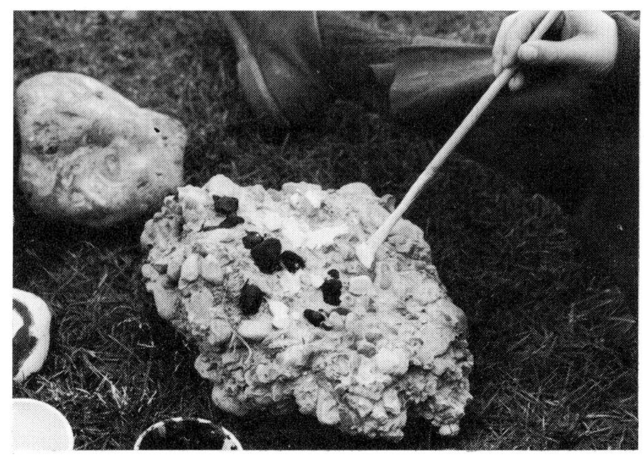

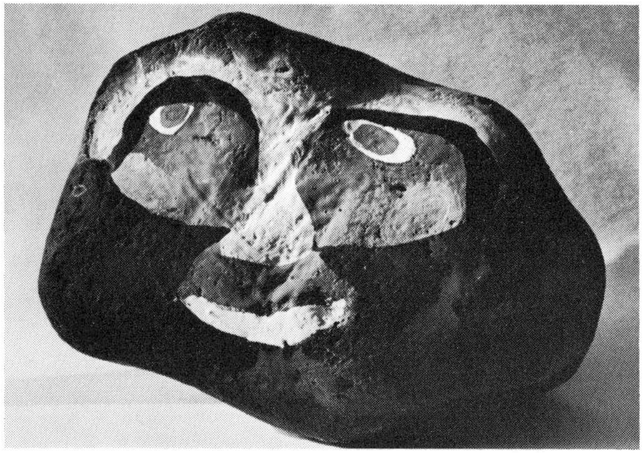

Left Here are some other stones which have been painted.

Top right A rabbit's tea party made by glueing small pebbles and shells together.

Below A painted walrus.

Bottom right A strange creature painted on stone.

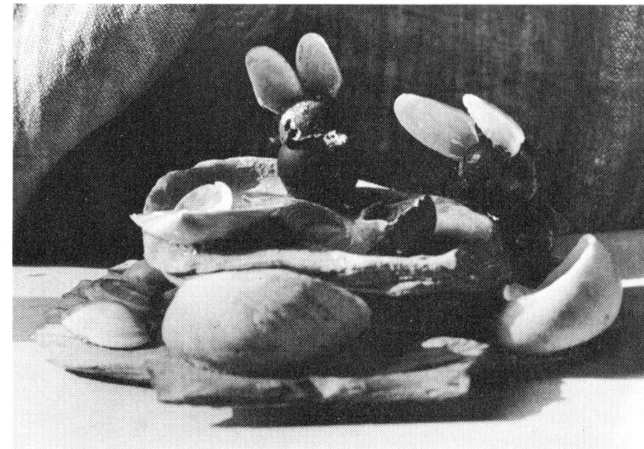

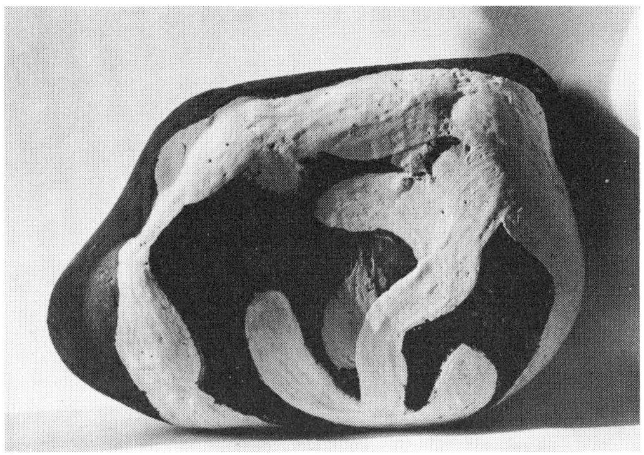

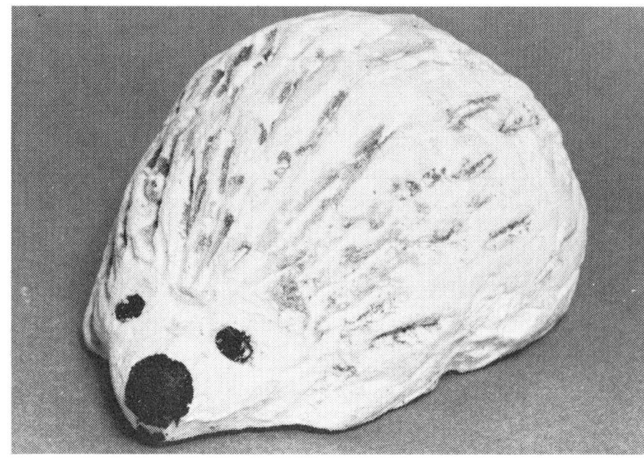

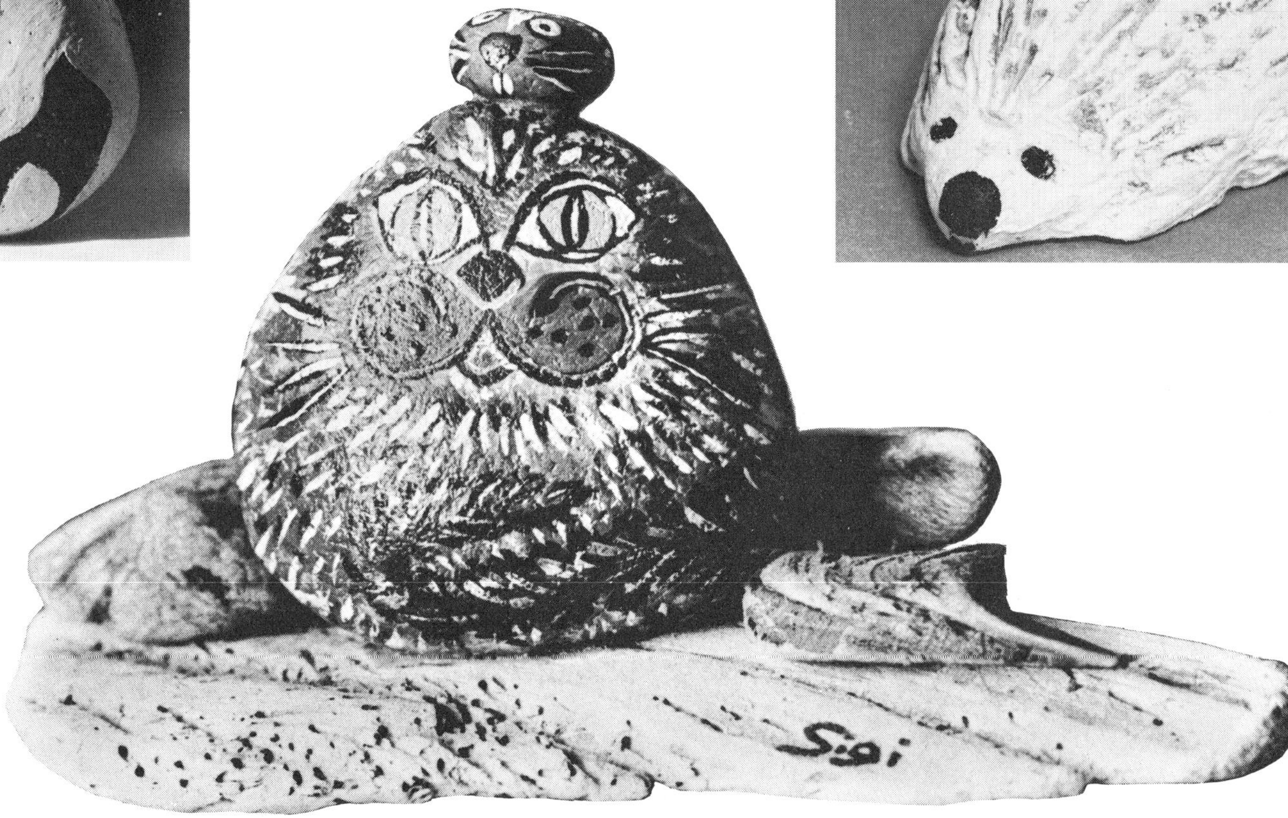

Wire

Wire is fun to use because it bends easily into shapes. Wire cutters will cut it and scissors will cut very thin wire.
You can join the shapes by twisting the ends around each other.

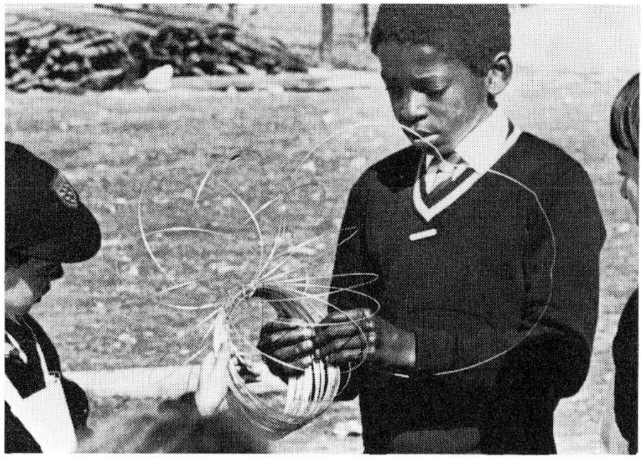

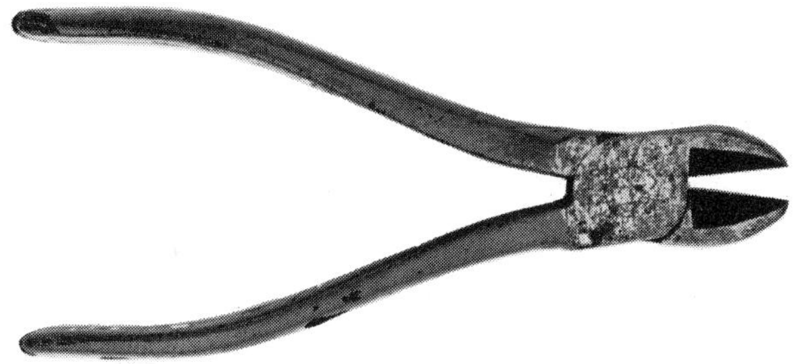

A man with glasses and a big nose.

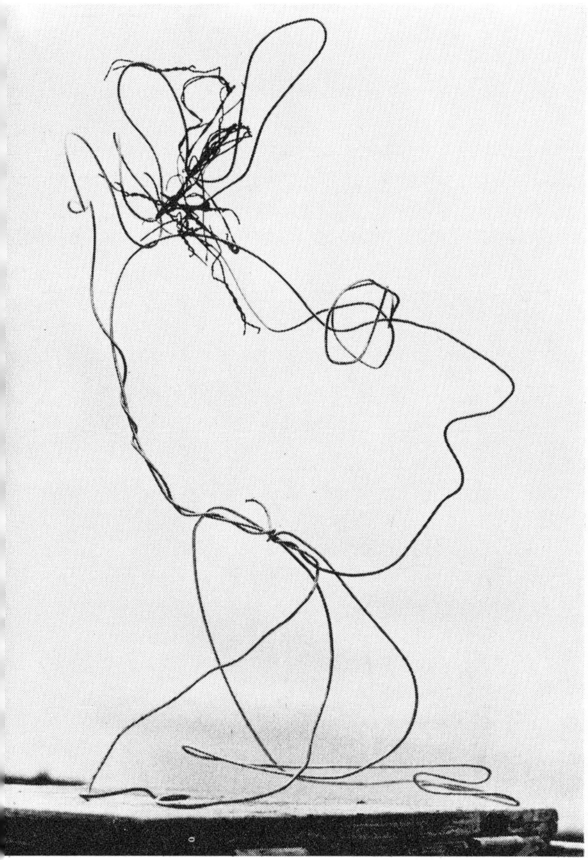

Another sculpture made with wire.

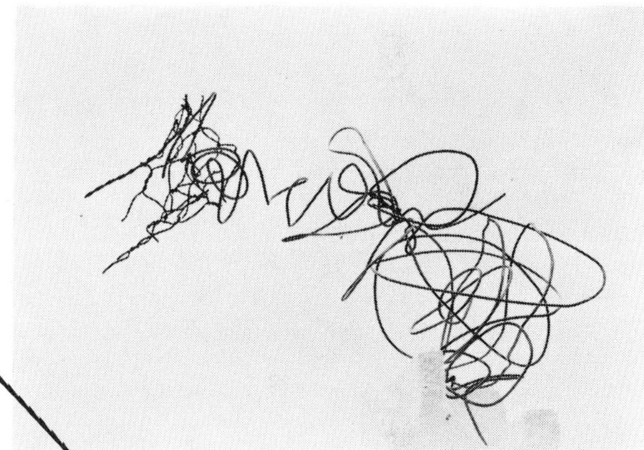

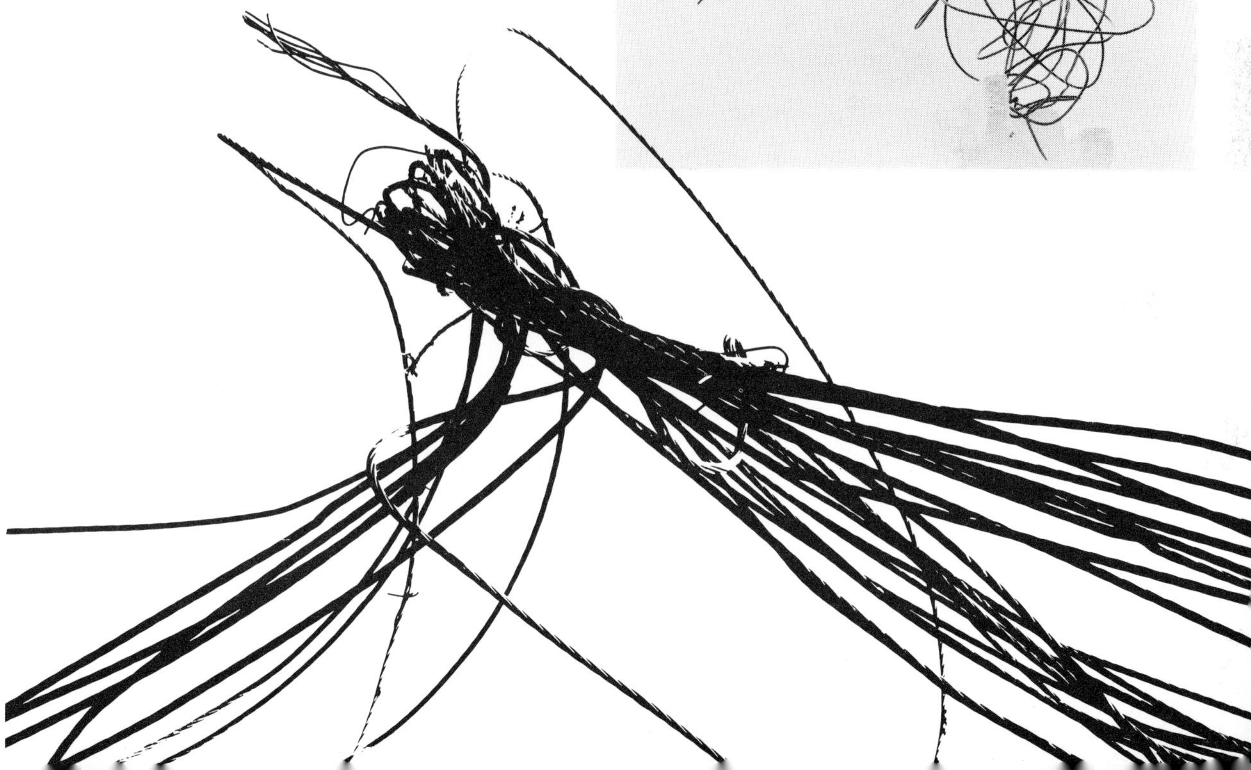

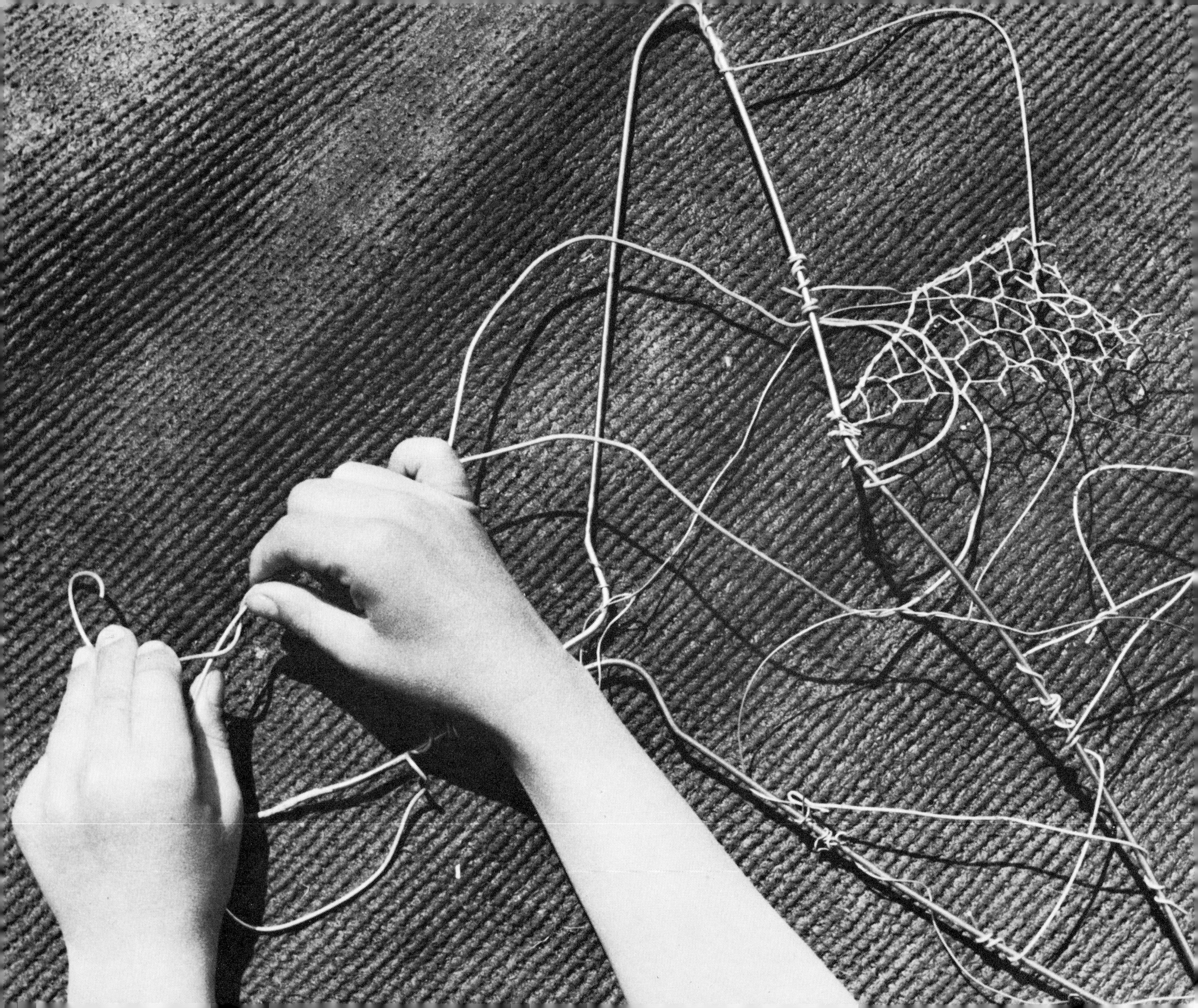

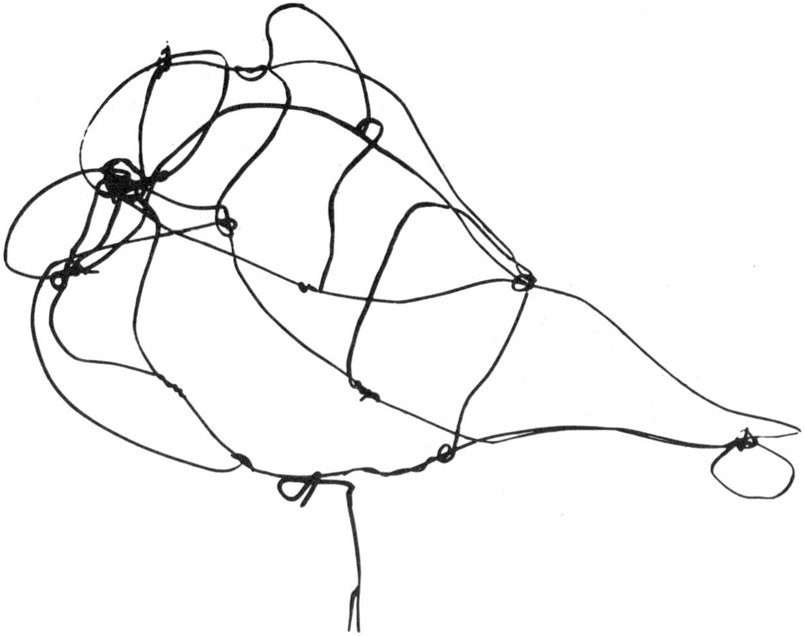

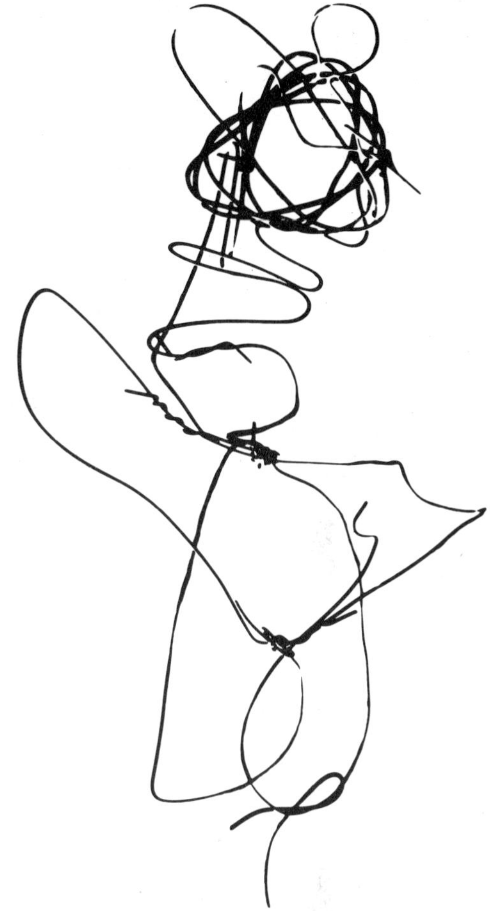

Here are various shapes made by bending and joining wire.

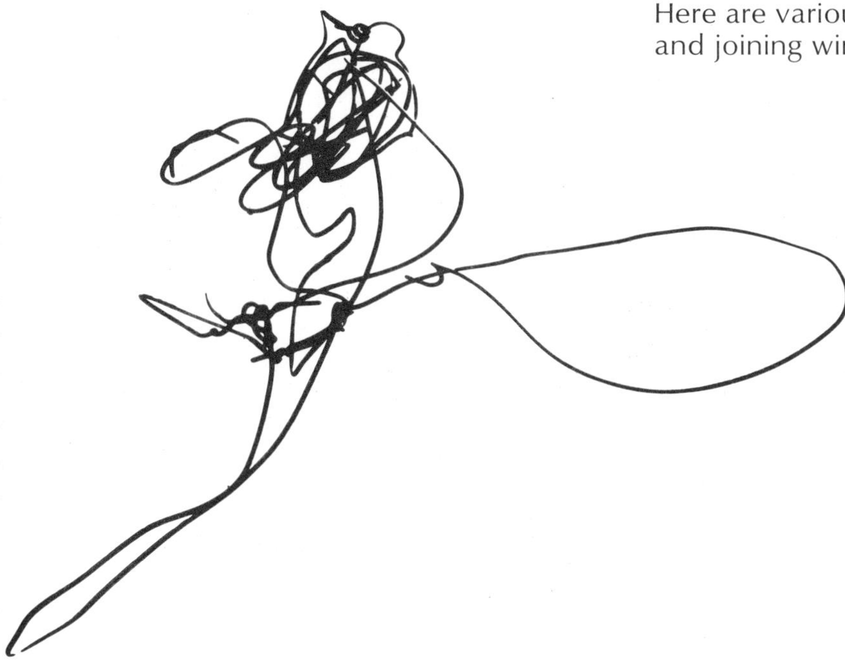

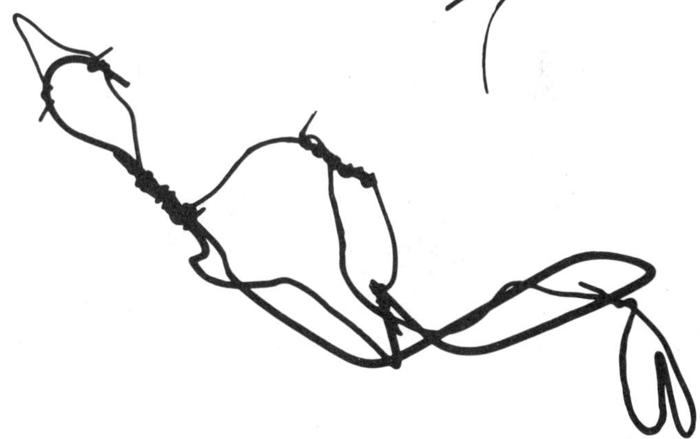

Polystyrene

Polystyrene (styrofoam) is very light and very strong when glued.

Shapes can be cut in it with a sharp knife. Pins can hold these shapes together while the glue dries.

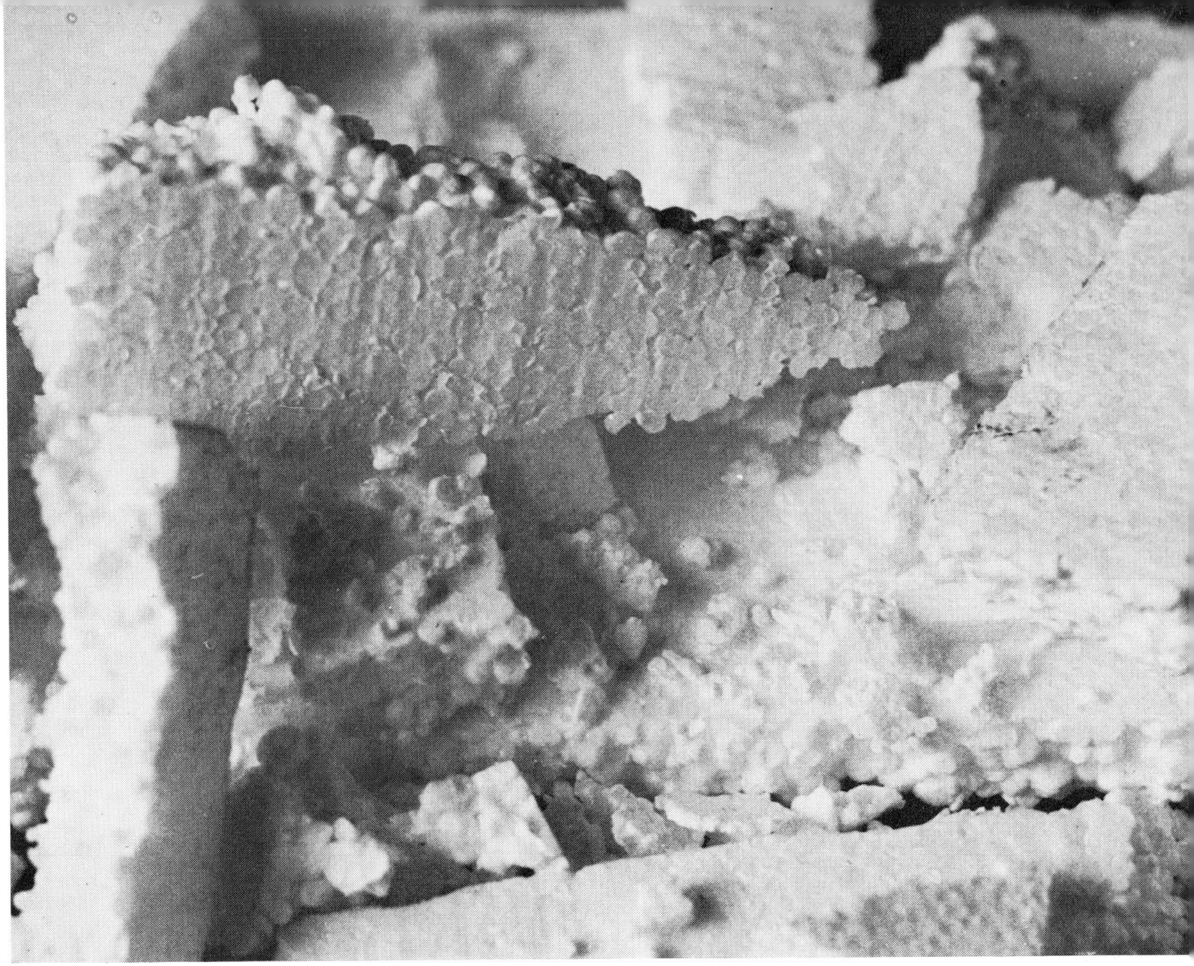

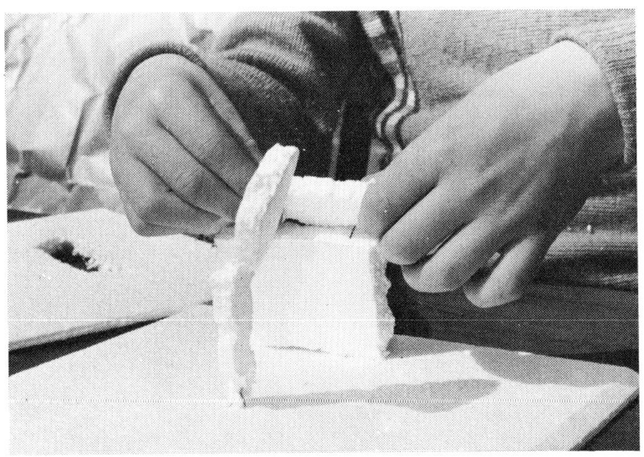

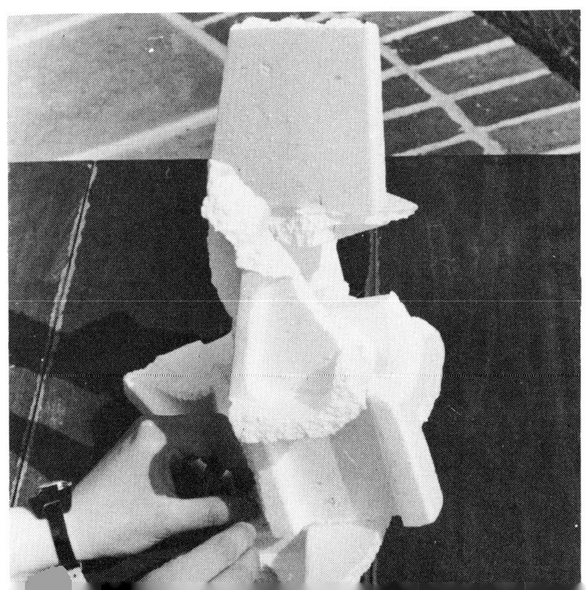

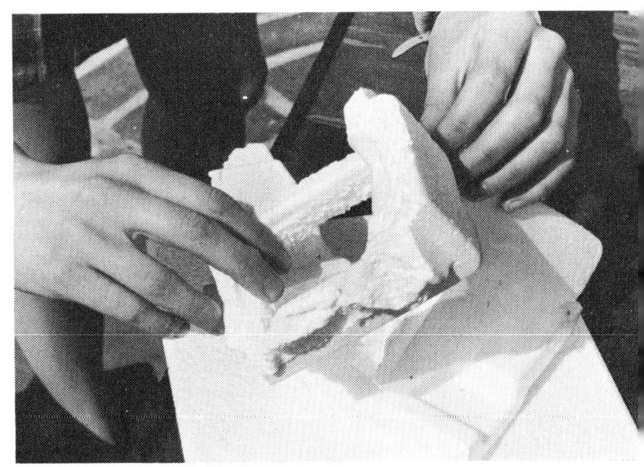

These polystyrene sculptures were made by glueing and pinning the pieces together onto a sheet of polystyrene.

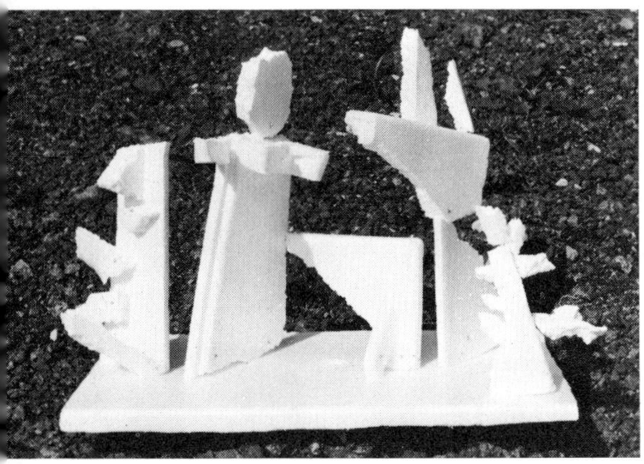

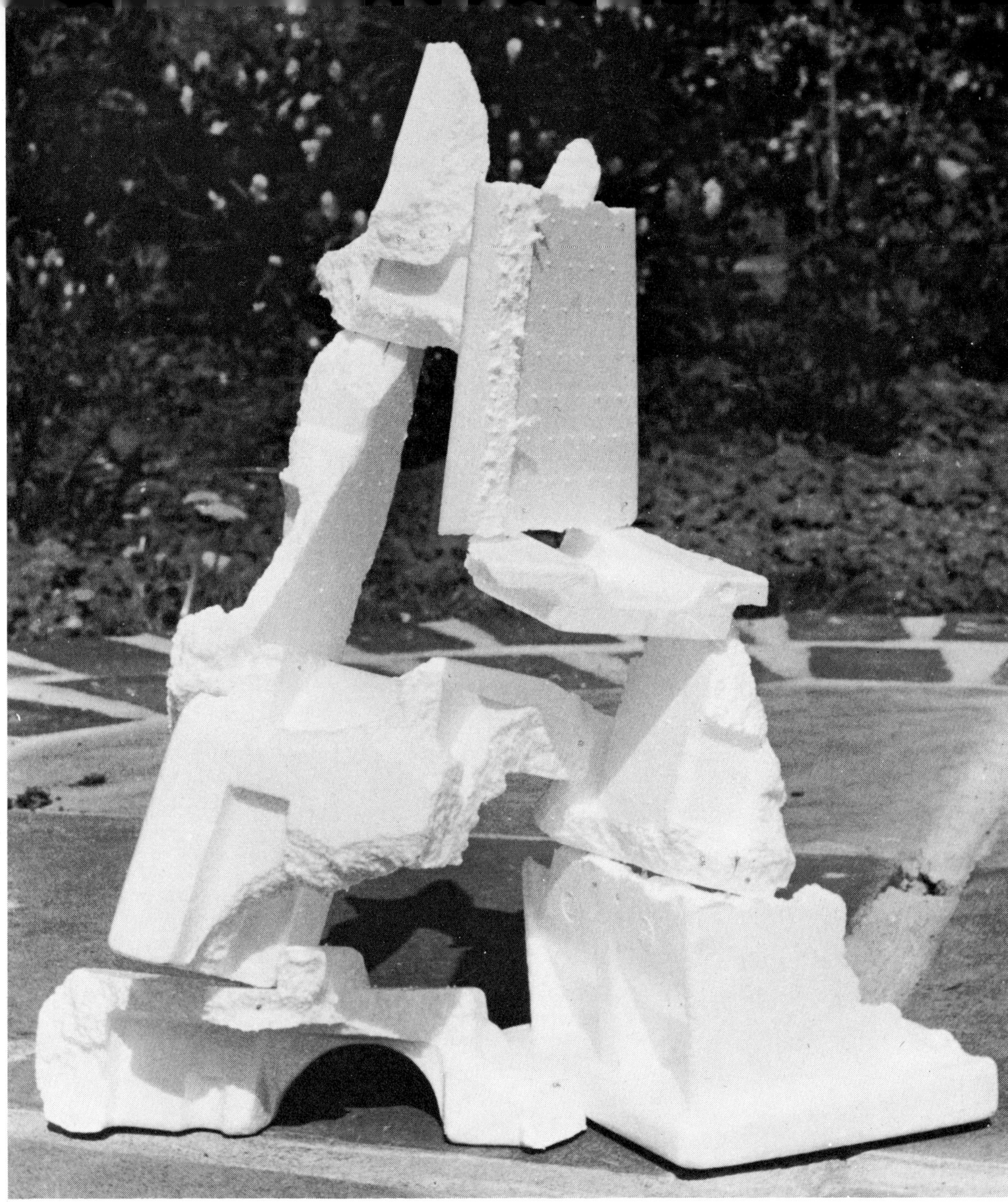

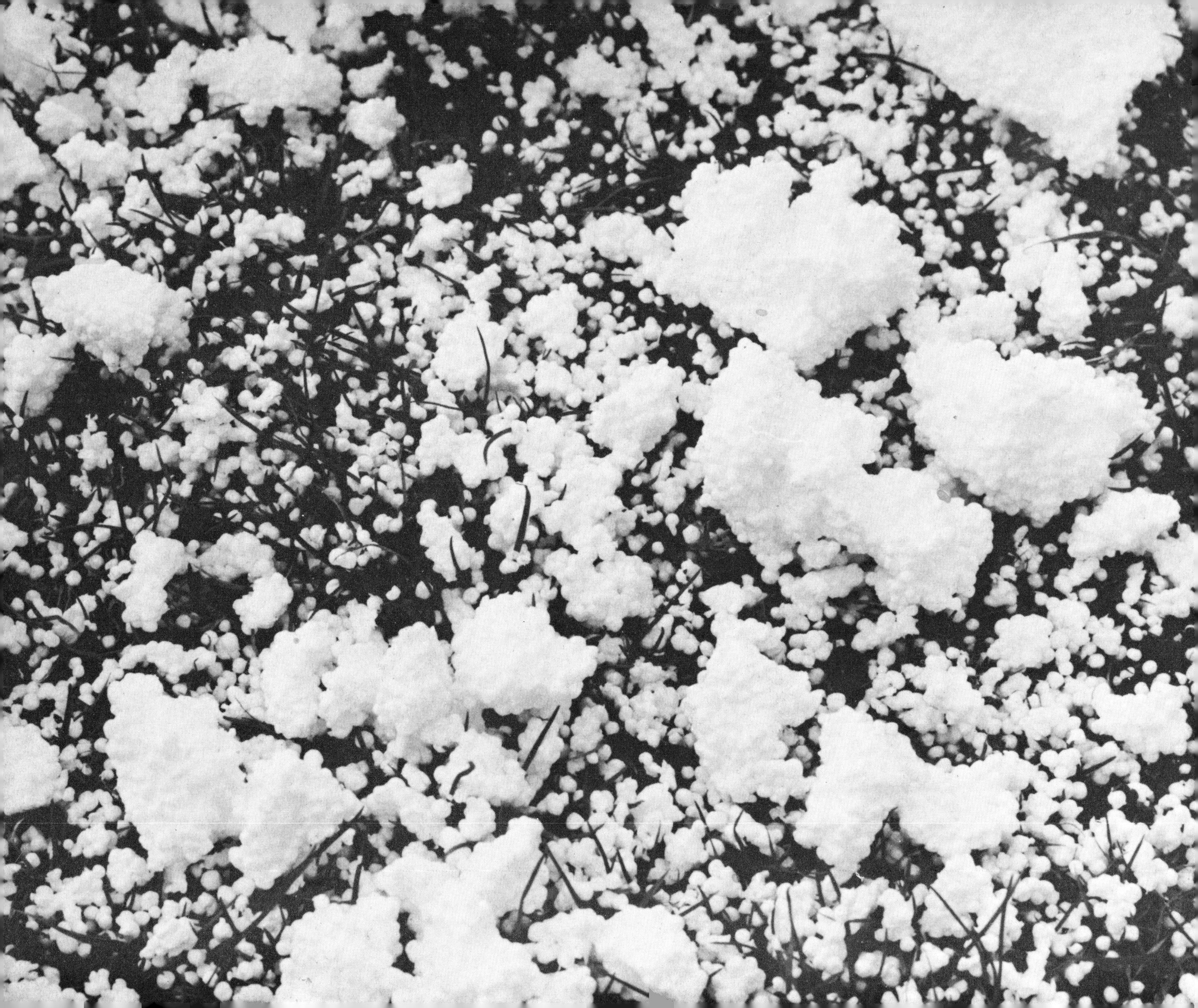

Polystyrene can be glued to many materials.

Below This sculpture was made by glueing the cardboard shapes together and then glueing bubbles of polystyrene to it.

Below right Another polystyrene and cardboard sculpture being made.

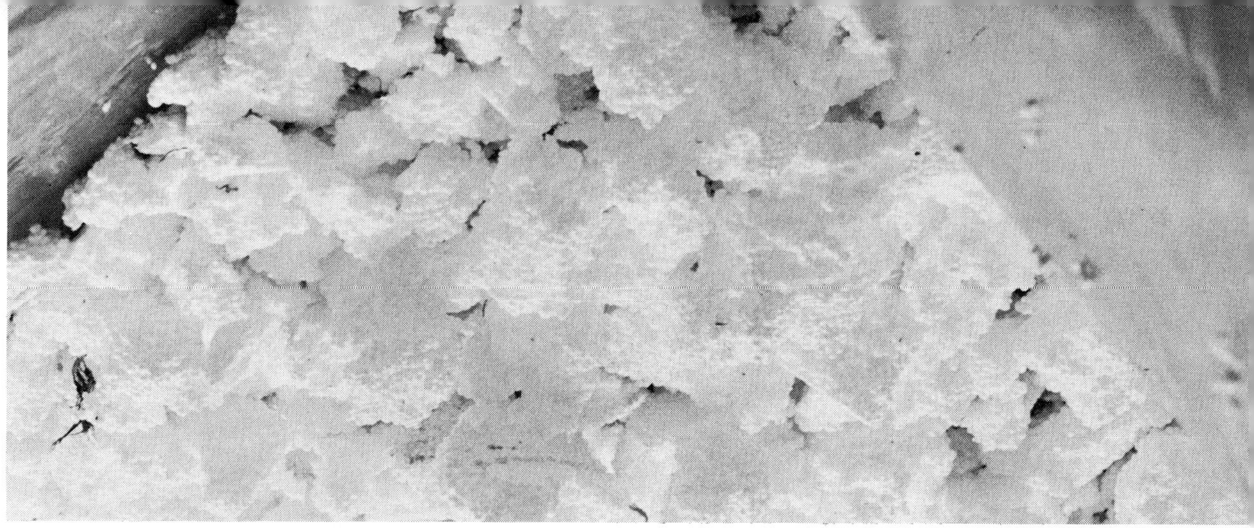

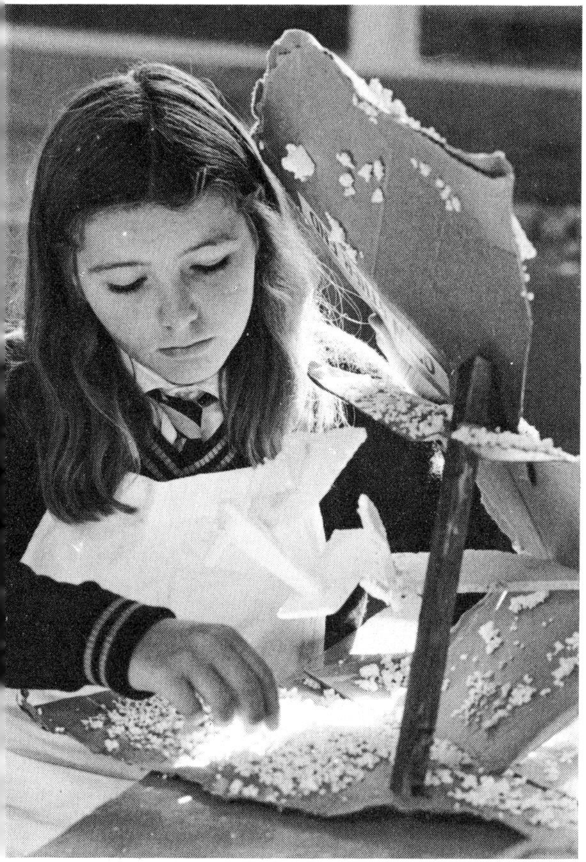

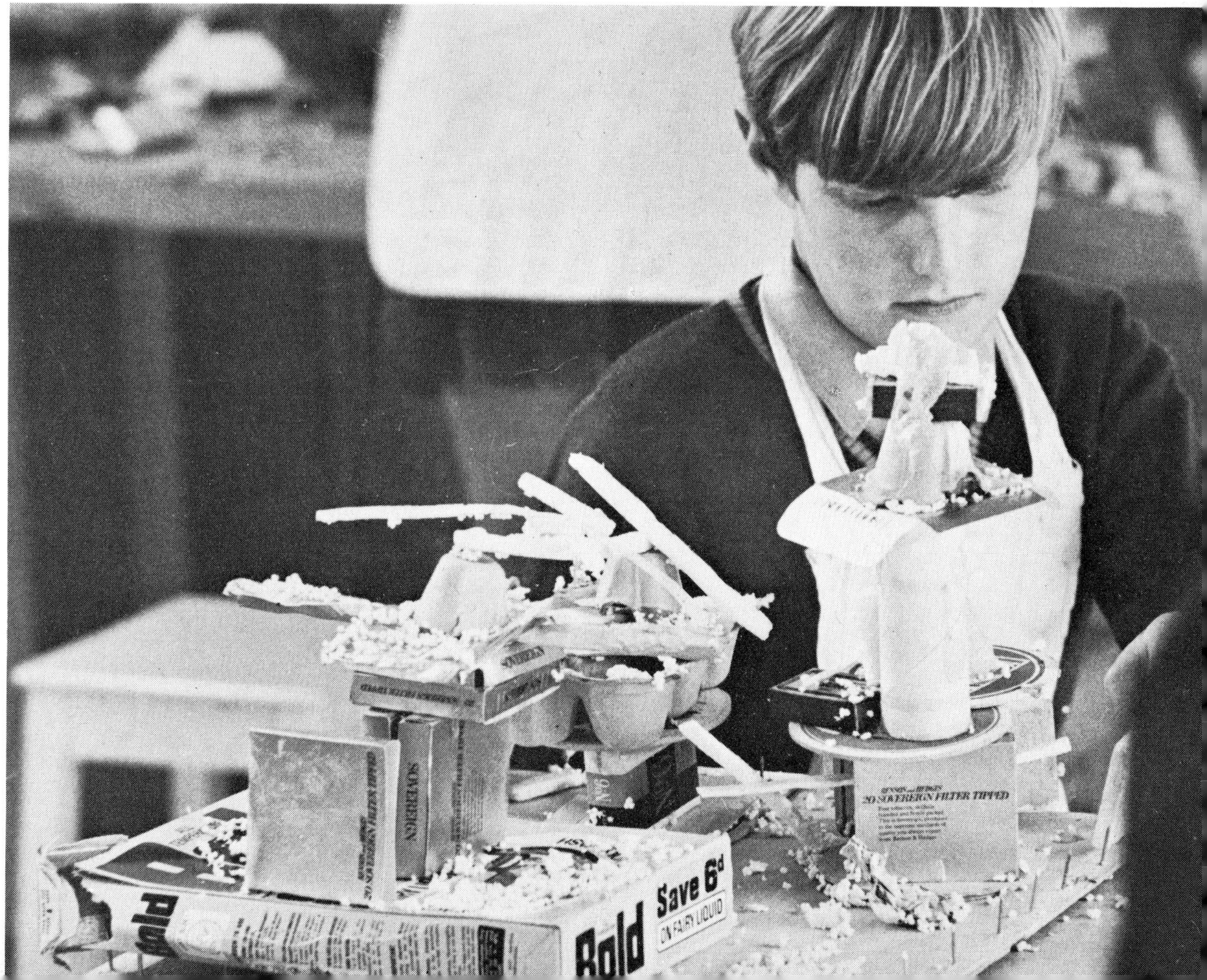

Paper

Paper is made from wood. When we add glue to it, it becomes strong again.
Paper is a very good material to use for sculpture. It is light and easy to cut and shape.

Bottom left This face is being made by glueing tissue paper over a cardboard box.

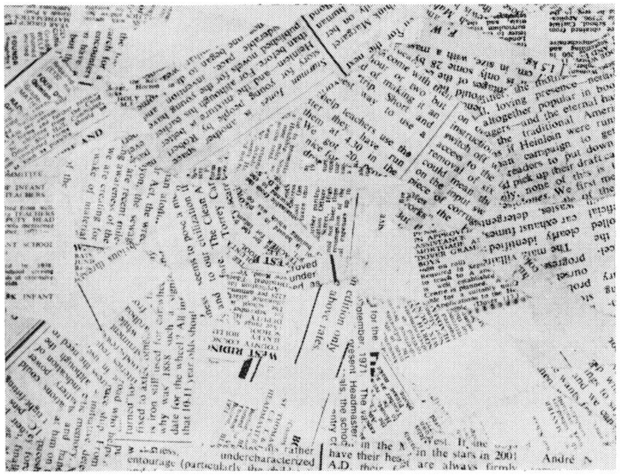

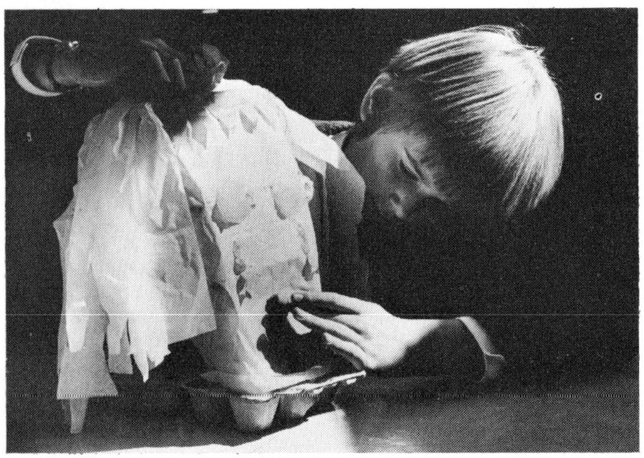

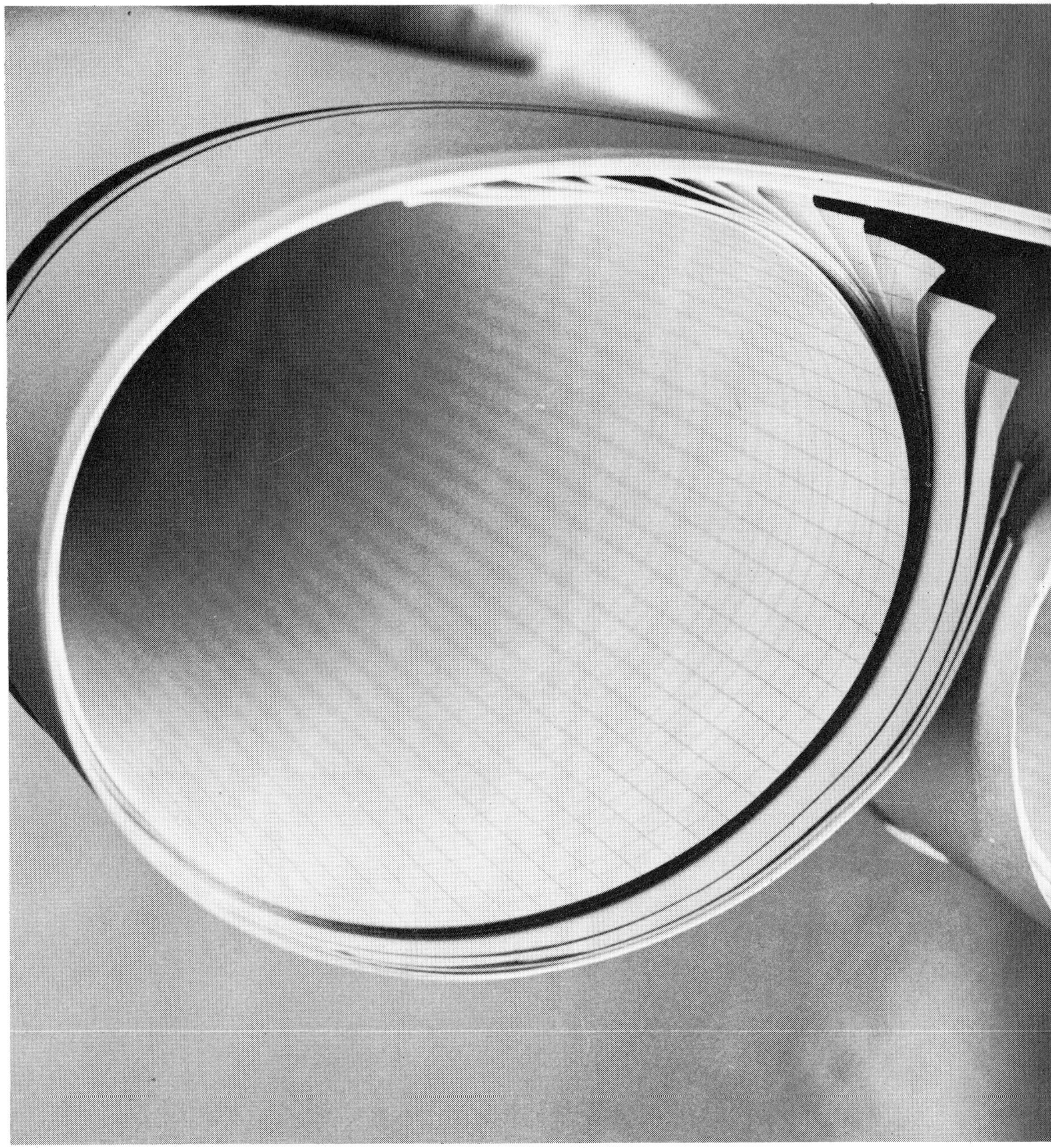

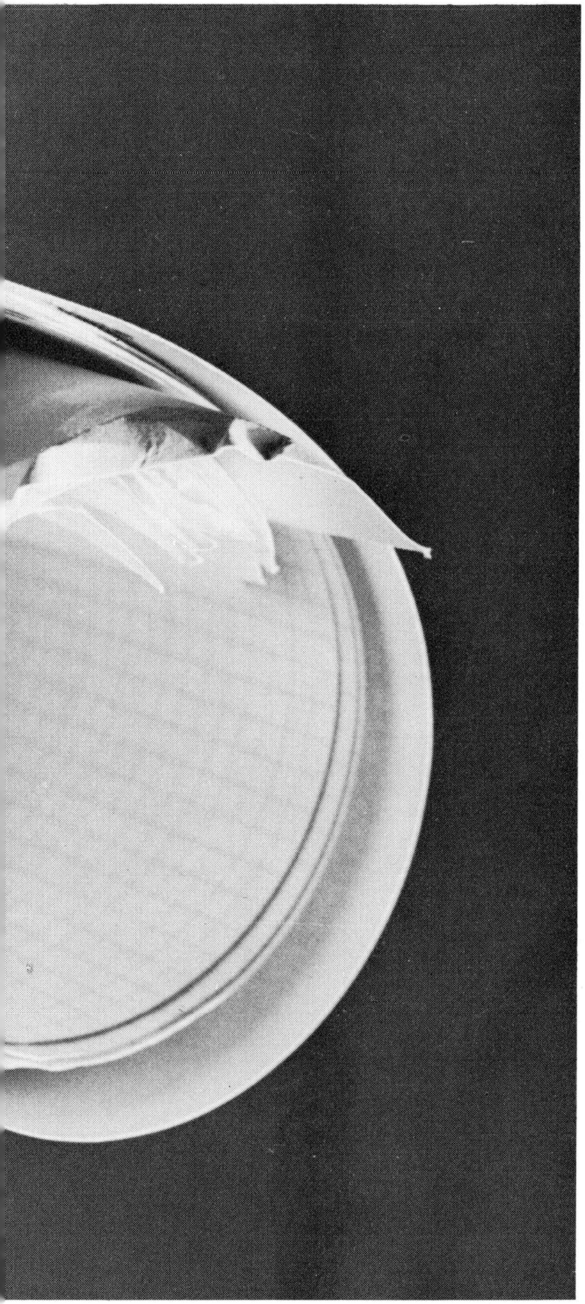

Right Here layers of newspaper strips are being wrapped around a balloon. The paper is first dipped in glue.
When it is dry, more strips are added. When the paper feels strong the balloon is burst with a pin.

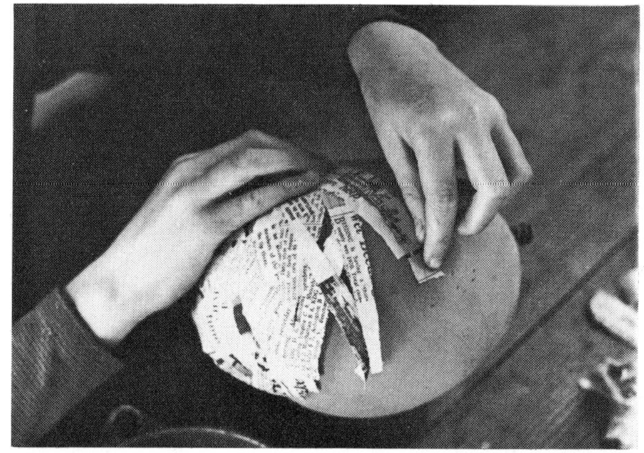

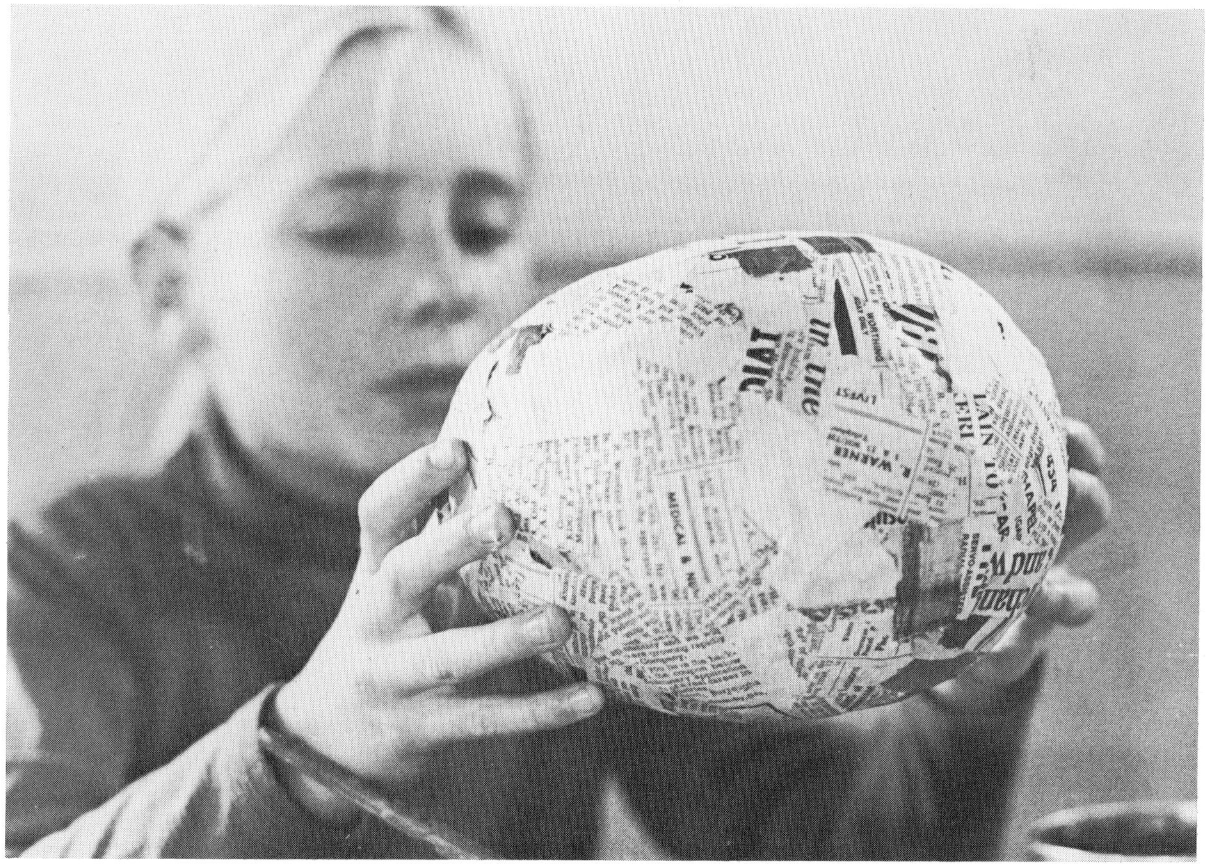

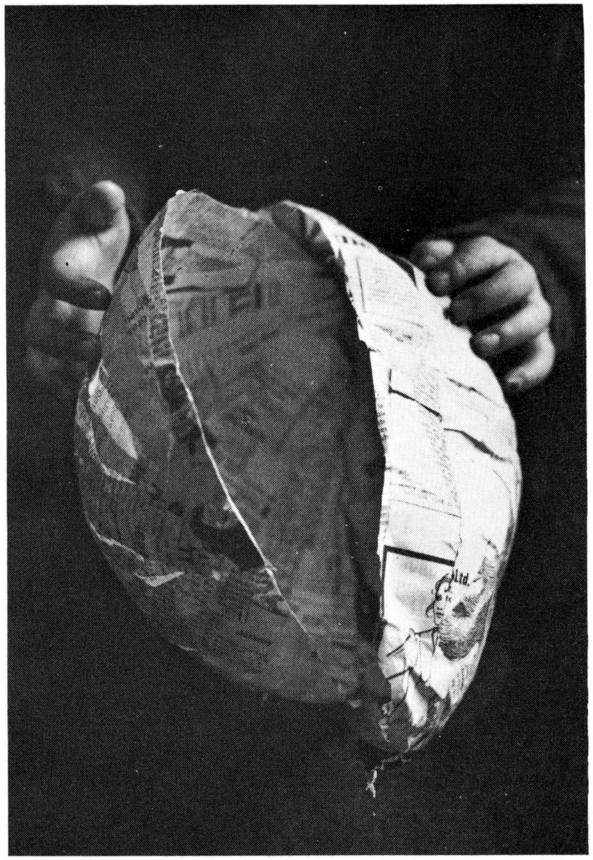

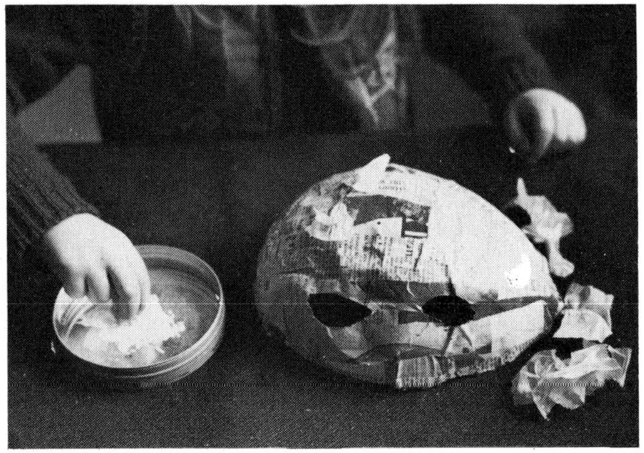

It is easy to make a mask from a paper balloon.
A paper balloon is cut in half with scissors.
Eyes are cut out and tissue paper is glued on to it.

Right A paper helmet with silver paper glued on to it.

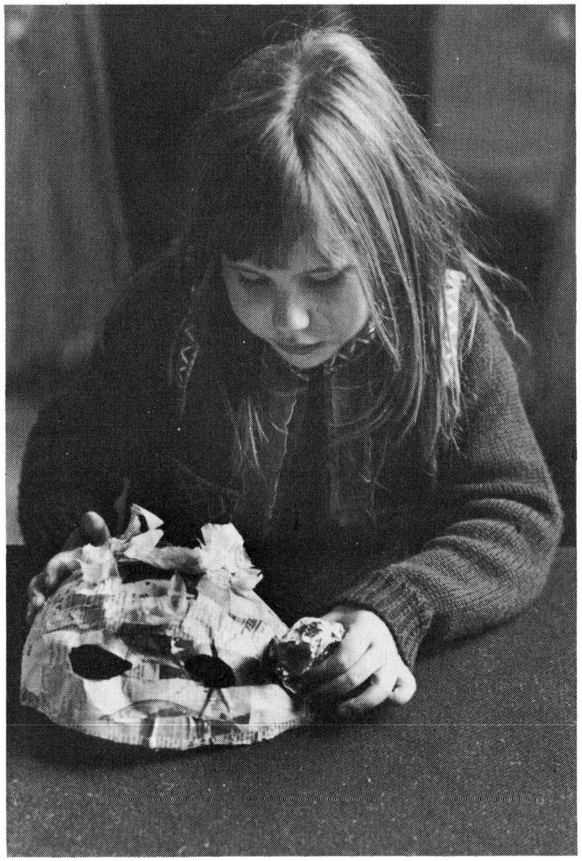

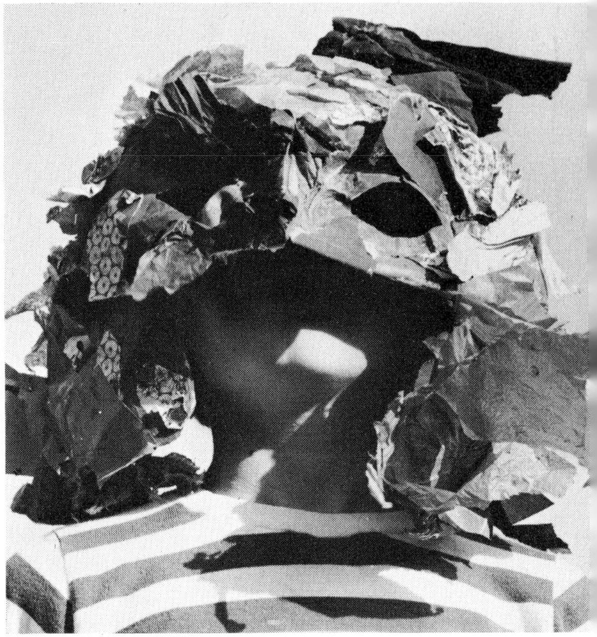

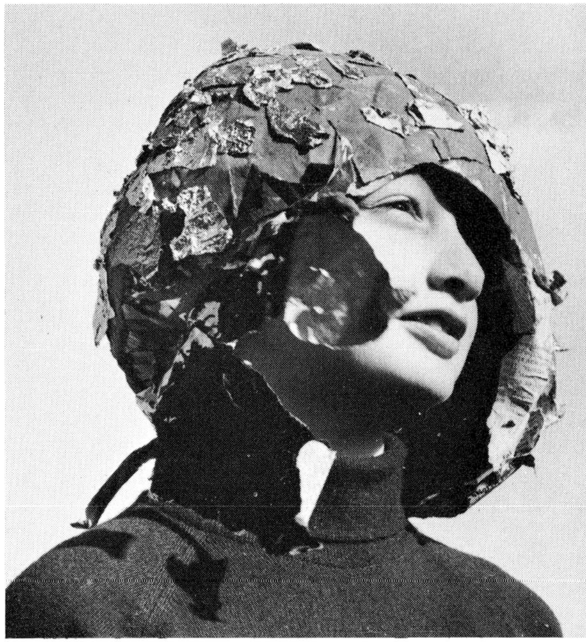

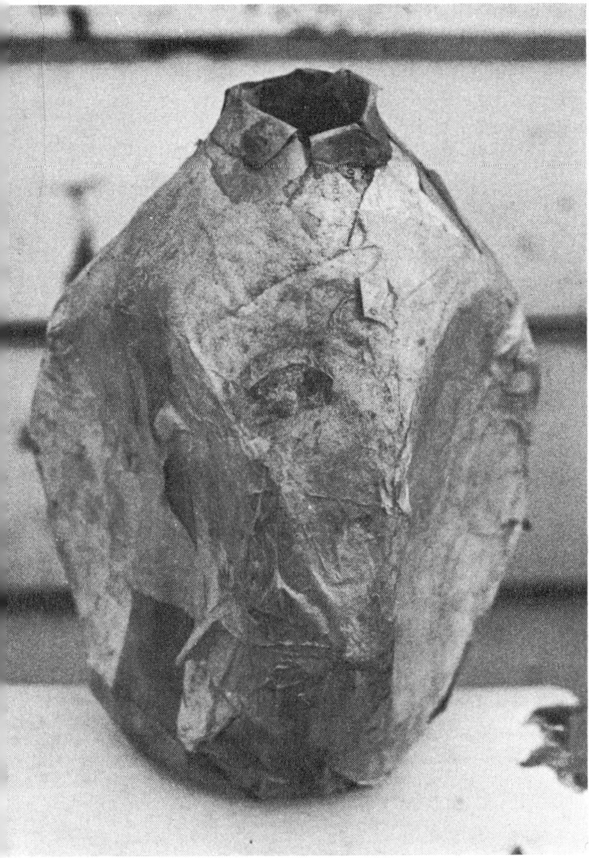

Paper can also be glued over other shapes.

Above You can easily make a paper shape of a bottle.
First grease a bottle with oil or Vaseline. Then glue layers of paper over it. When it is dry, cut the paper down the sides of the bottle and gently remove each half from the bottle. Glue the two halves together by adding more paper.

Right This paper head was made by glueing strips of paper over a head of clay after it was greased. When it was dry, it was painted.

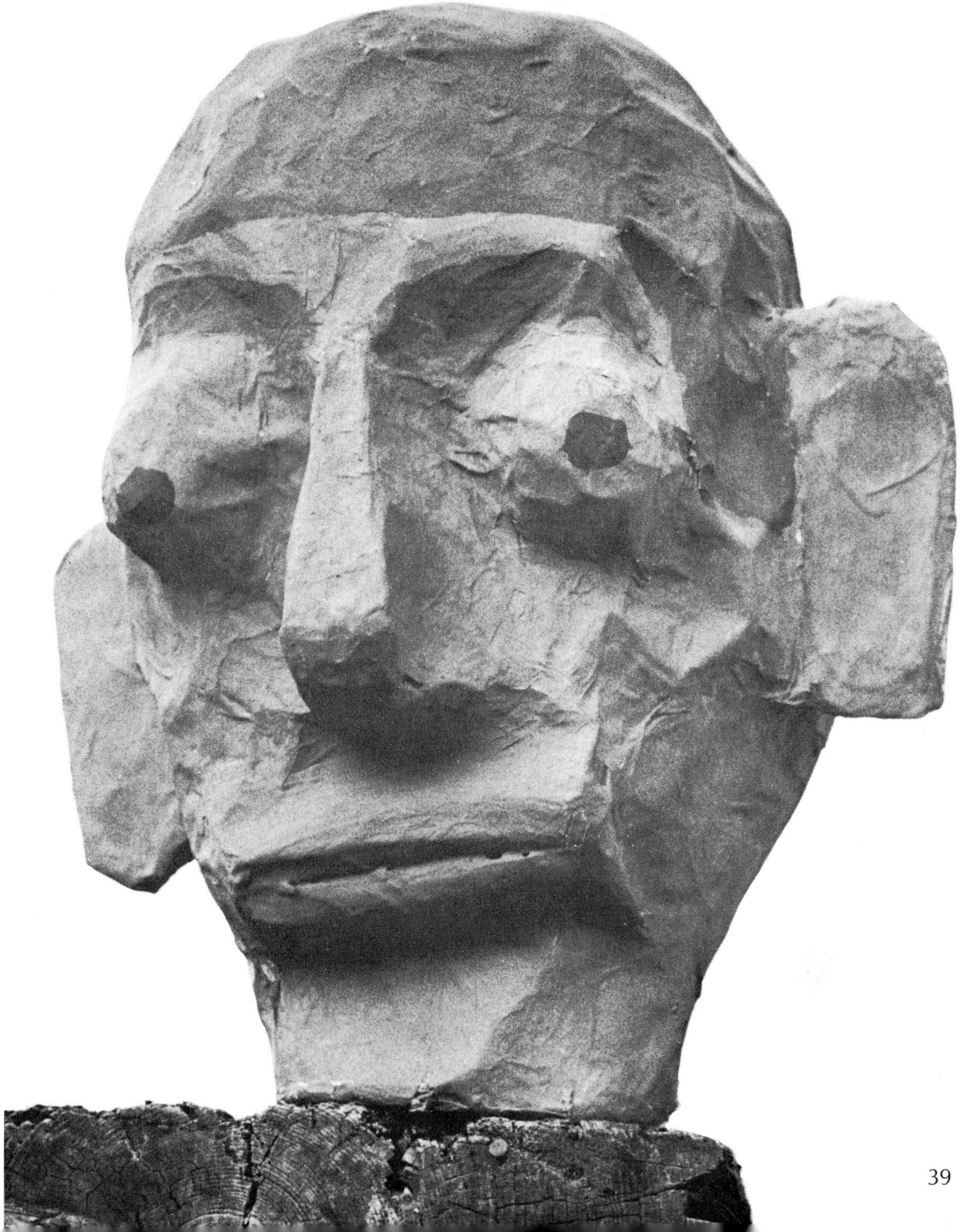

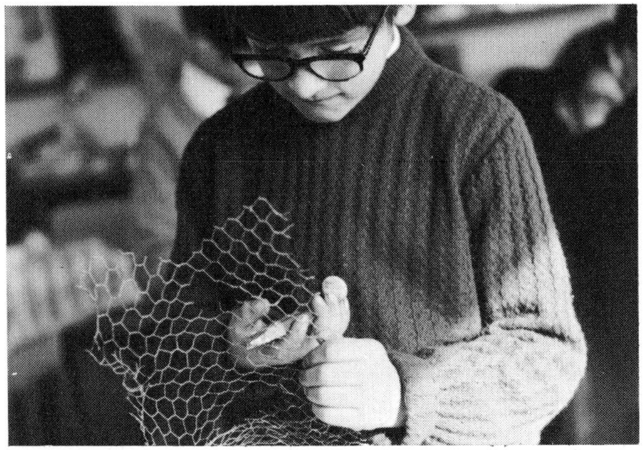

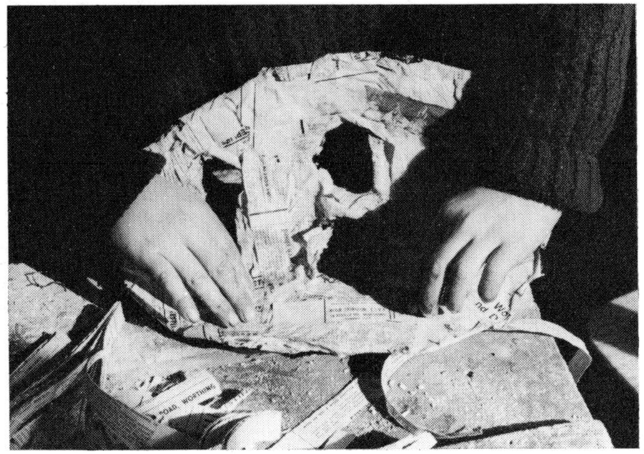

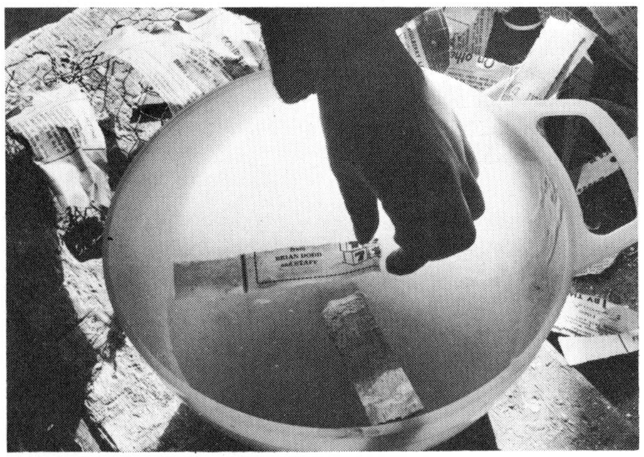

You can make paper masks and shapes using wire as a base.
First make a wire shape and cut out holes with wire cutters.
Dip strips of newspaper into glue and cover the wire shape with enough layers to make it strong.
When the paper dries, it can be painted.

Right The finished paper mask.

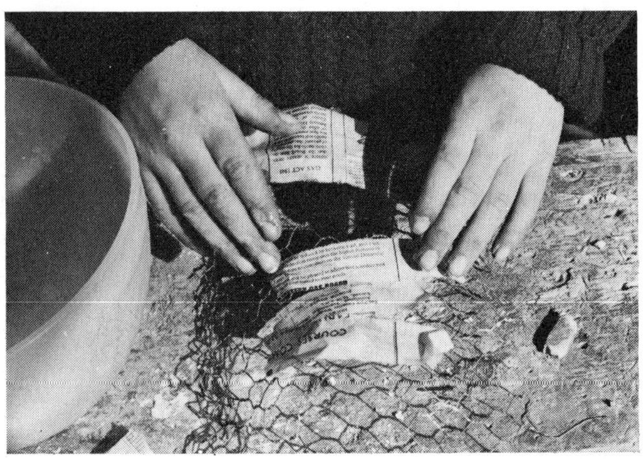

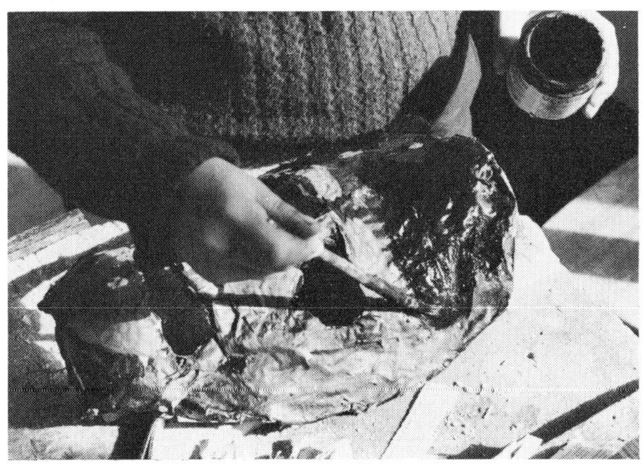

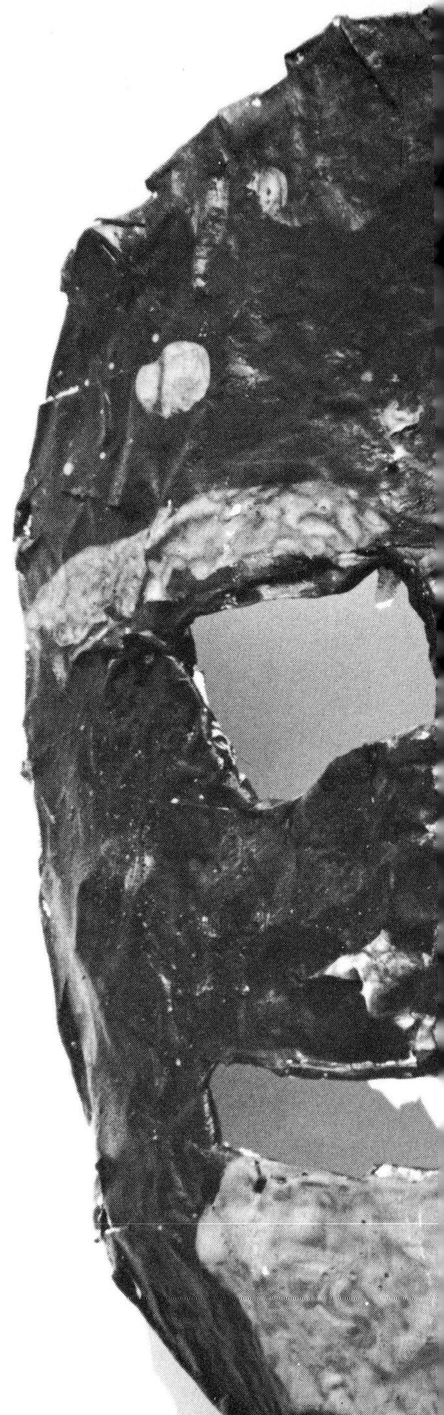

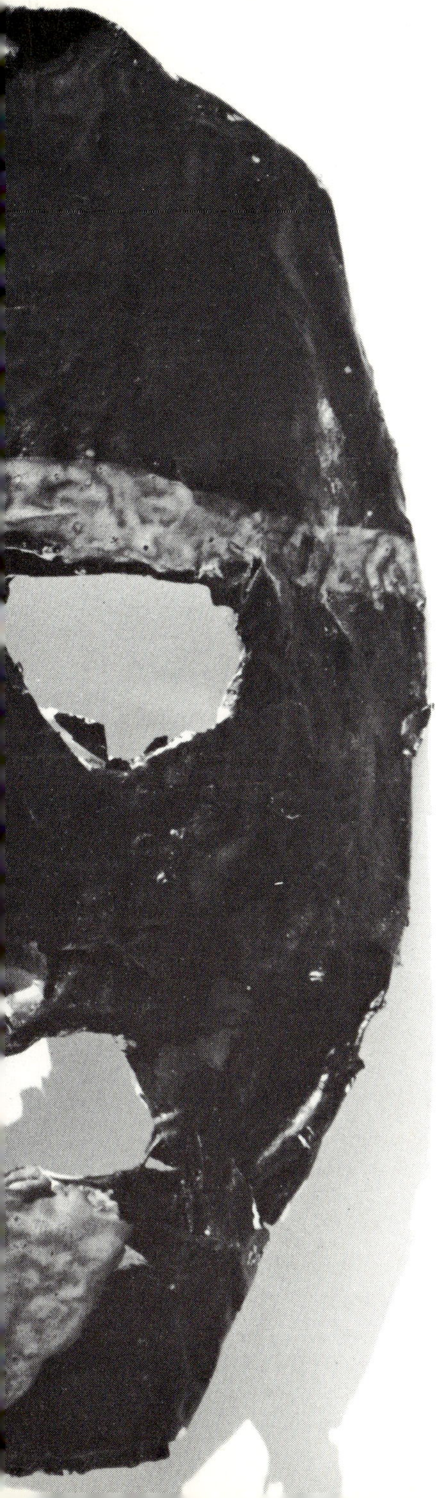

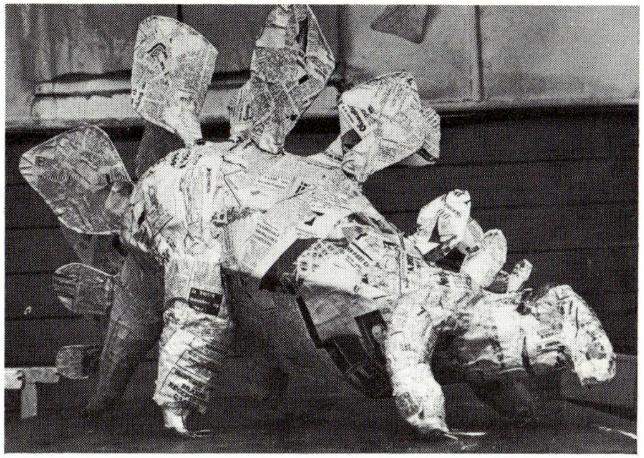

Above A dinosaur made by glueing paper over wire.

Below A cat made in this way with bits of fur glued on and wire whiskers.

Right This giraffe was also made by glueing strips of paper over chicken wire. Here it is being painted.

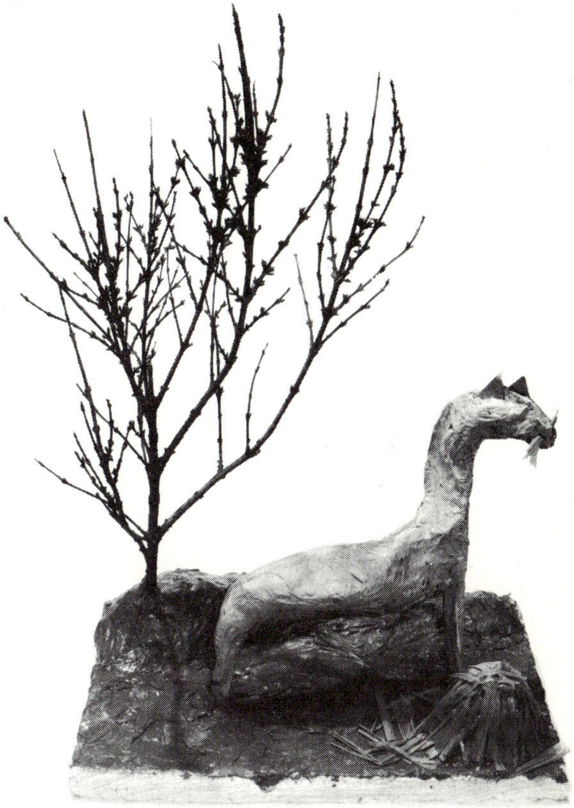

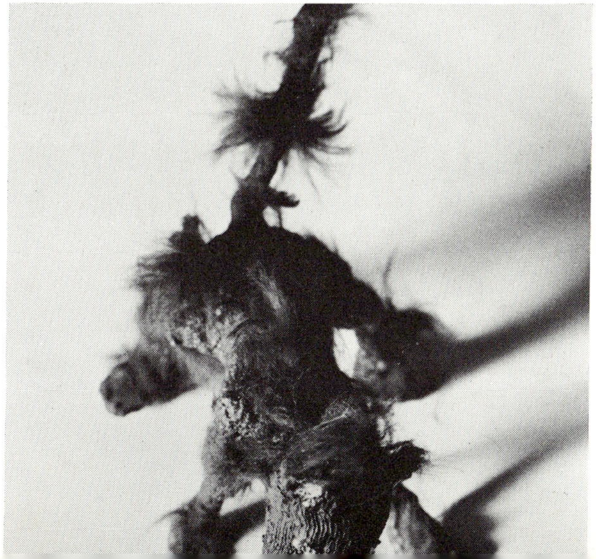

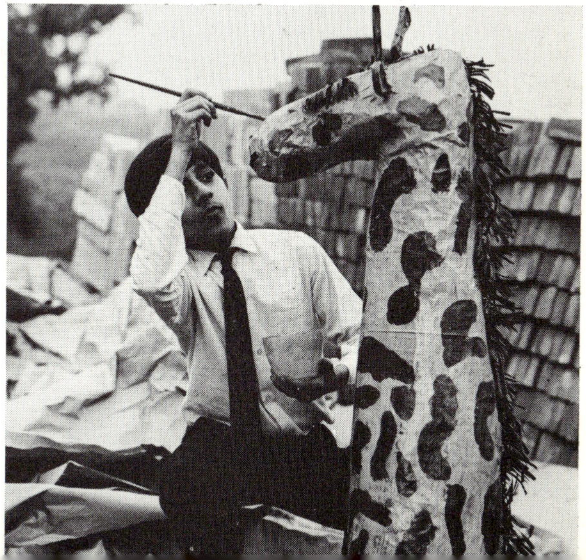

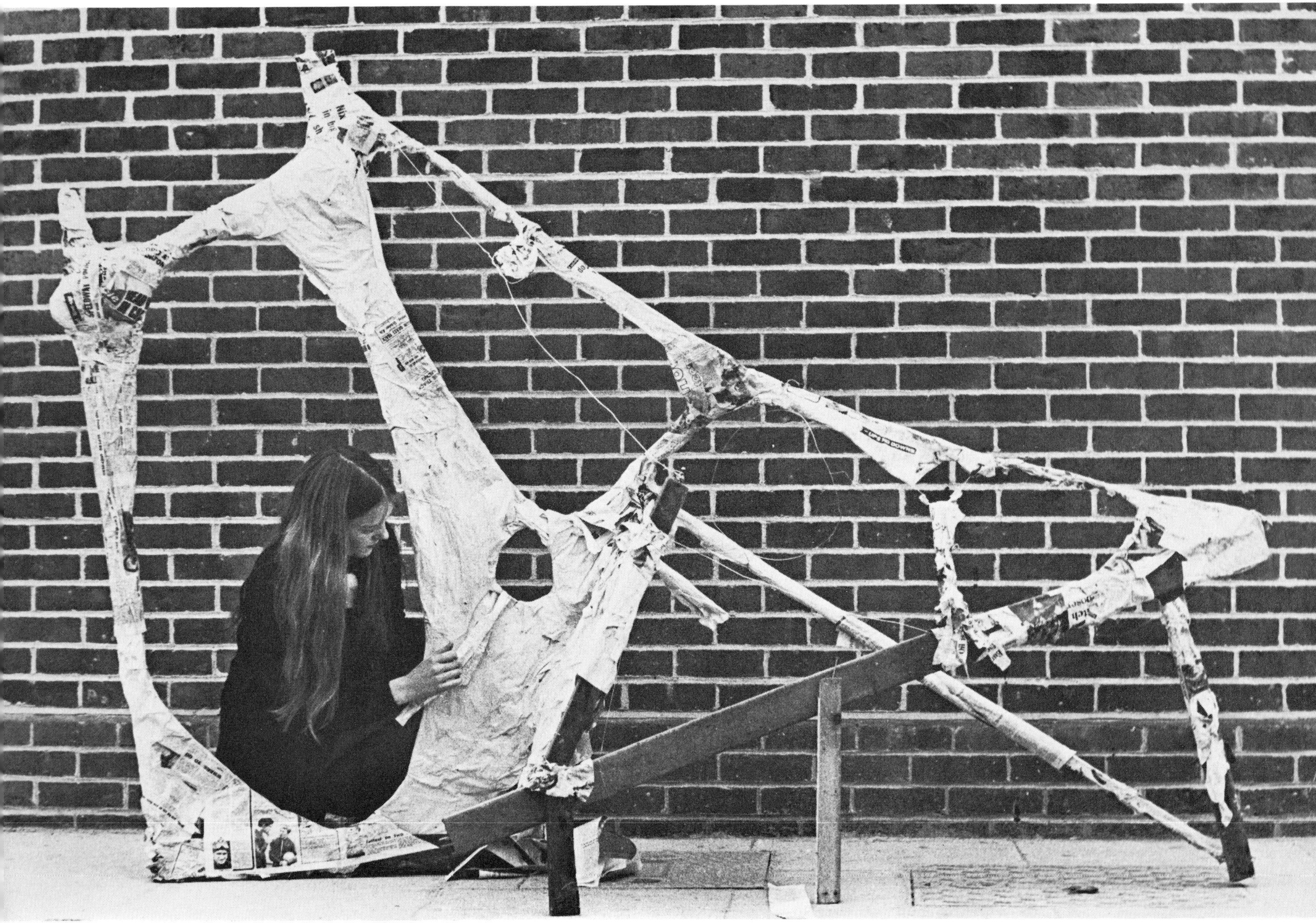

Opposite You can use paper and wood too. This was made by nailing together old scraps of wood.
Paper is being wrapped around the wood with glue.

This bird costume is made with crêpe paper, cardboard, glue and tape. It was designed by eleven-year-old David Glass.

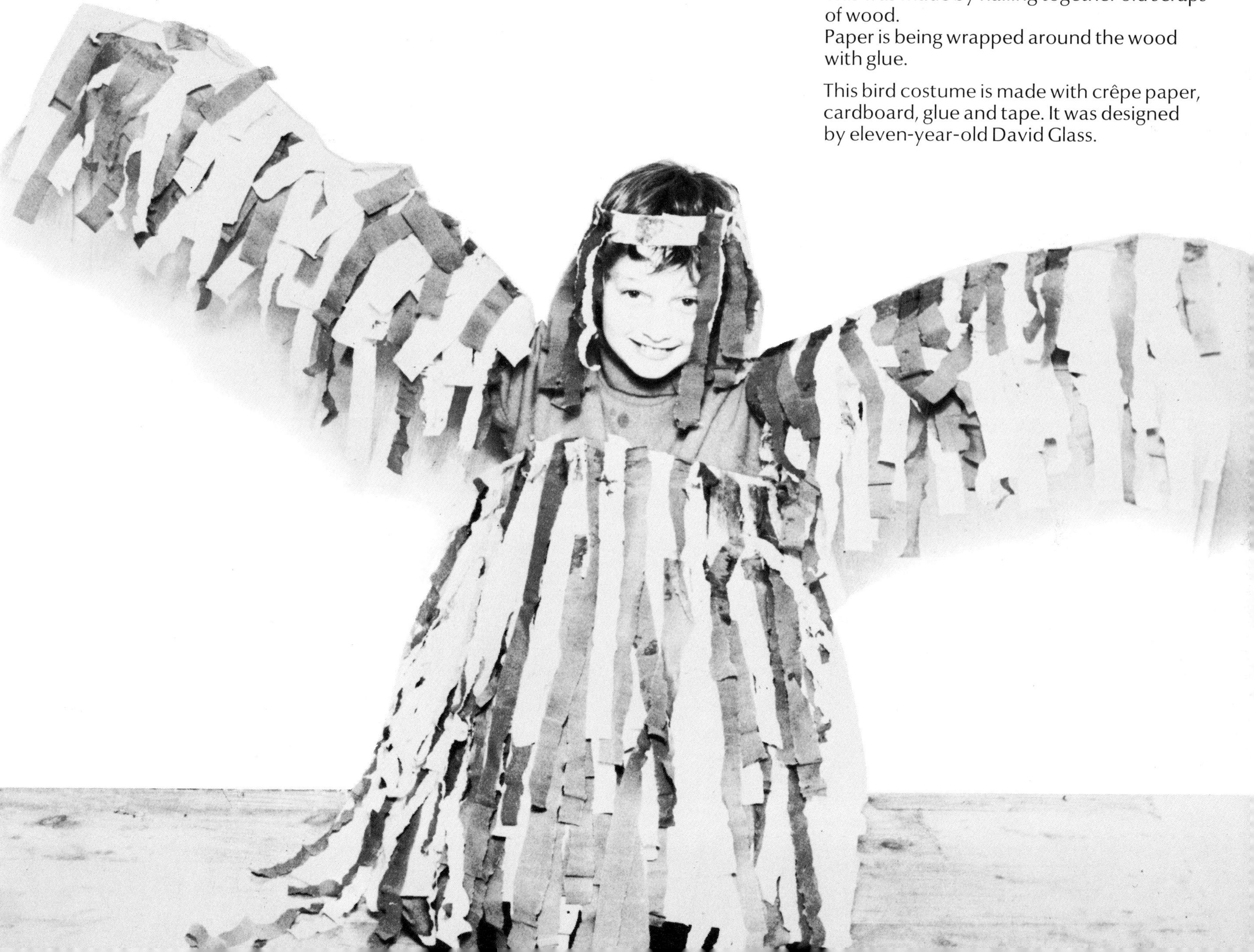

Wood

Scrap pieces of wood can be made into sculpture with a hammer and nails.

Here wood sculpture is being made.

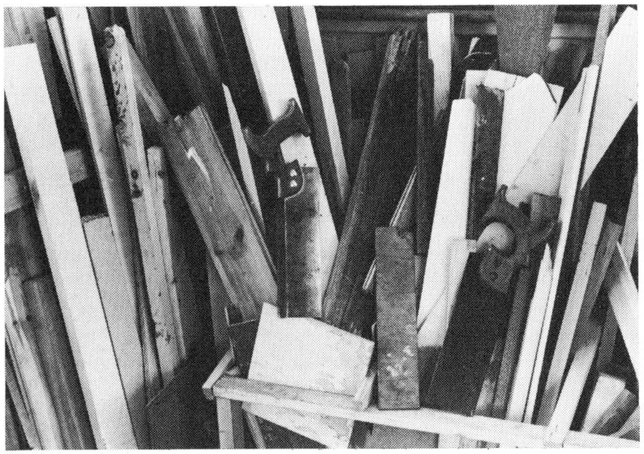

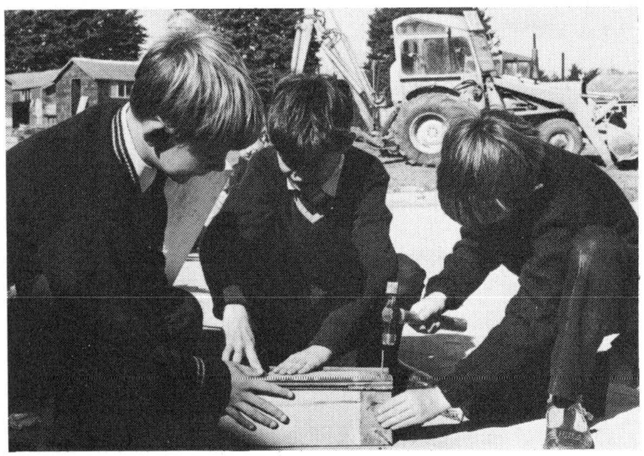

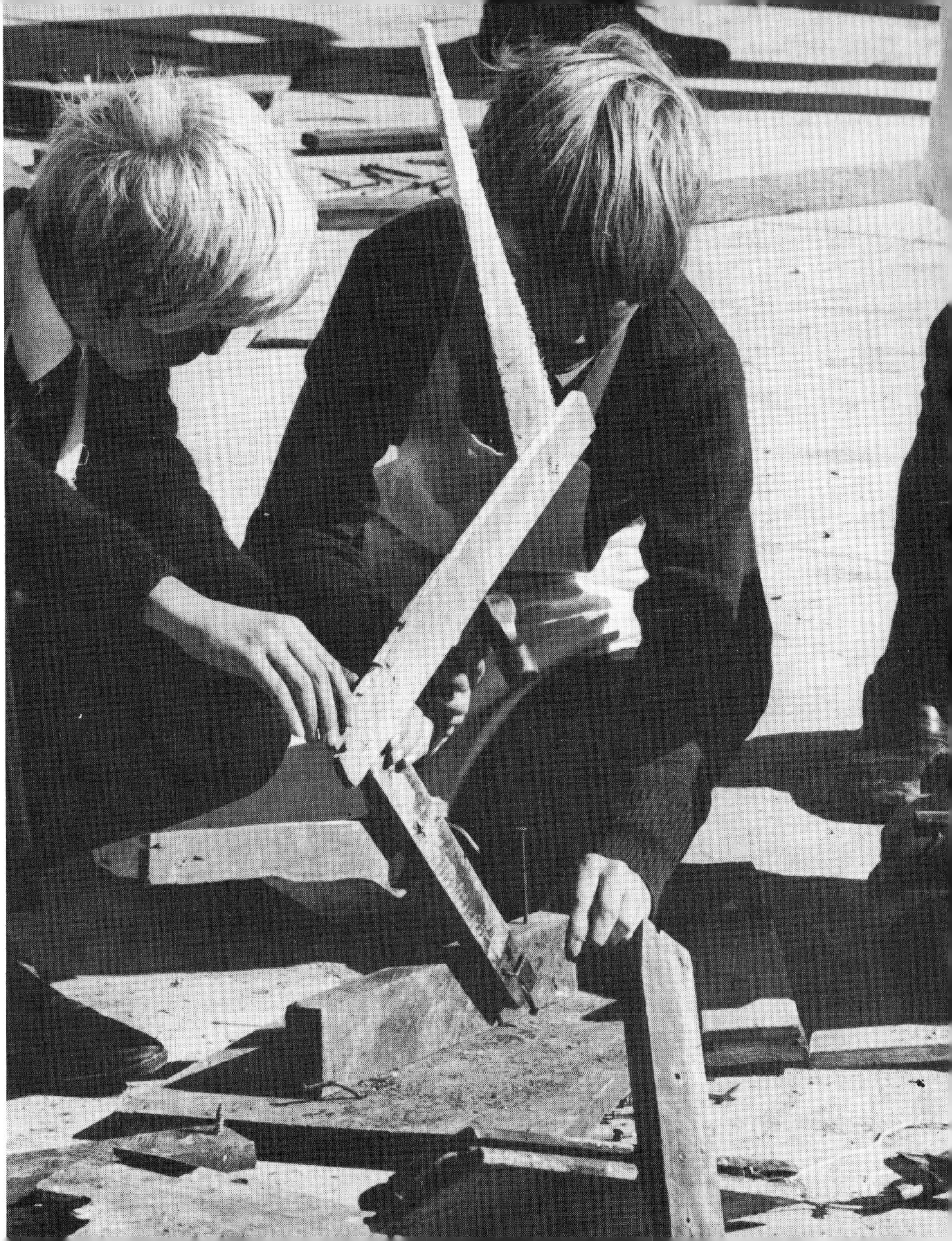

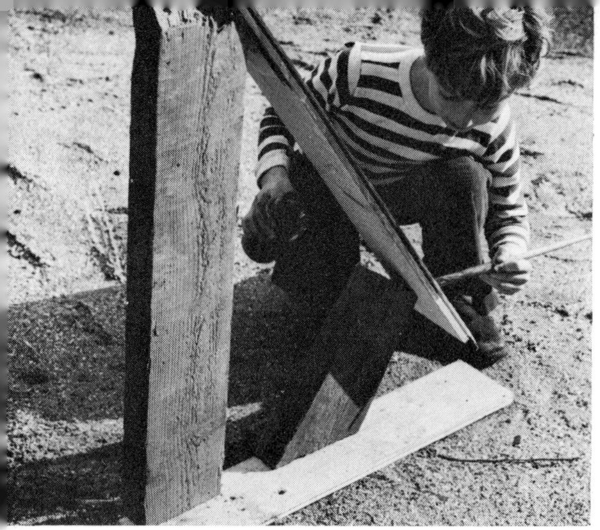

Left Pieces of wood have been nailed together and now they are being painted.

Right and below A second sculpture piece in wood is made.

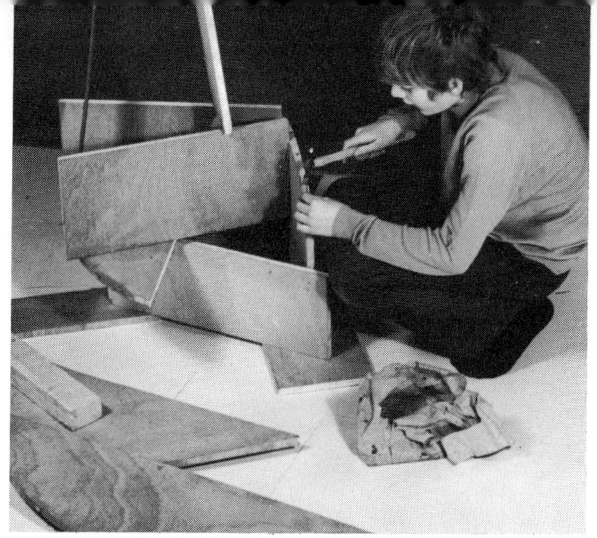

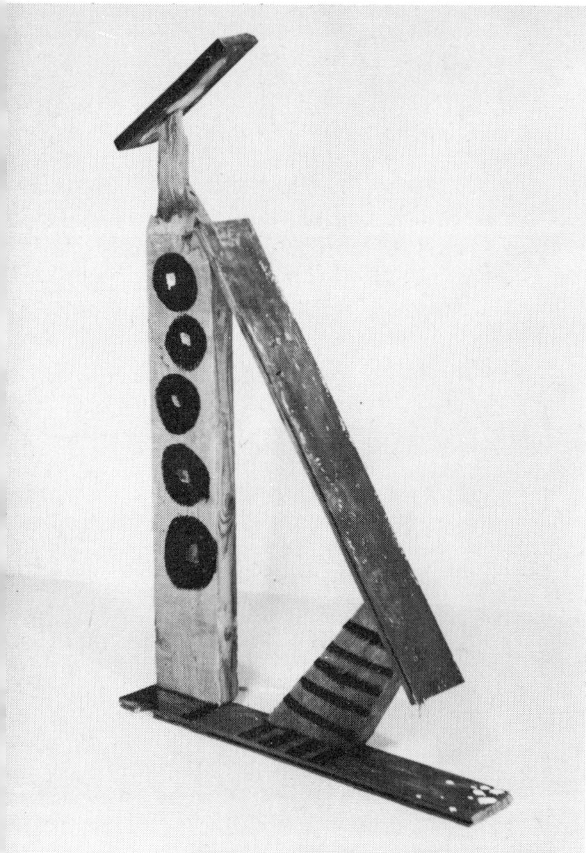

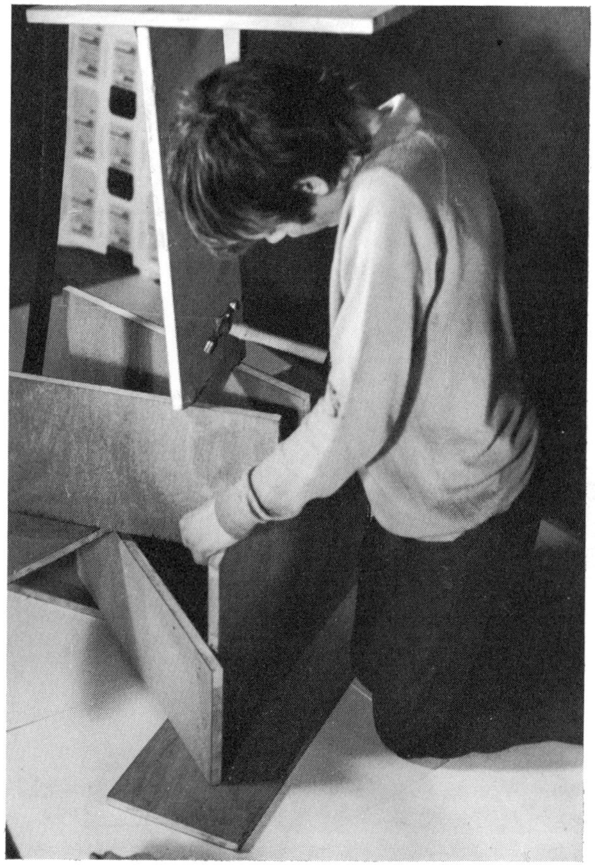

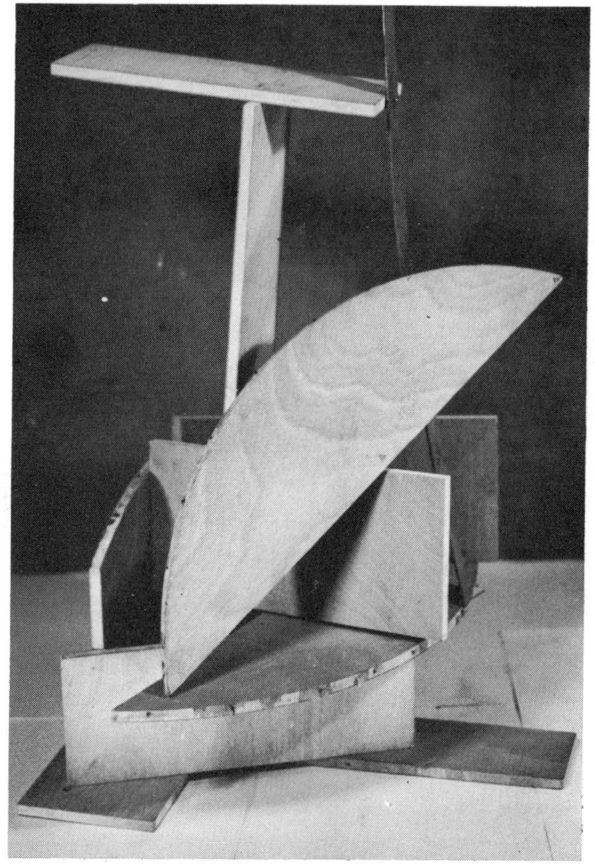

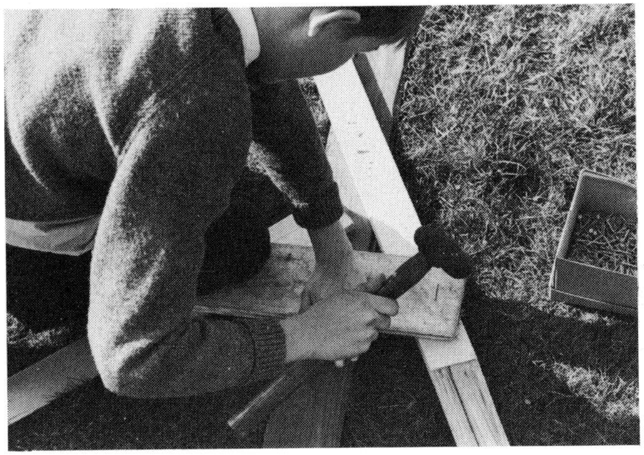

Large pieces of wood are nailed together by a group of children working together.

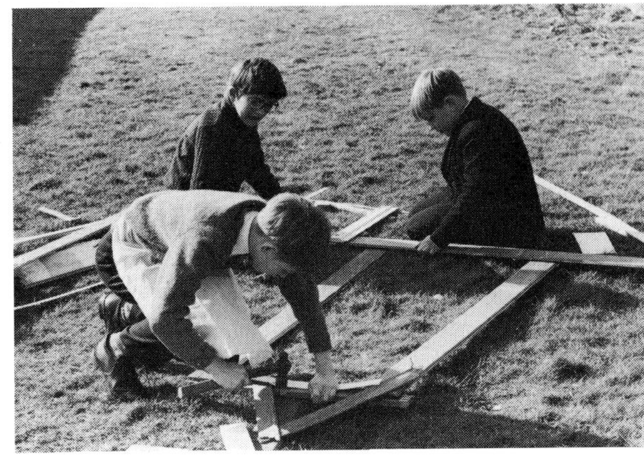

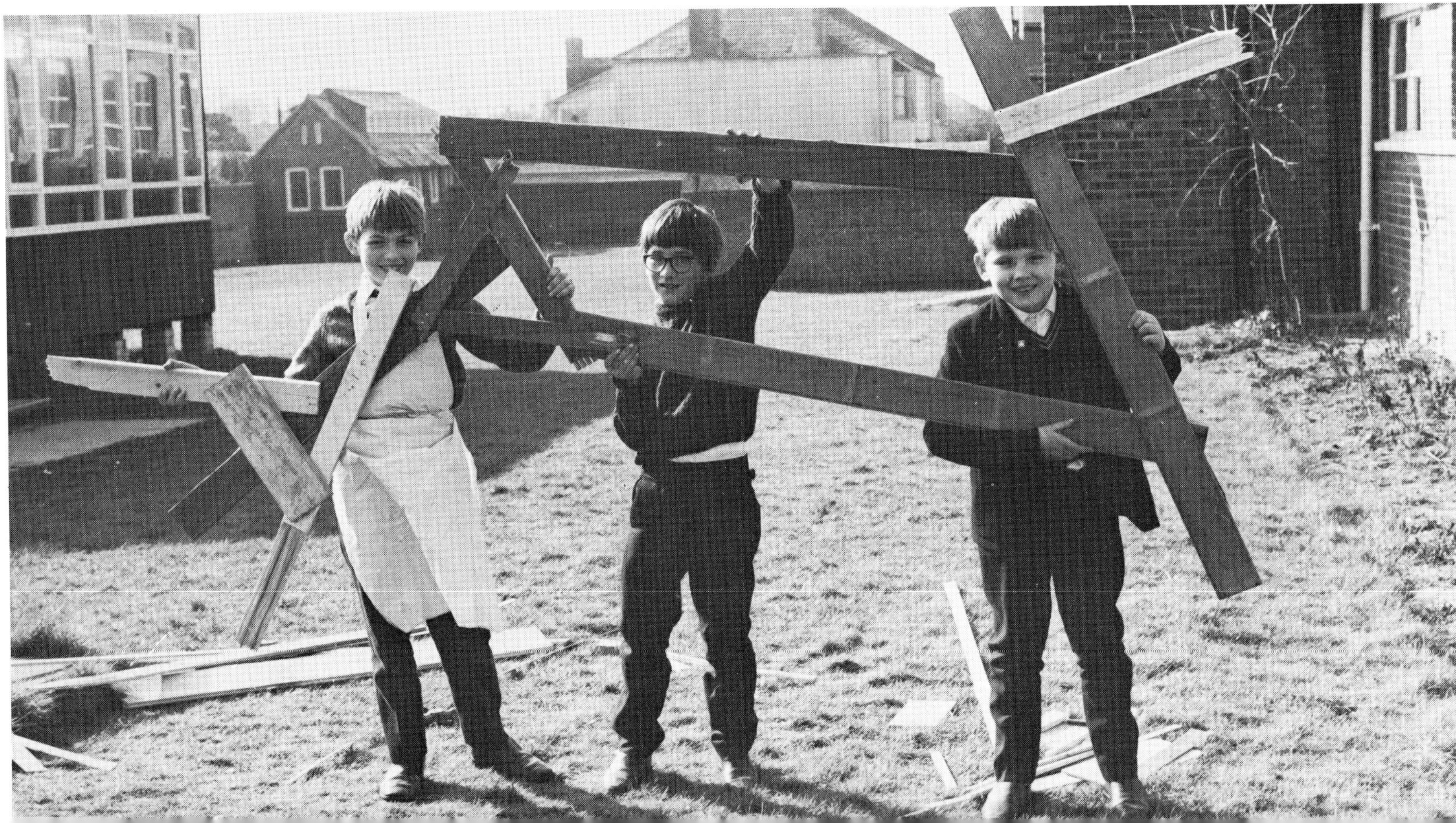

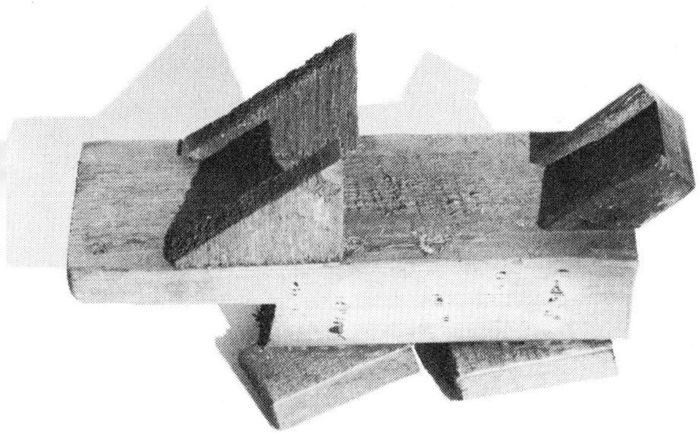

Above An animal shape in wood.

Below A wood sculpture, "Construction 1932" by David Smith. The Solomon R. Guggenheim Museum.

Right The sculpture piece is called "Abesti Gogora III" and it was made by Eduardo Chillida. Reproduced by courtesy of Galerie Maeght, Paris.

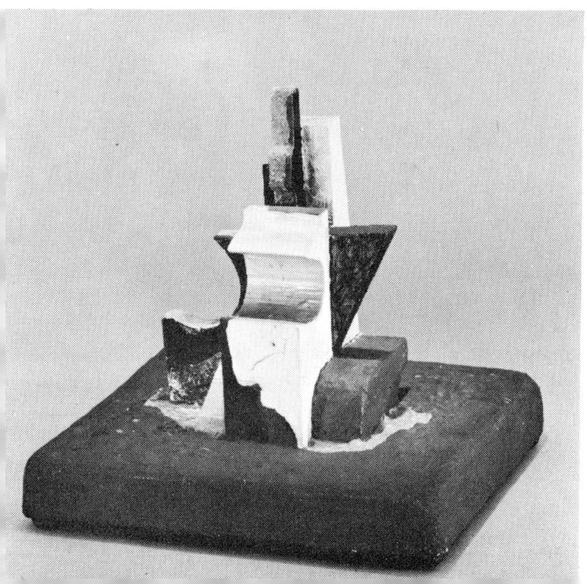

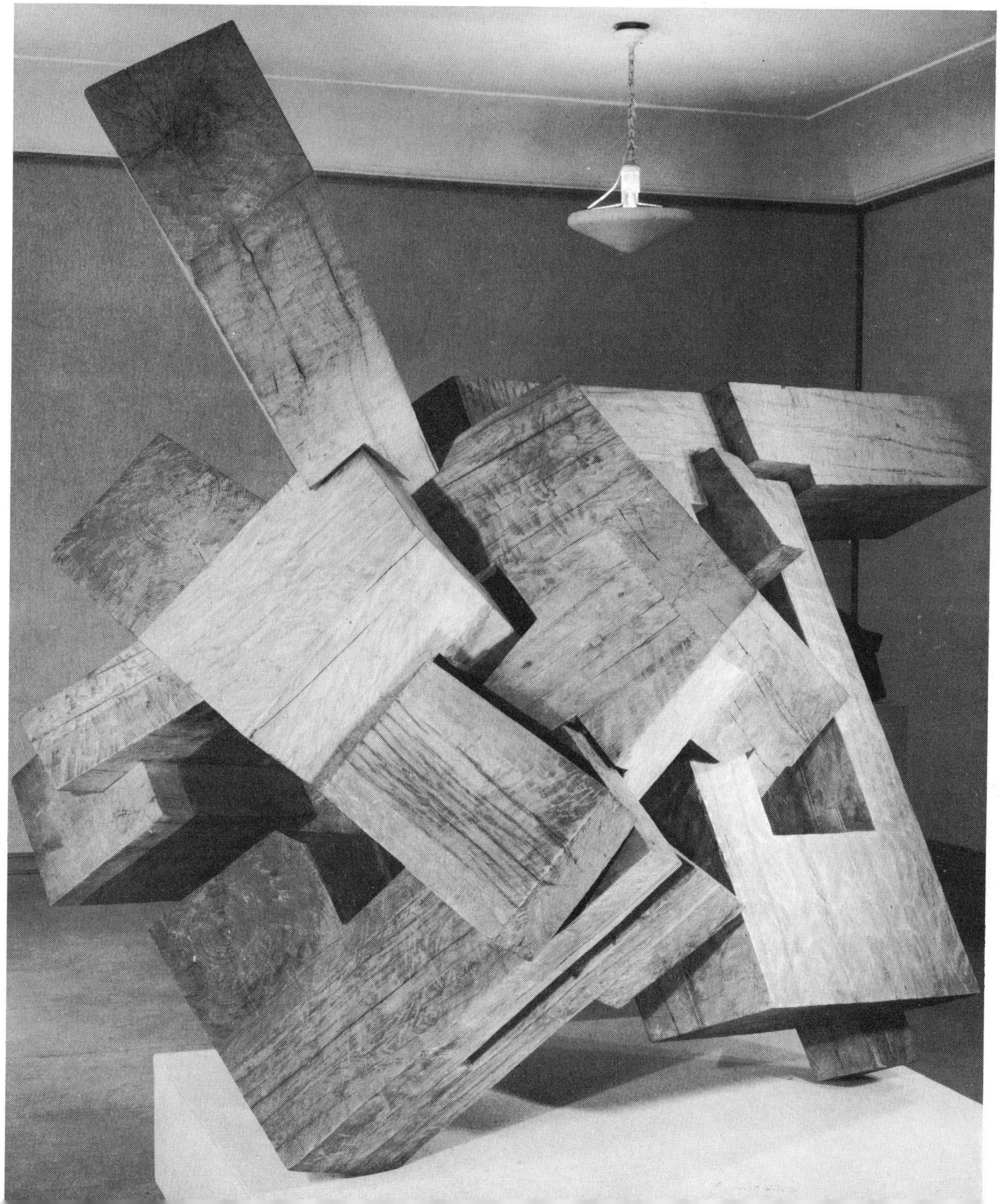

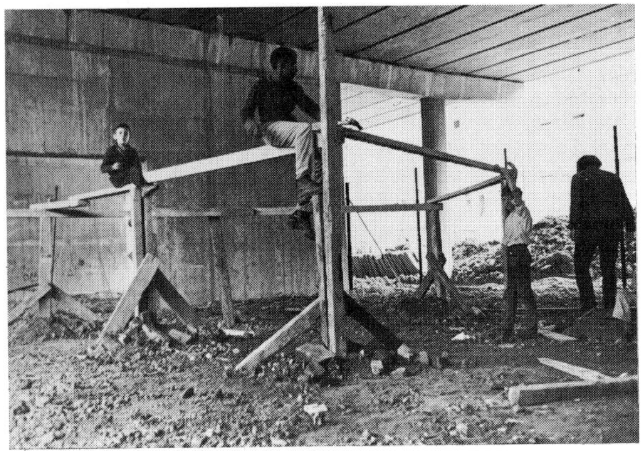

Children in London build a large wooden frame to make a sculpture of Gulliver in an Inter-Action Drama-Scape. Gulliver is made from rags which have been tied around the great wooden frame. He is forty feet long. His tongue moves.

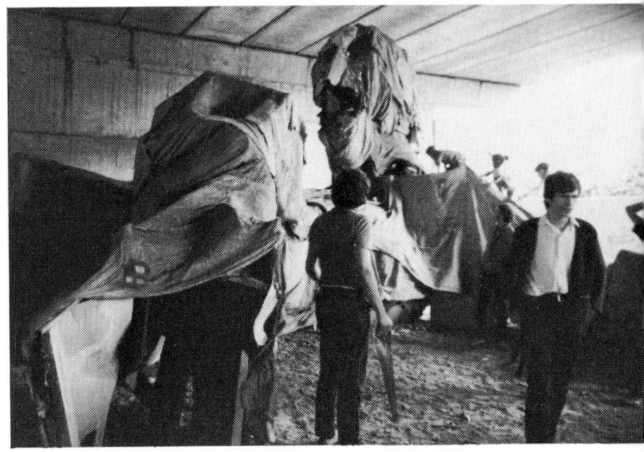

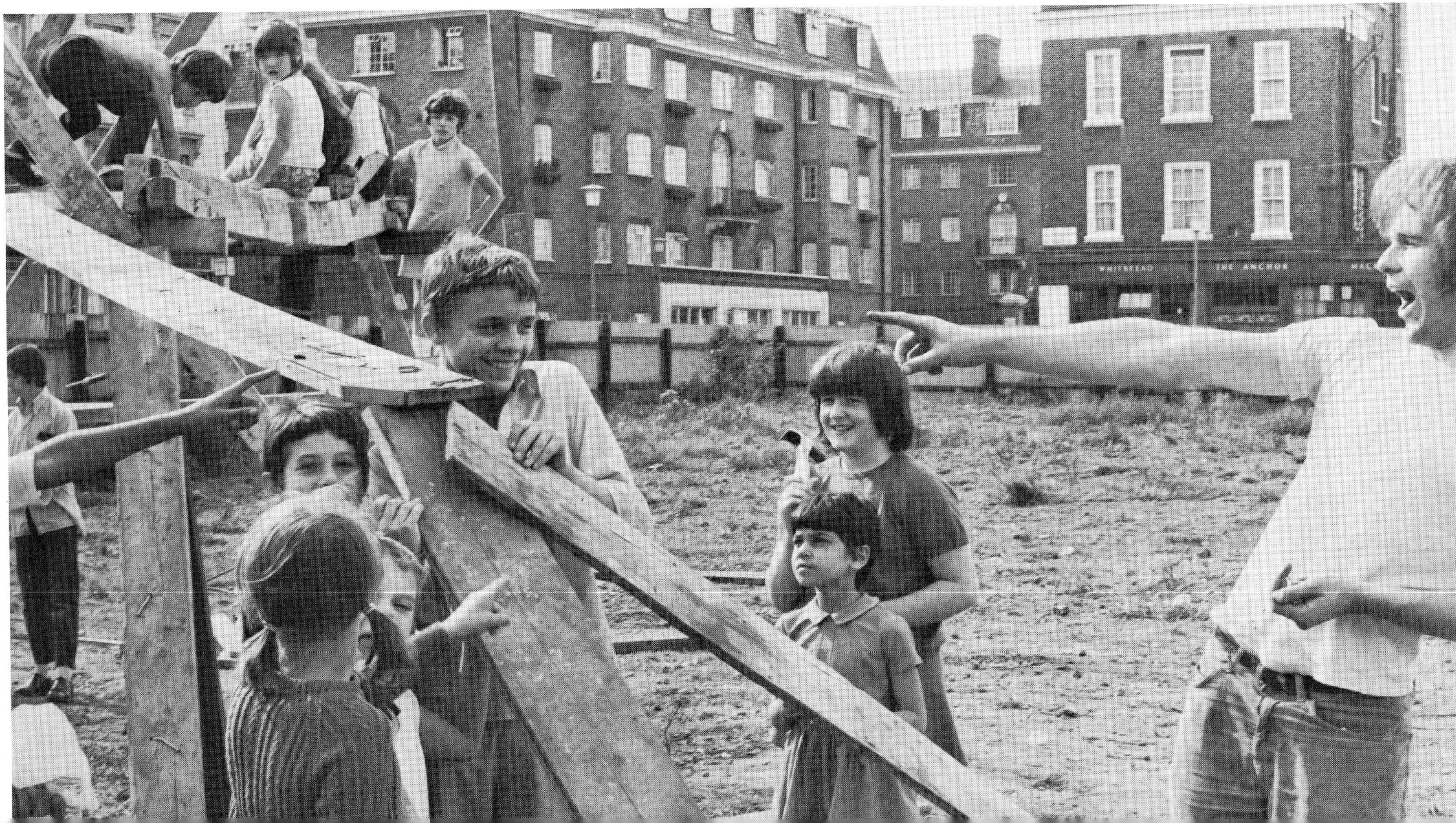

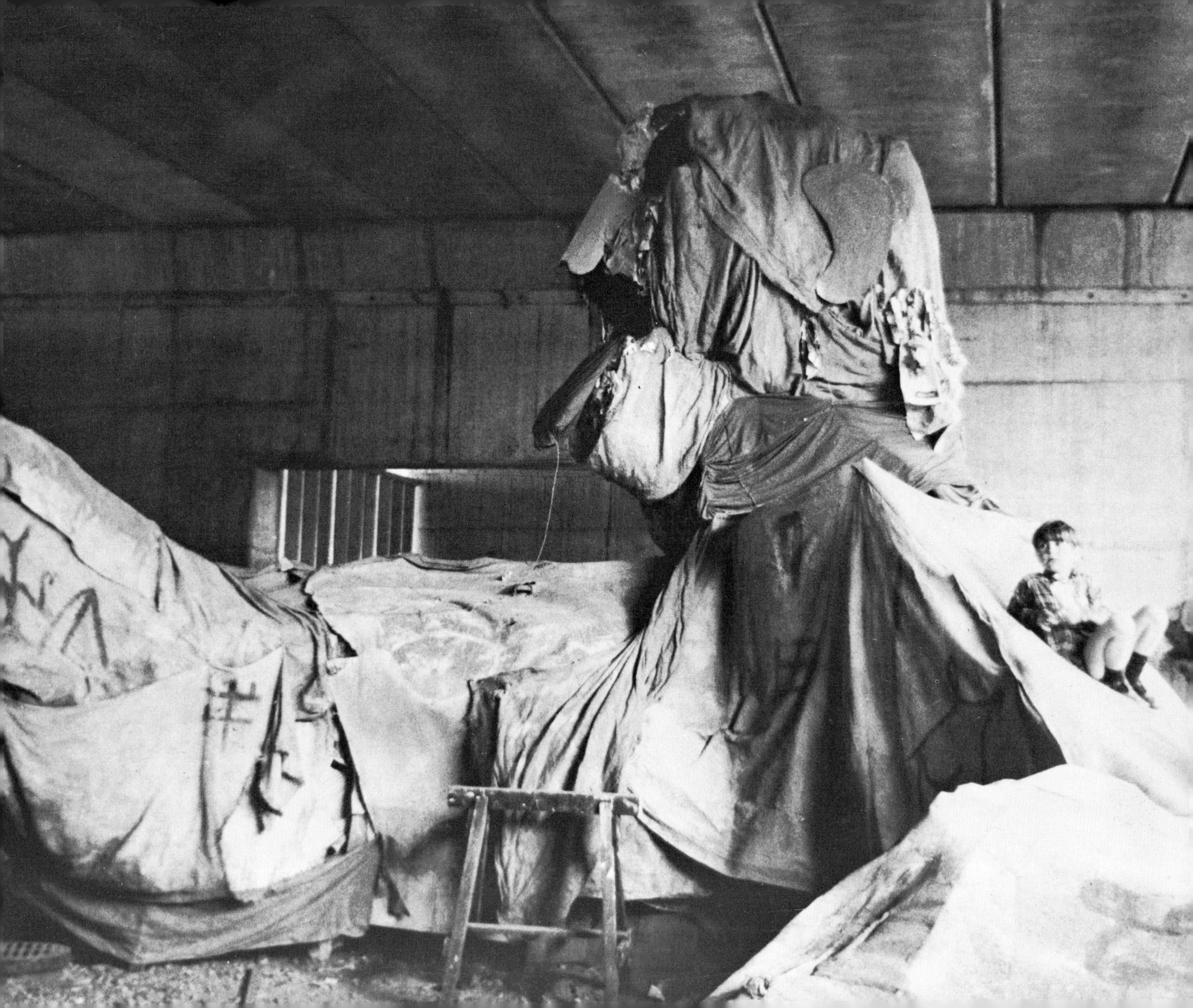

Junk

Sculpture can be made from almost anything. Old cereal boxes, rags and plastic bottles which are usually thrown away can make very good sculpture.

Below Children glueing and painting egg cartons, cardboard, paper and tins to make junk sculpture.

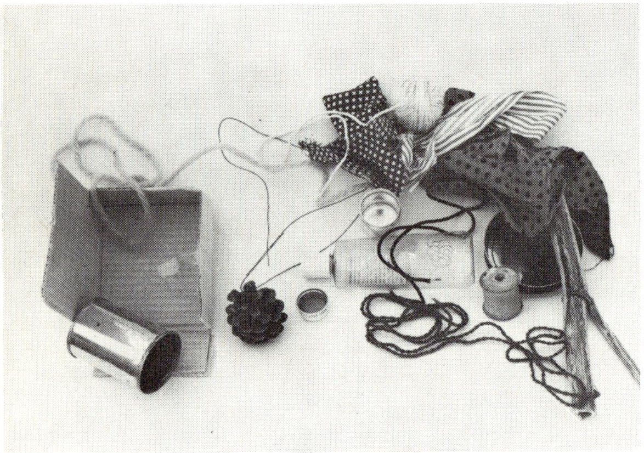

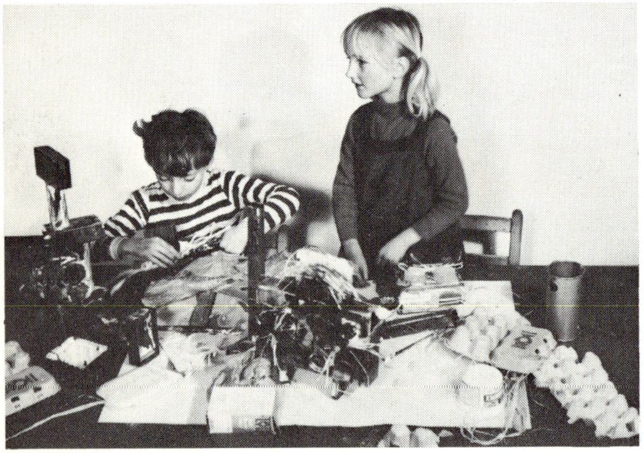

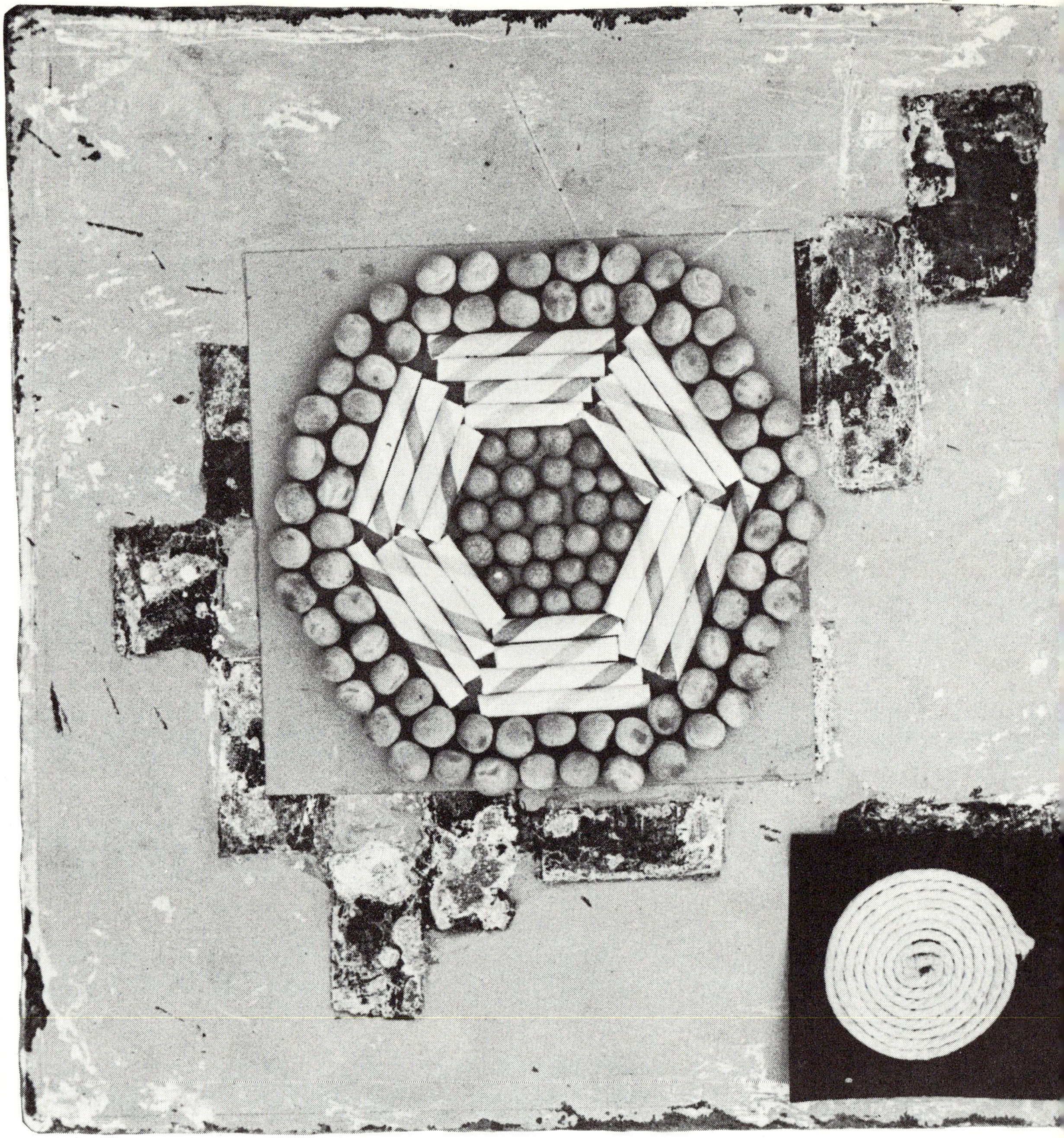

Left Straws, string and dried peas make this design.

Top right A plastic egg carton, bits of string, and cardboard were glued to make this sculpture piece.

Bottom right A design made with rice, dried peas, noodles and paint.

Below A design in string and cardboard.

Bottom Sculpture made from an old lid, a straw, pieces of cloth, a plastic wheel, and a meat carton.

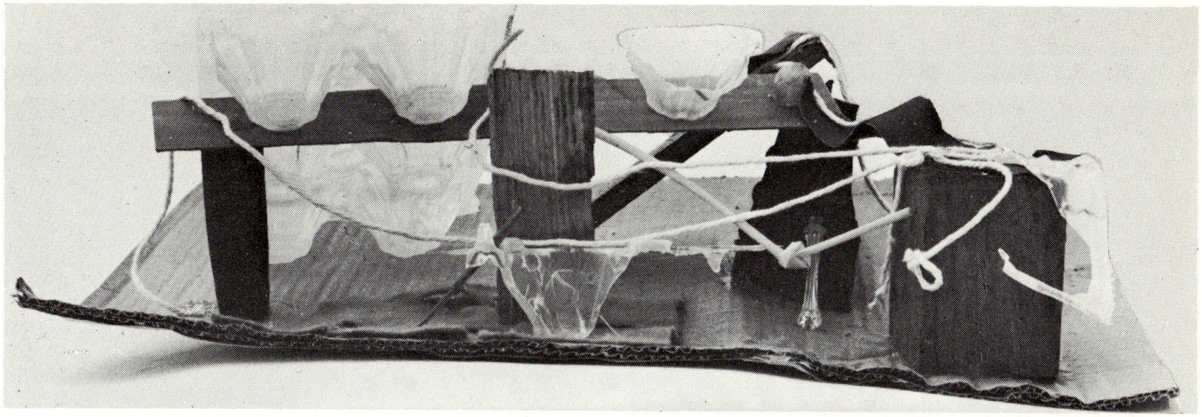

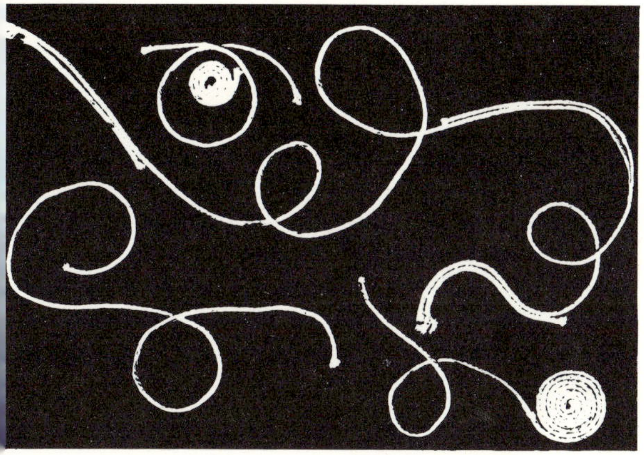

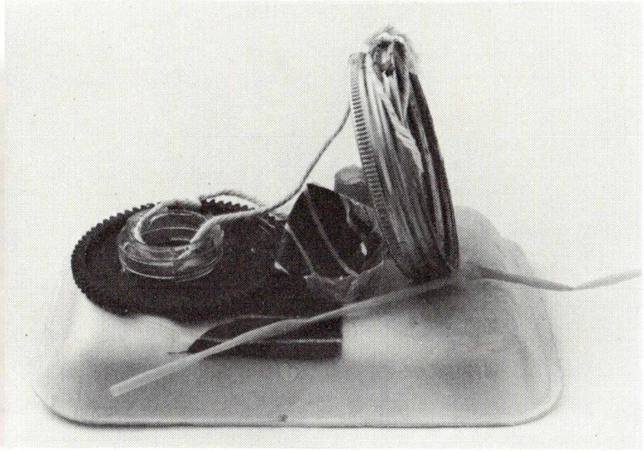

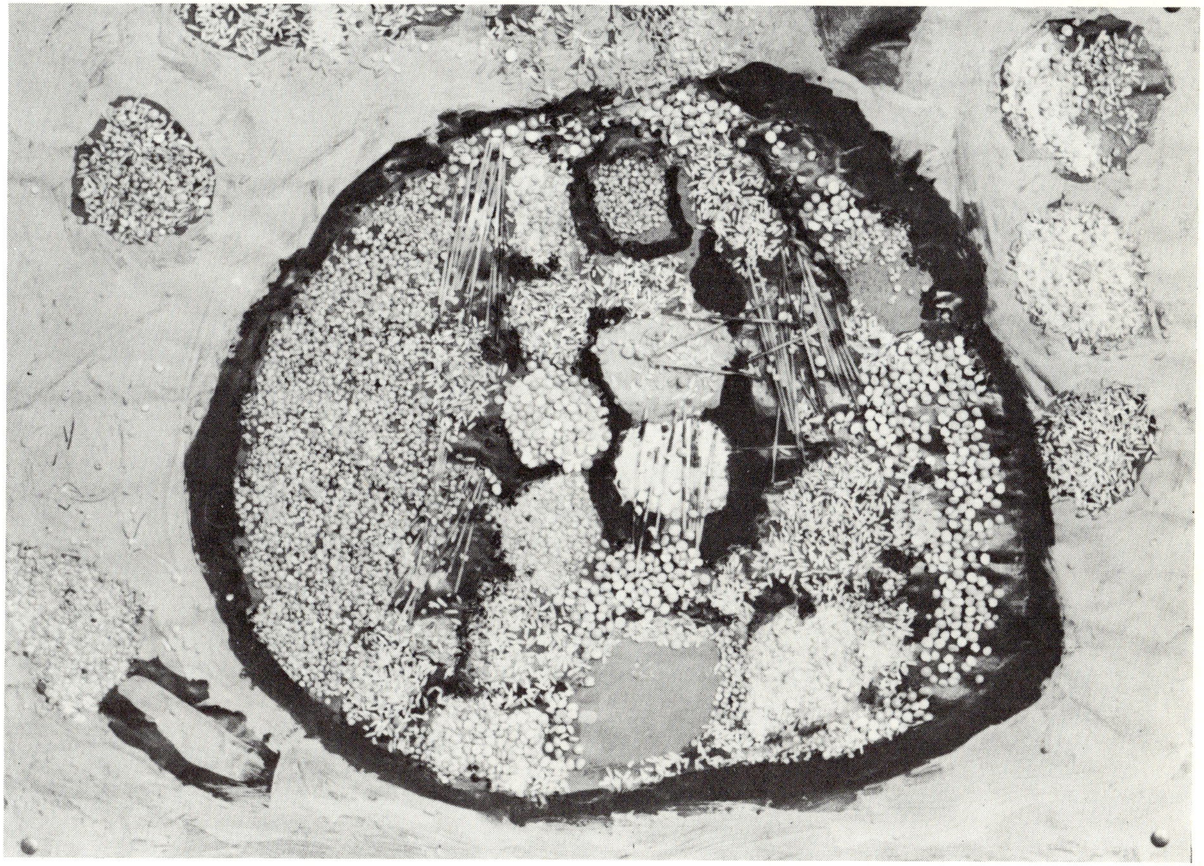

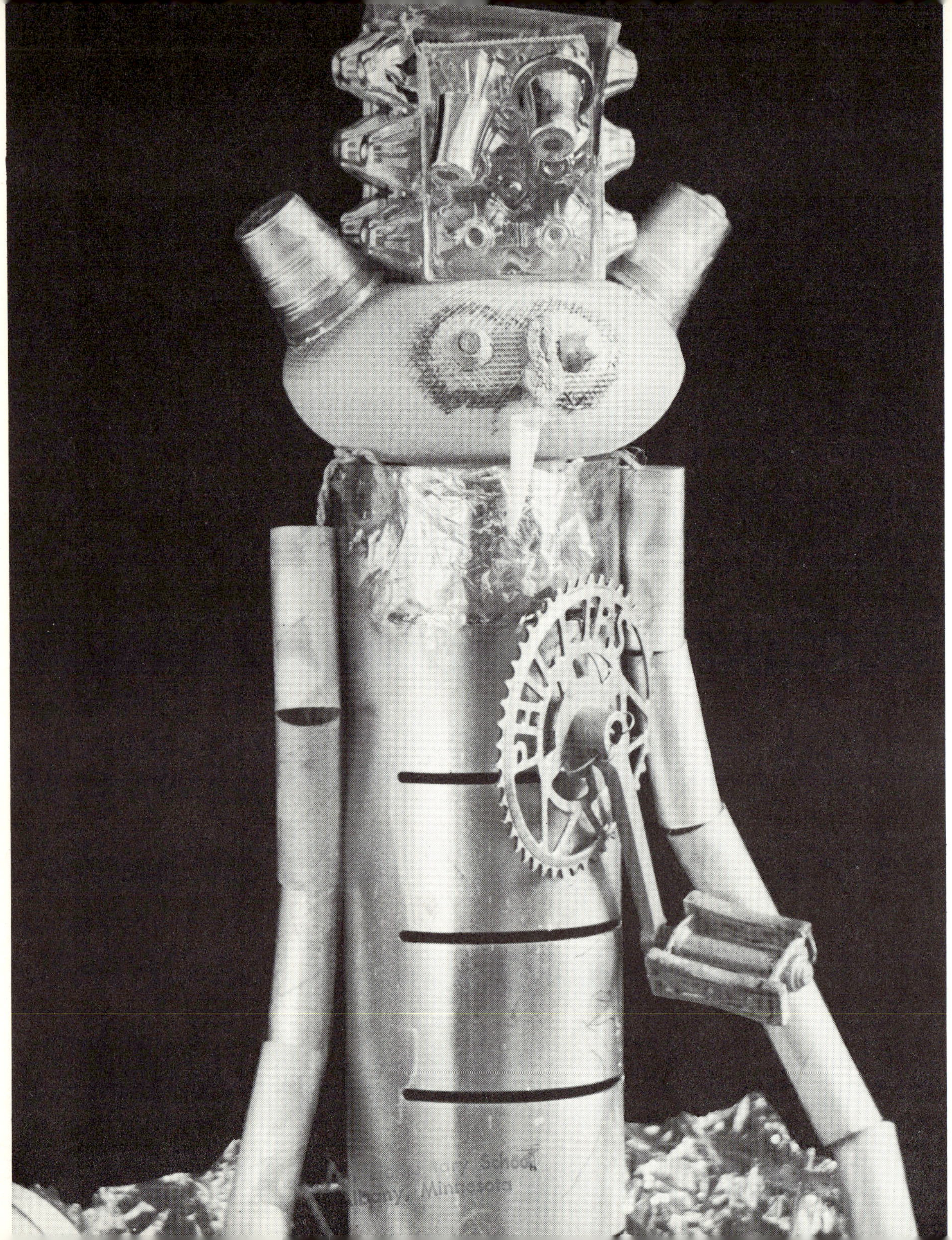

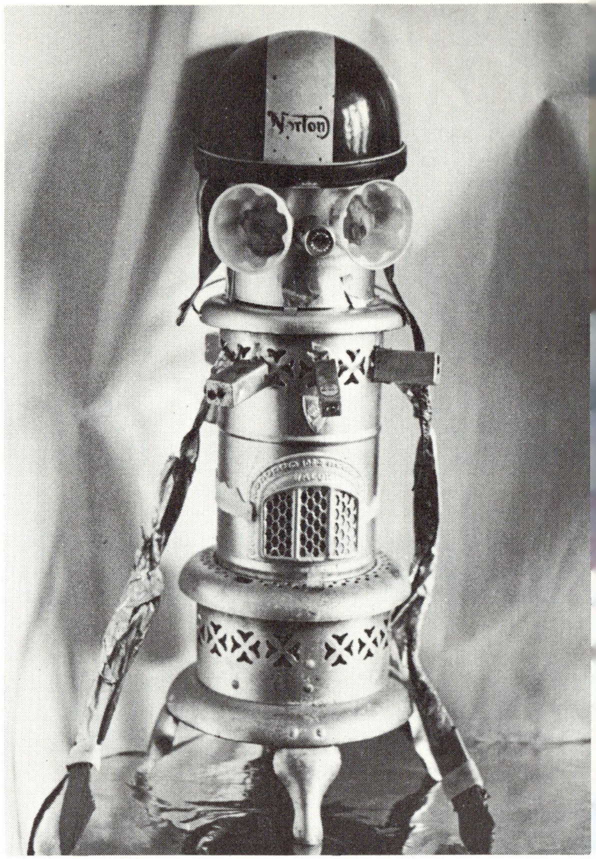

These junk sculptures were made by parents and children working together. You will recognise most of the materials that have been used.
Left Pieces of metal were glued to a metal rod and stuck into a wooden base.
Above A monster made from an old oil stove, with plastic ice-cream cones for eyes.
Top right Nails and potatoes were stuck together to make this creature.
Right A figure made with an old light bulb, wool, cloth, rope, a plastic bottle and glue.
Far right Another monster made from tins with cardboard flower pots for arms.

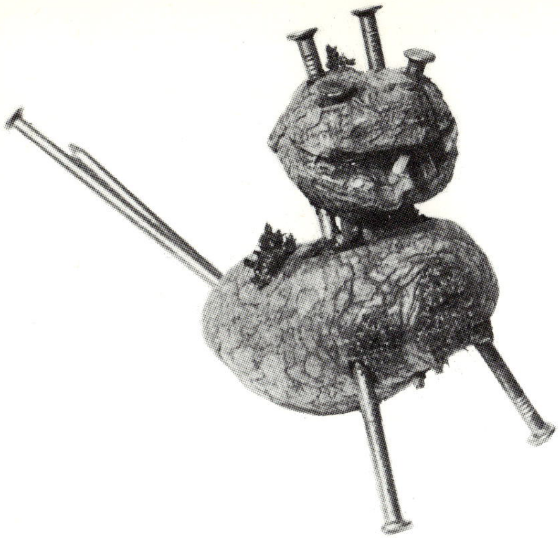

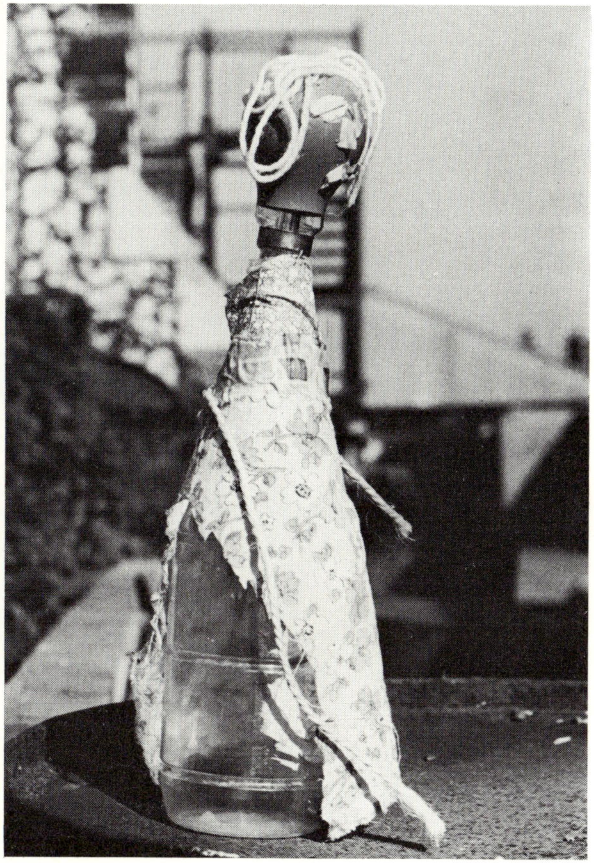

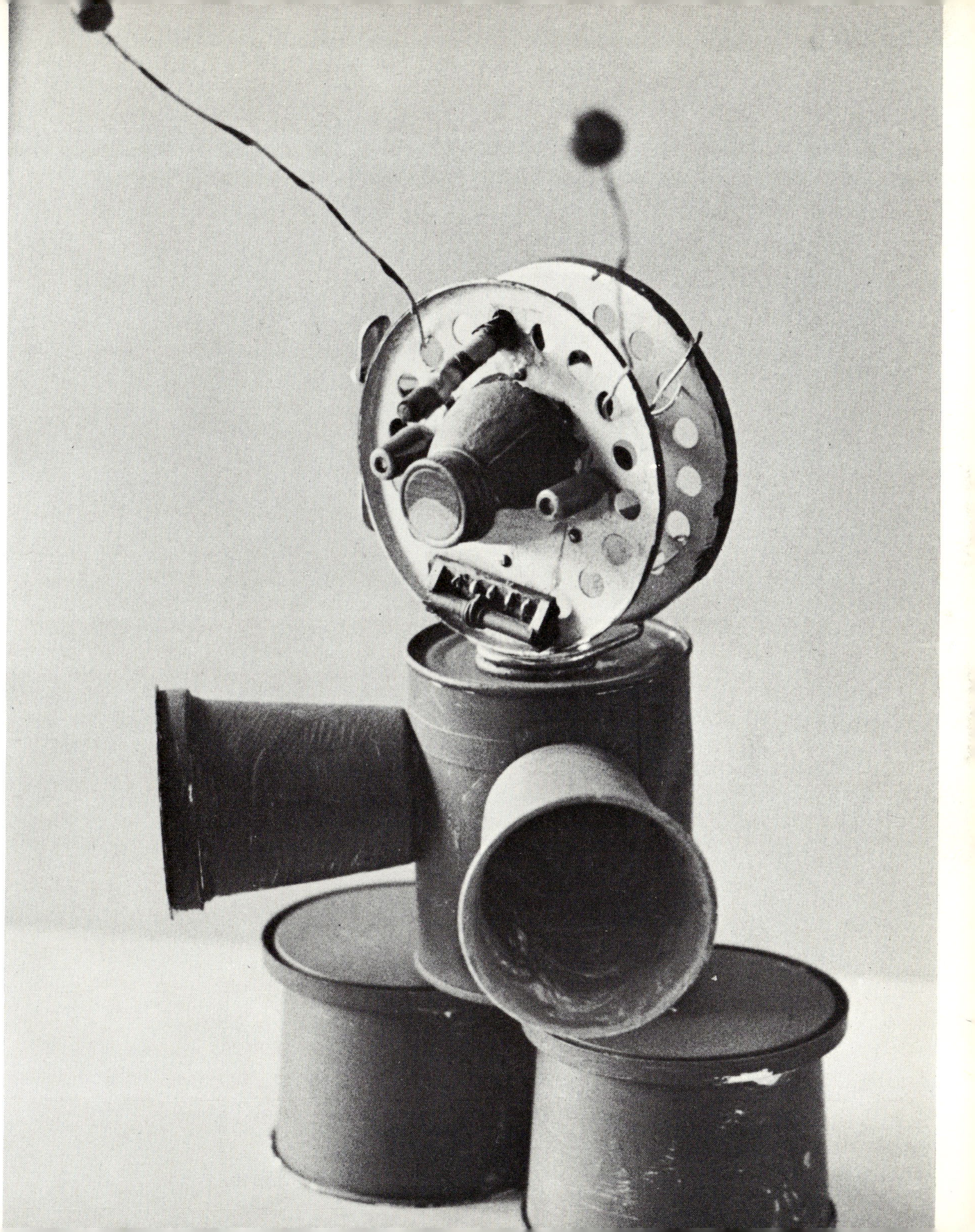

2 MODELLING

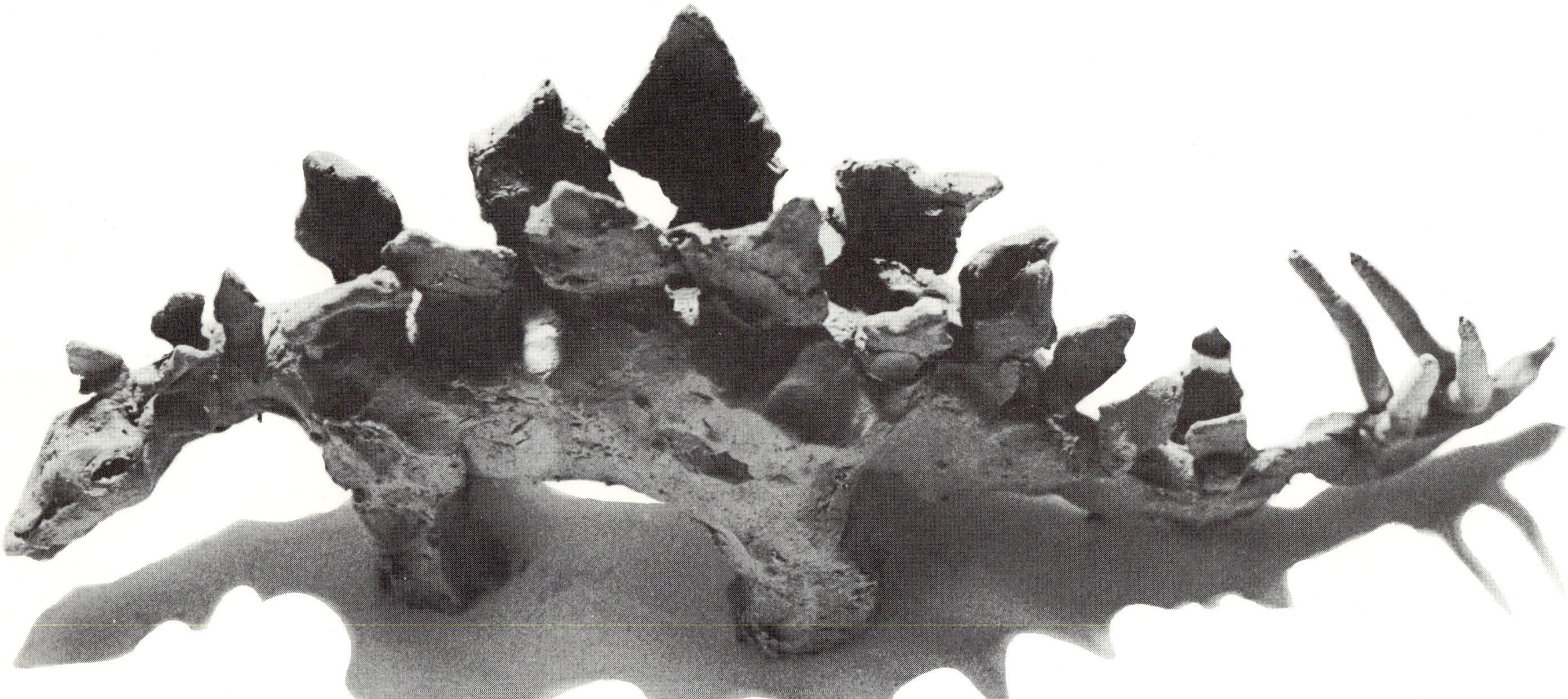

Clay

Modelling is the building up of shape with one material. You can model with clay, sand, mud, snow and plastiscene. Clay is probably the best as it is very soft and easily shaped.

Here a coil of clay is being rolled.

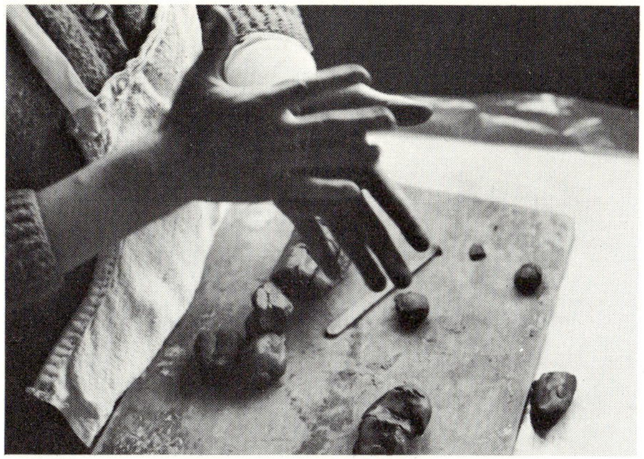

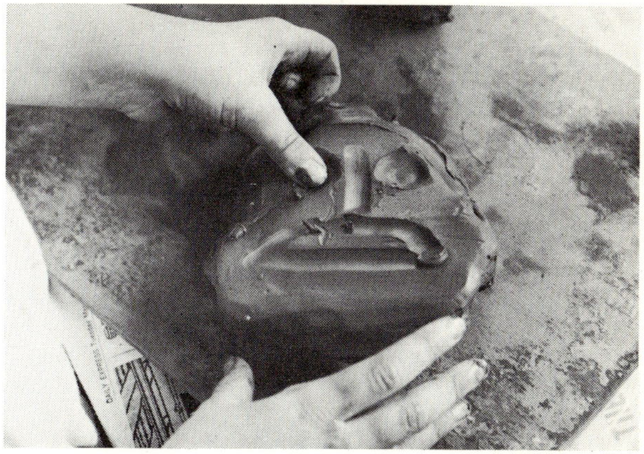

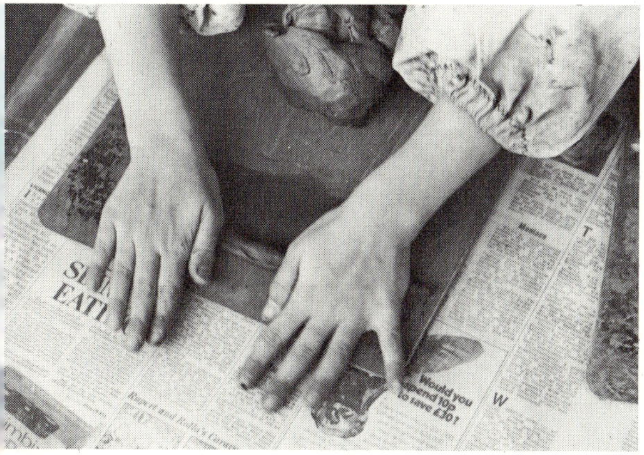

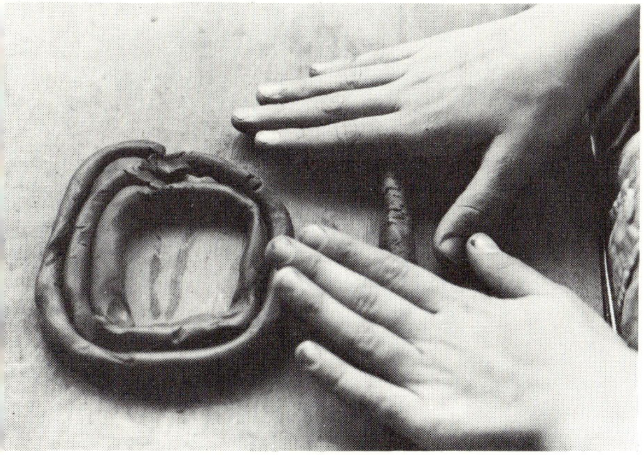

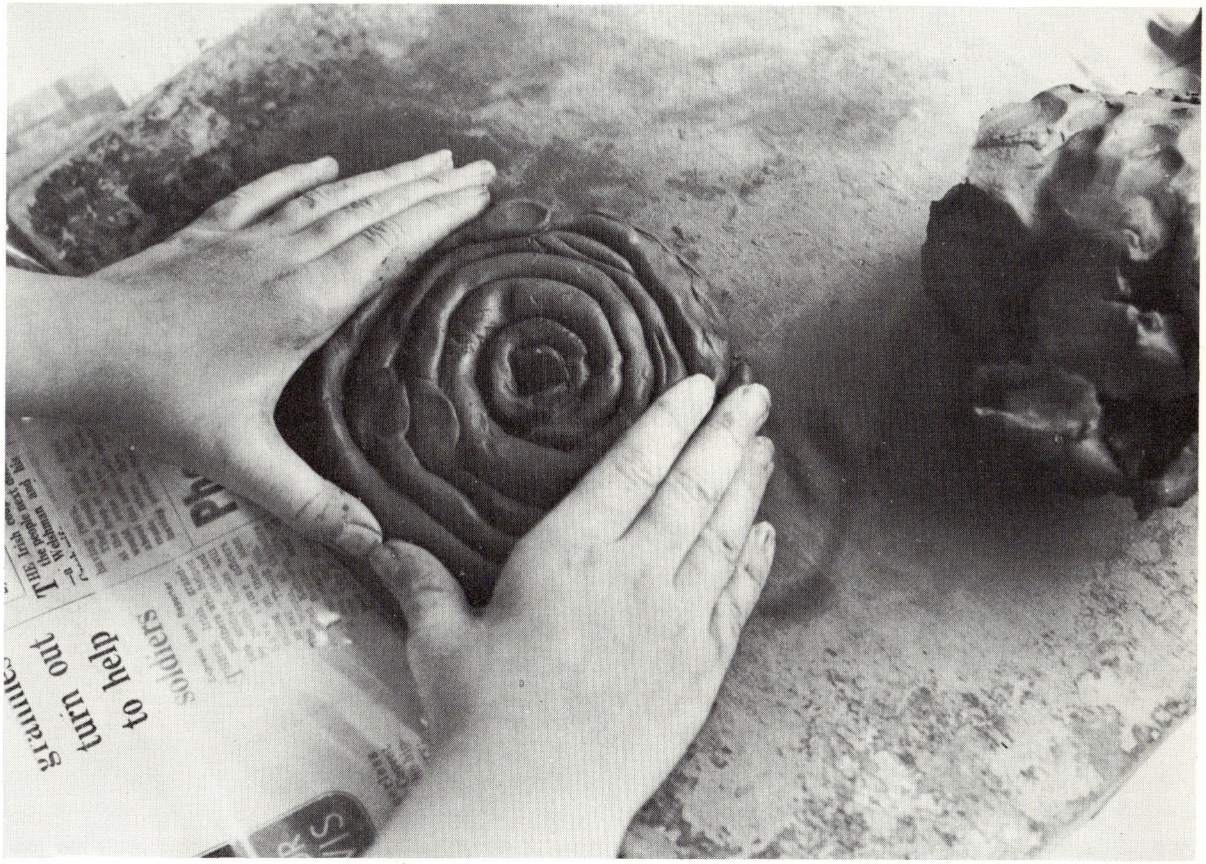

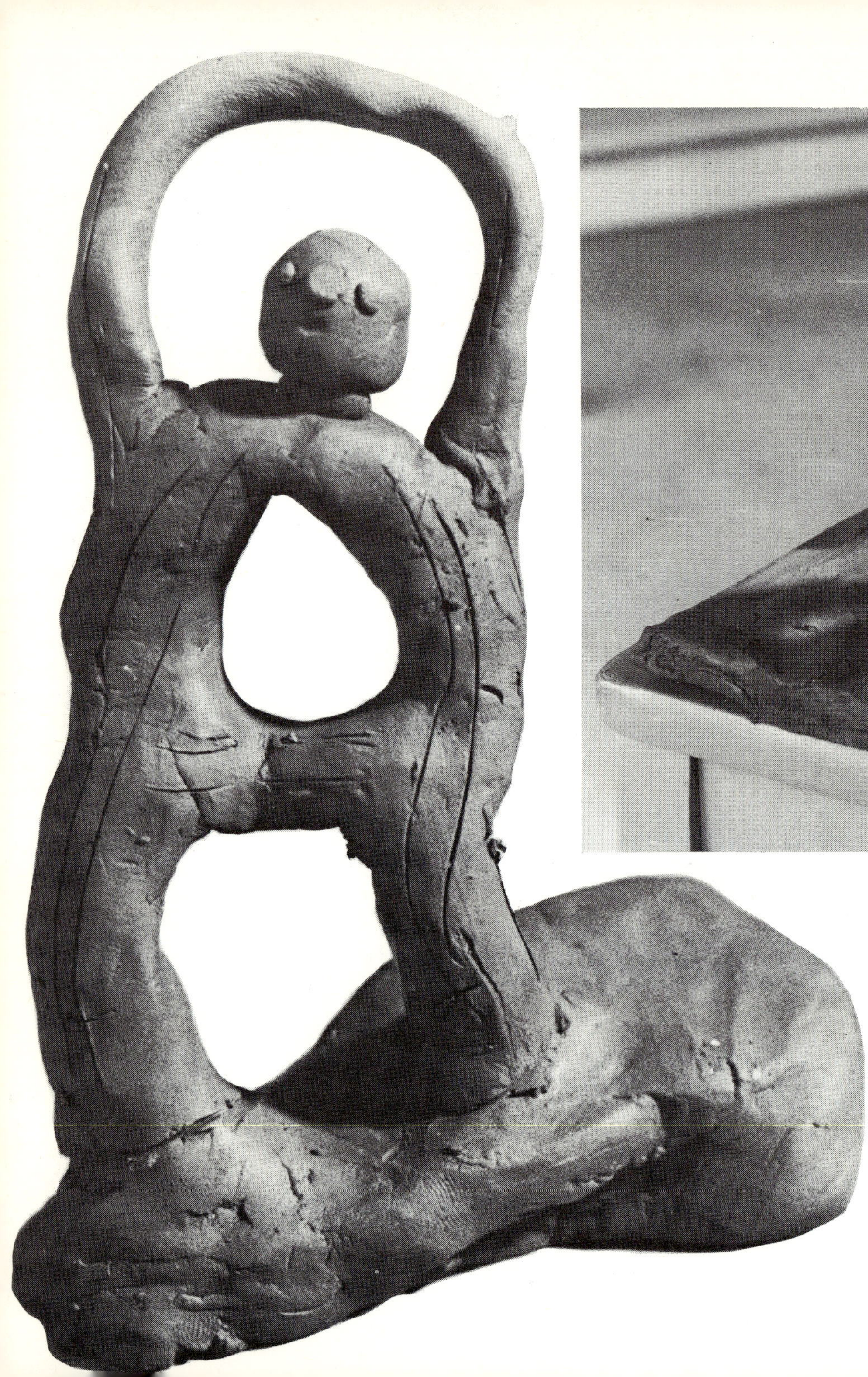

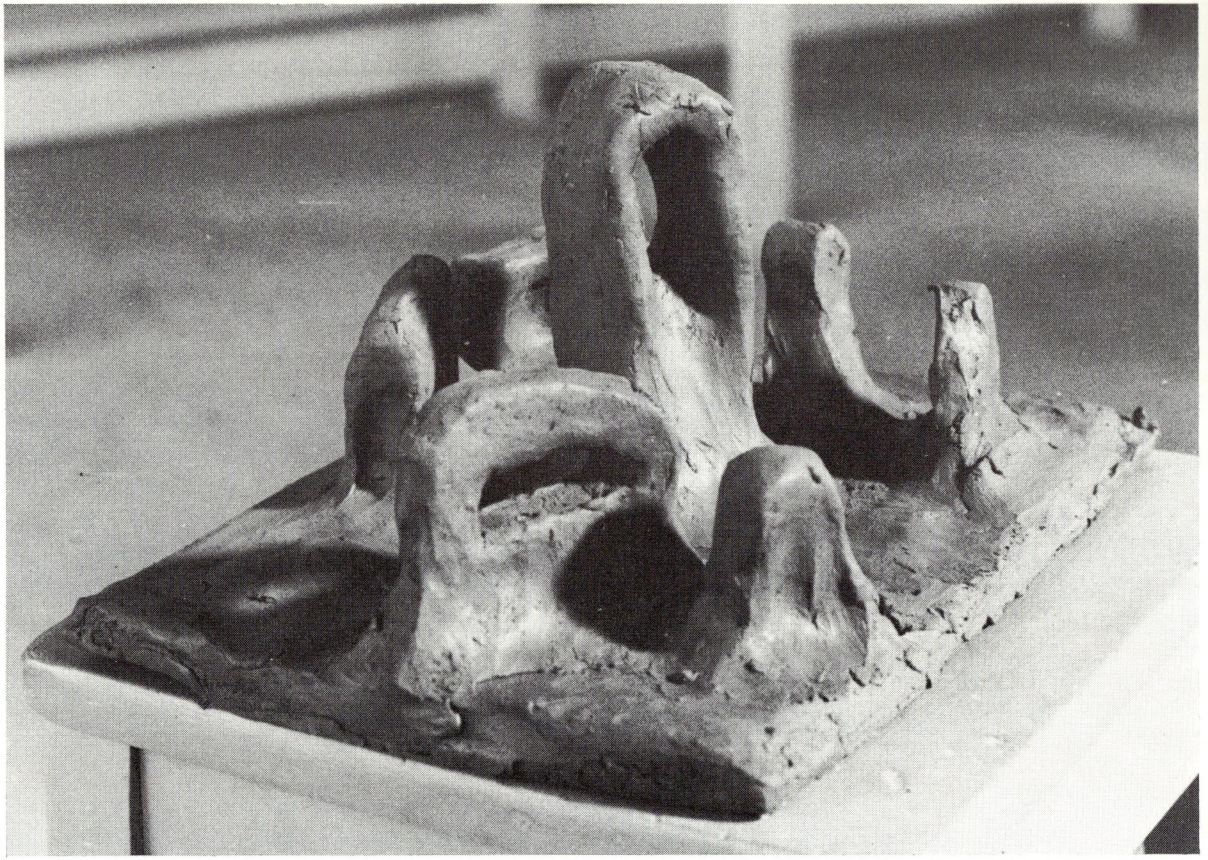

Left A coil figure in clay.

Above Clay shapes.

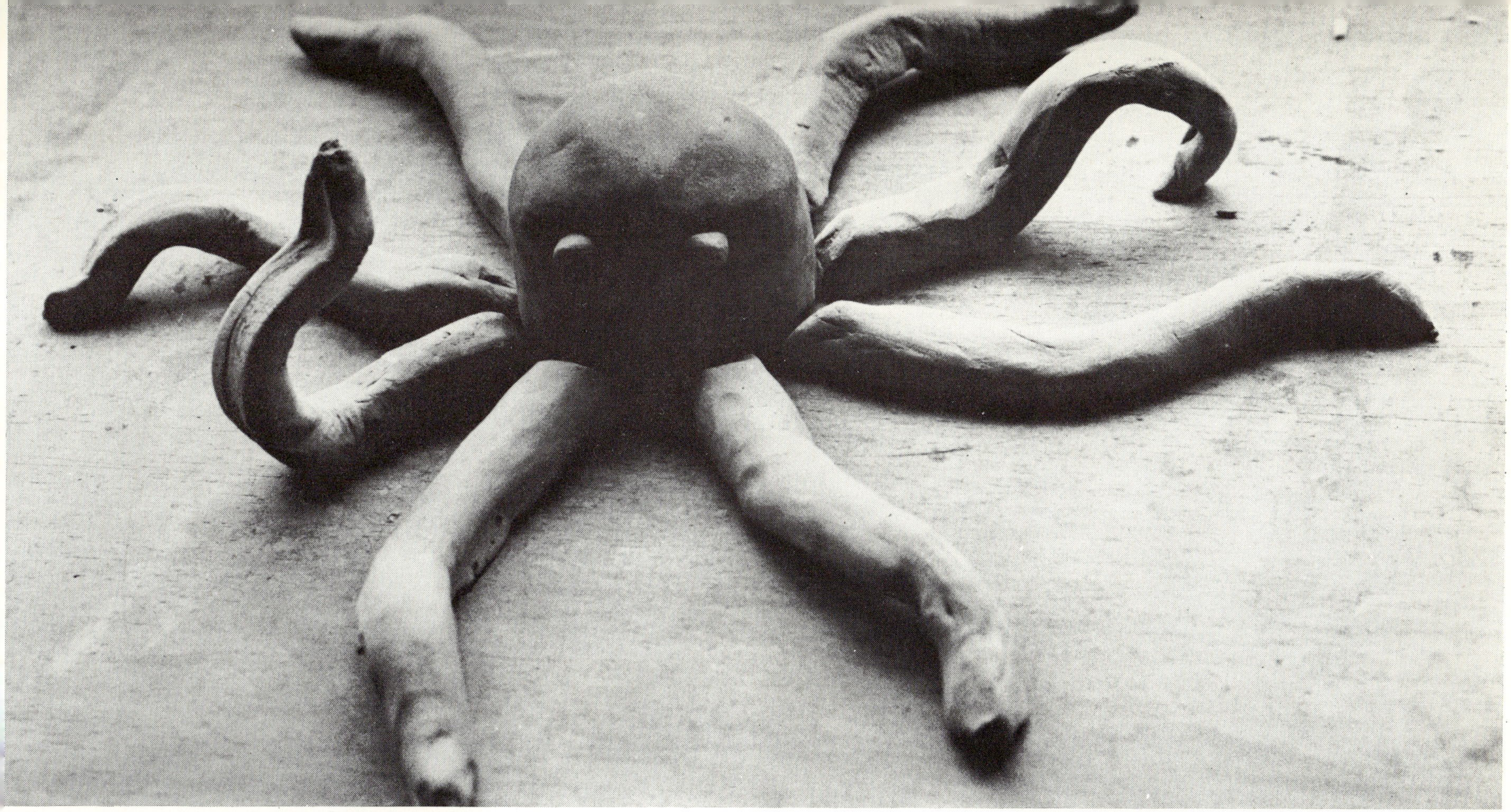

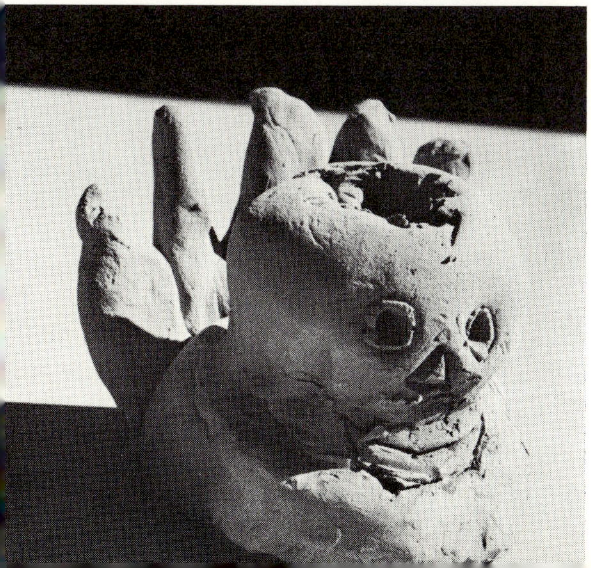

Above An octopus made with coils of clay.
Left A clay Humpty-Dumpty.
Right A clay dinosaur.

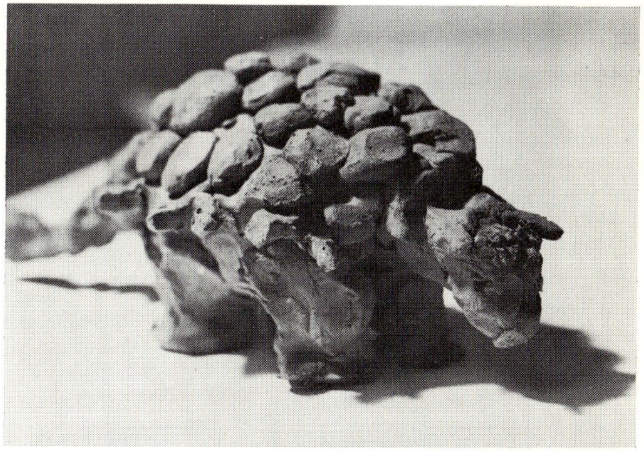

Relief

A relief is a kind of sculpture which is like a painting or drawing because it is flat with shapes marked on the flat surface.

Clay can be flattened with a rolling pin. A design can be drawn into the clay with different shaped tools and sticks of wood.

Right Another design in clay made with screws, bolts and pencils.

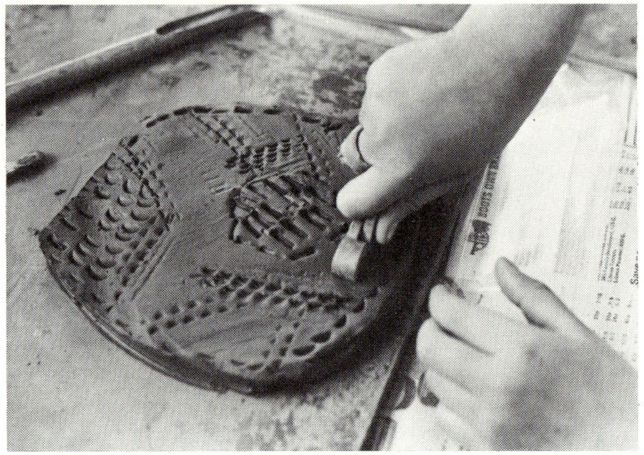

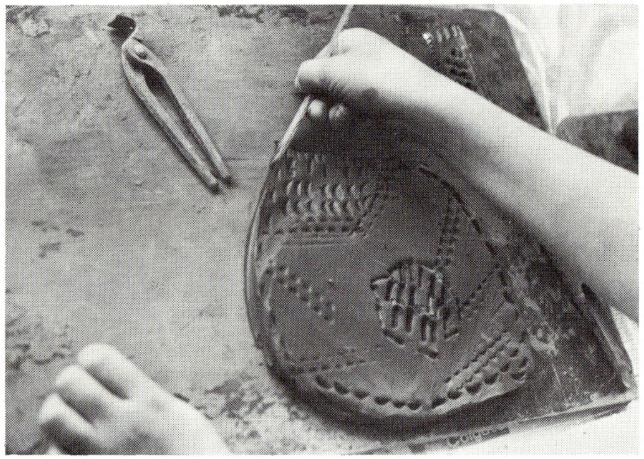

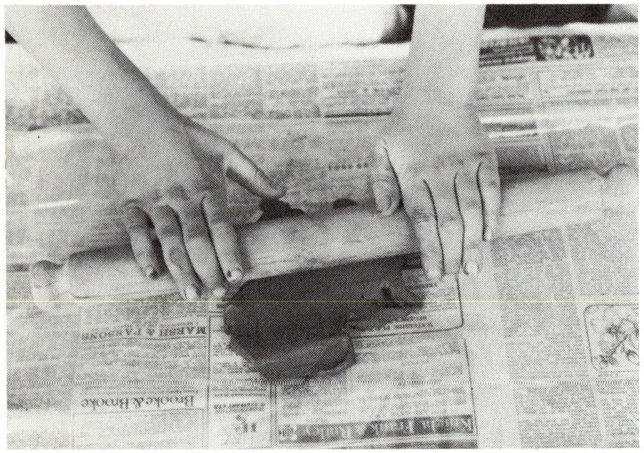

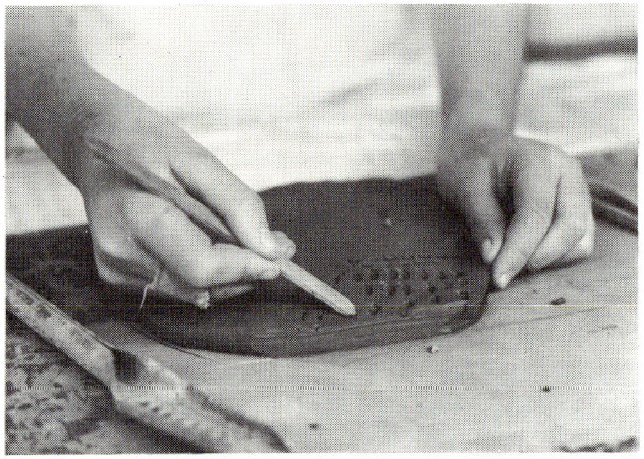

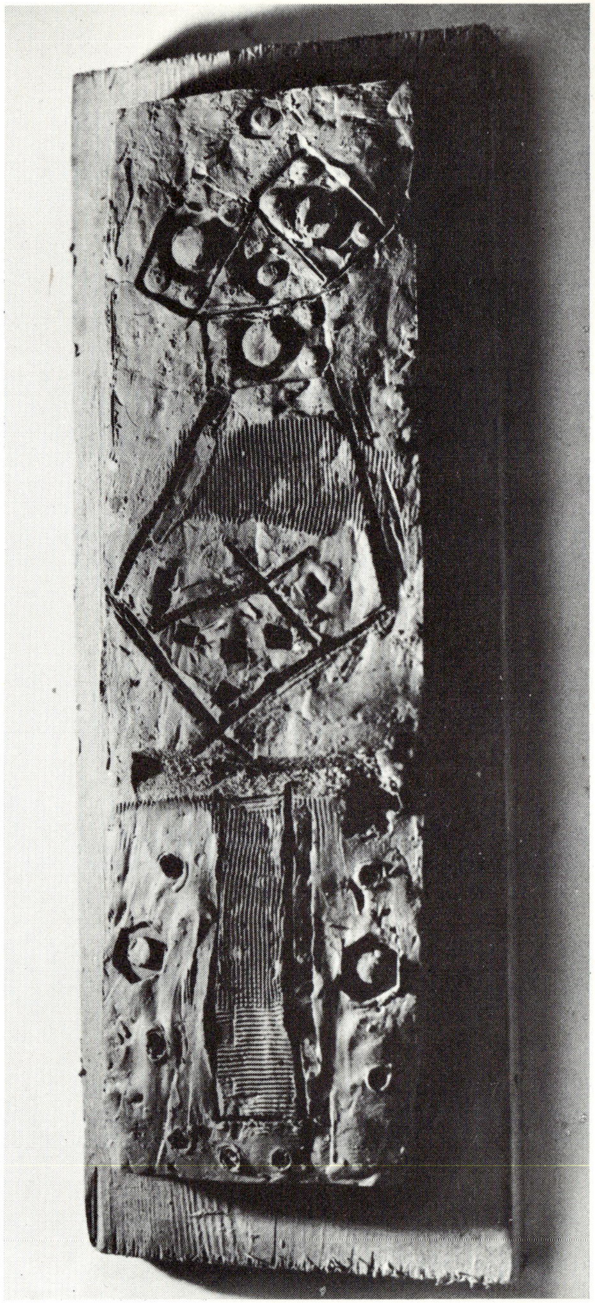

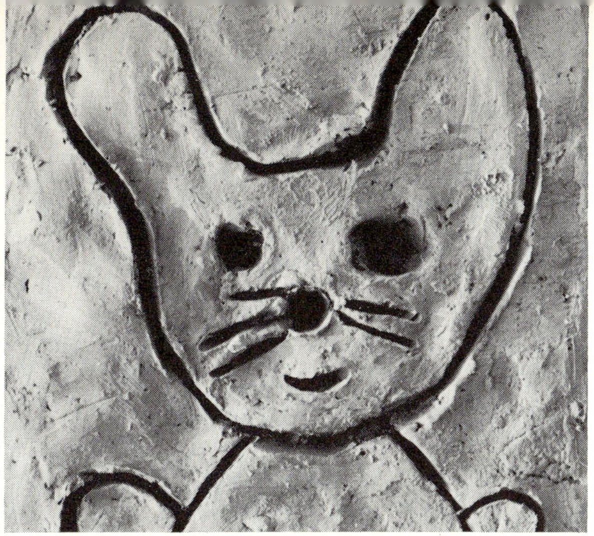

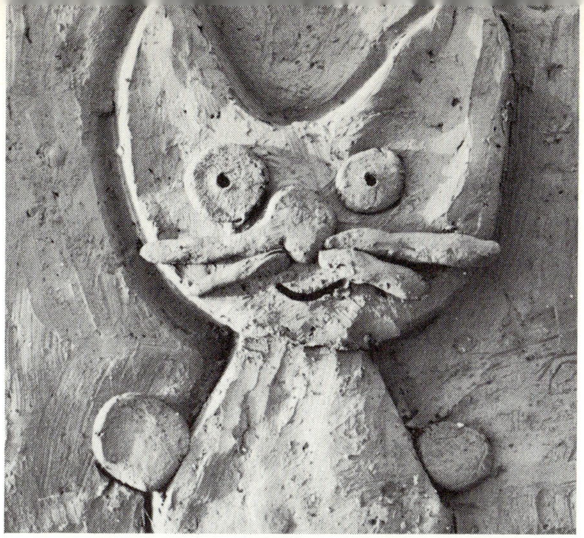

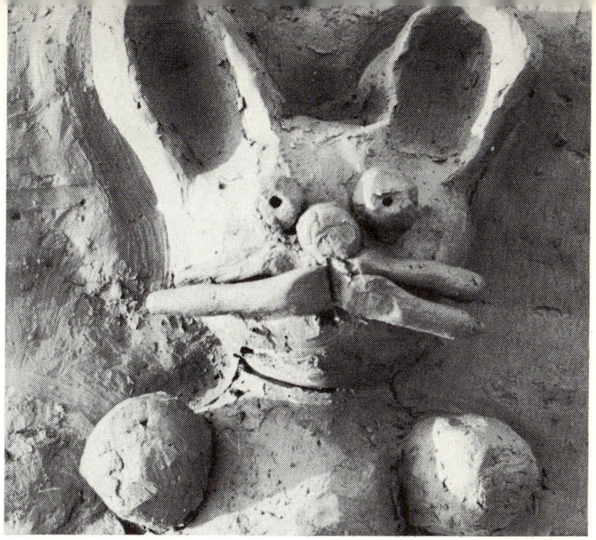

A relief can be drawn on clay. You can build it up a little or even higher.

Here are some heads which are reliefs because they are flat.

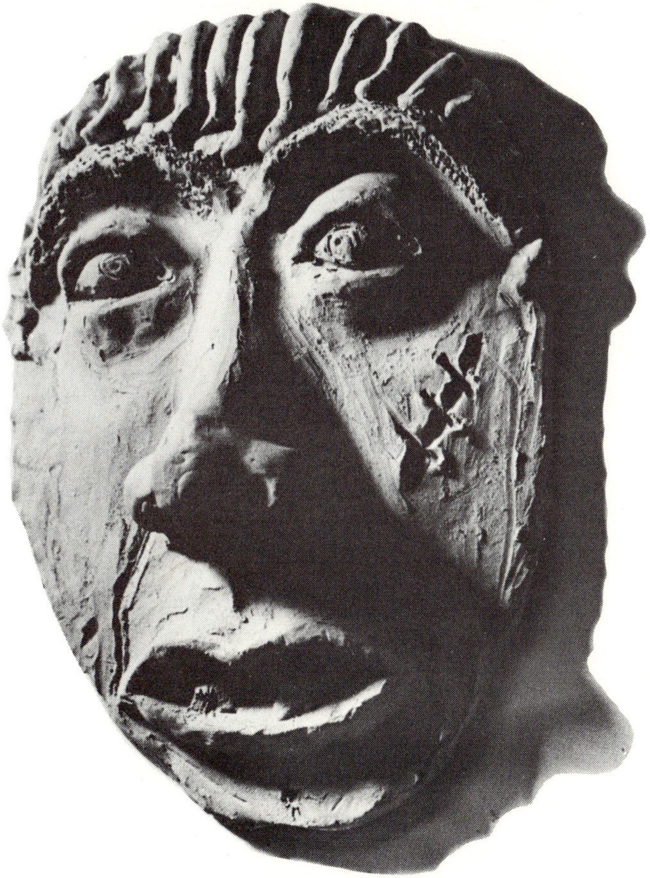

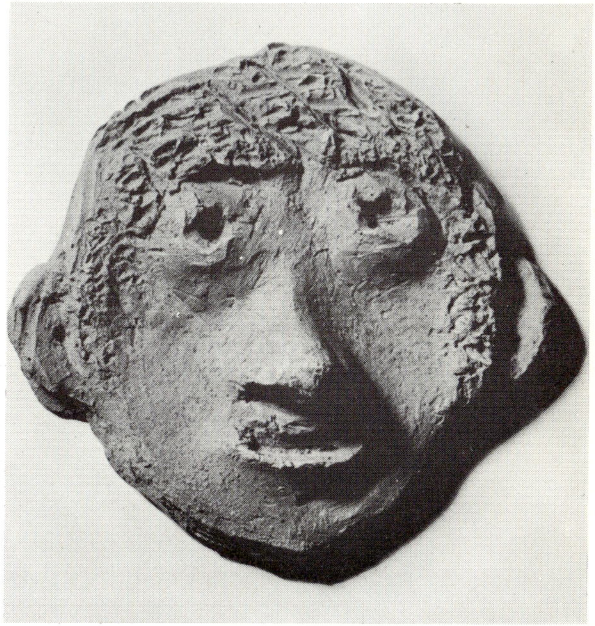

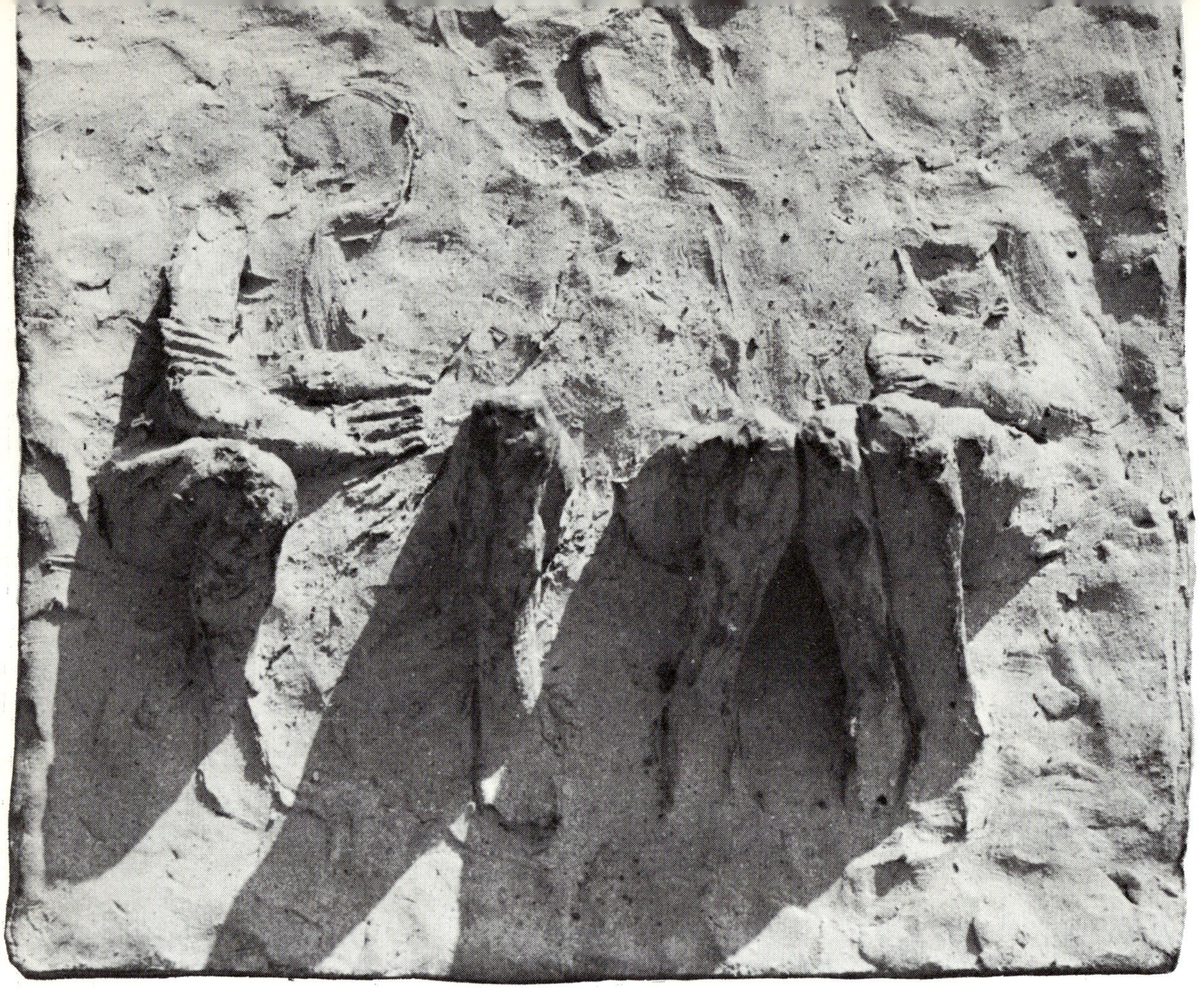

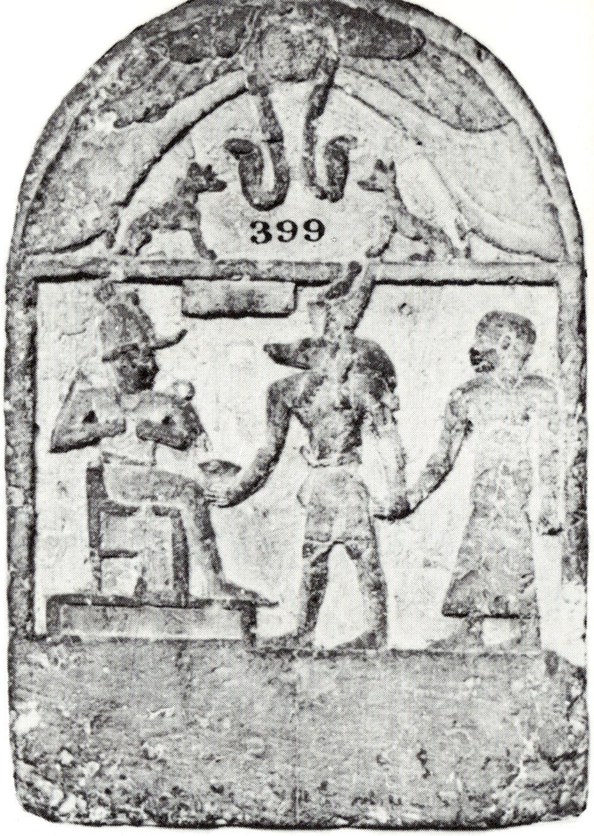

Opposite Here is a relief which was made by the Greeks over 2,000 years ago. Many reliefs like this one were built into houses and temples. This one was on the Parthenon Temple in Athens.
Far right This relief of a head was carved on a tombstone in Egypt over 2,000 years ago.
Above right Another Egyptian relief.
Above A clay relief of three figures by the author.
Right "Icarus". A relief by Michael Ayrton. Reproduced by kind permission of the artist.

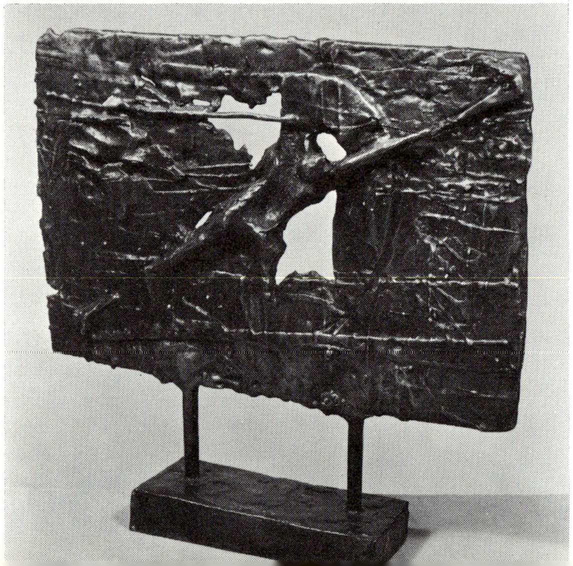

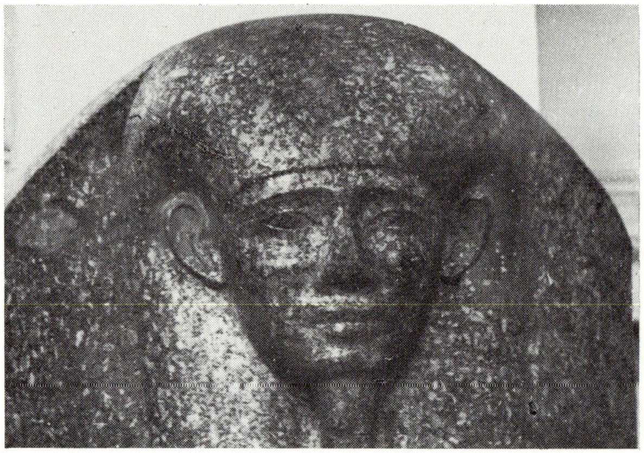

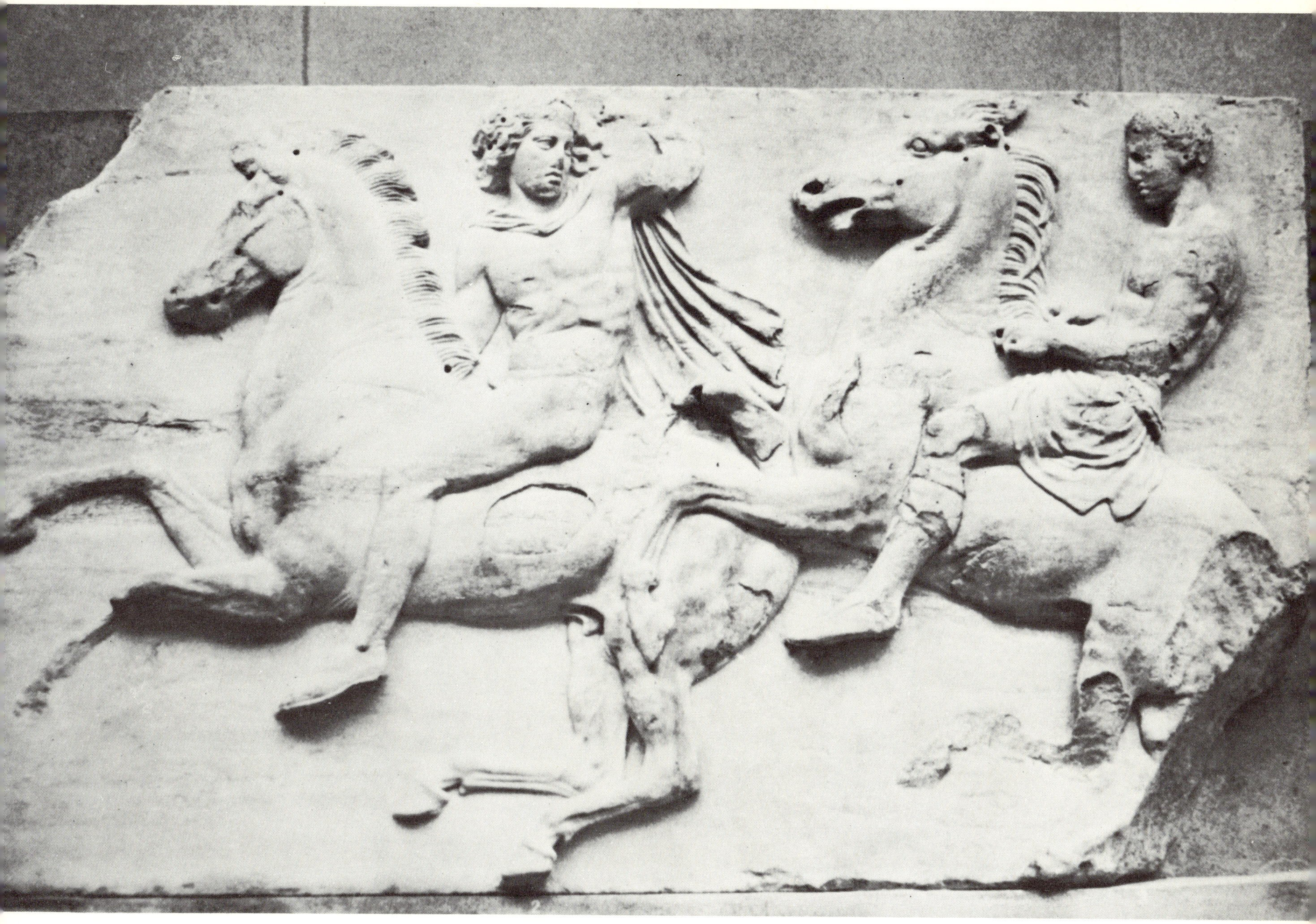

3 WORKING WITH PLASTER

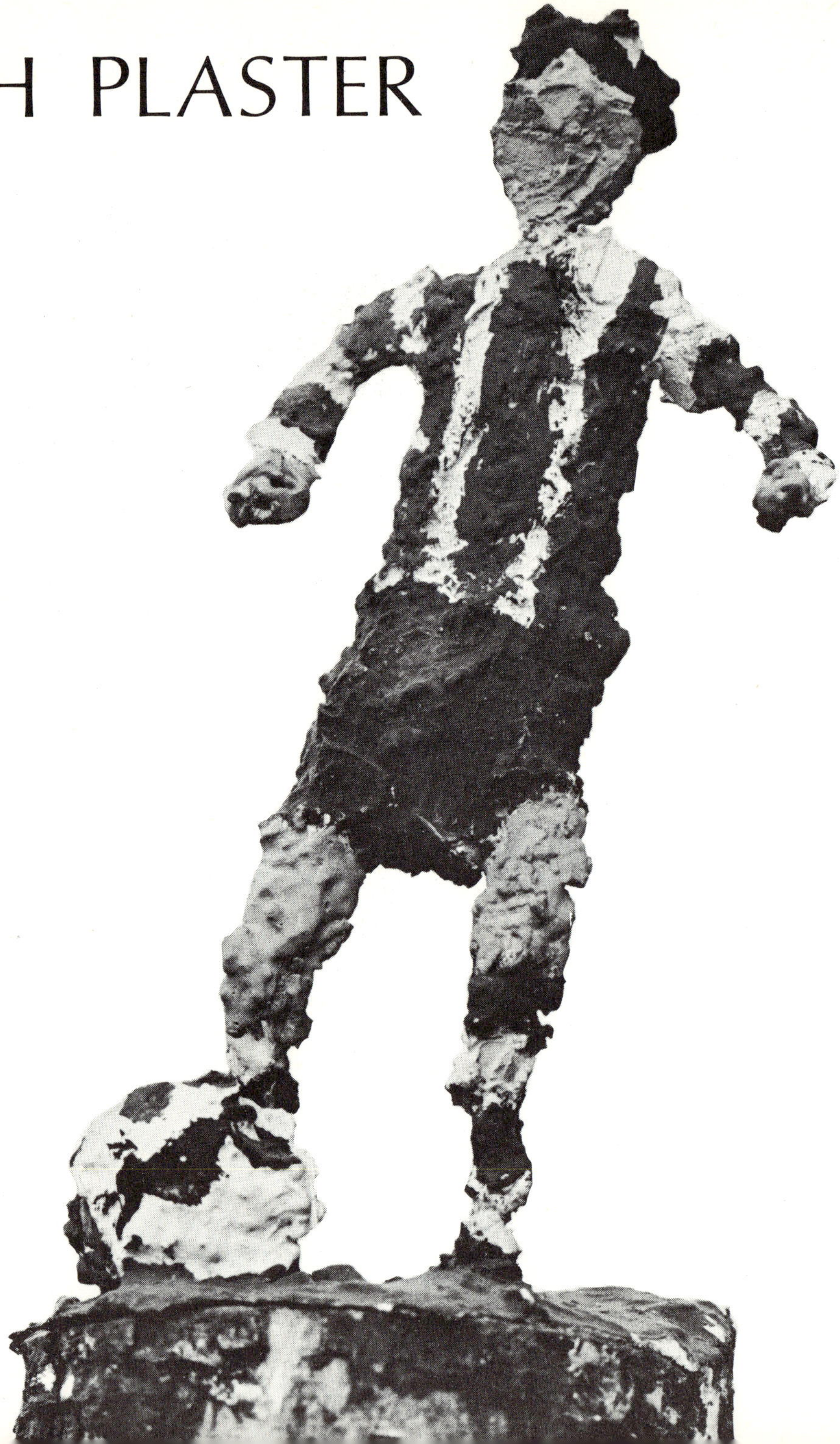

Plaster has been used for many hundreds of years. The Egyptians and the Greeks used it in making sculpture. Plaster is fun to use and there are many ways to work with it.

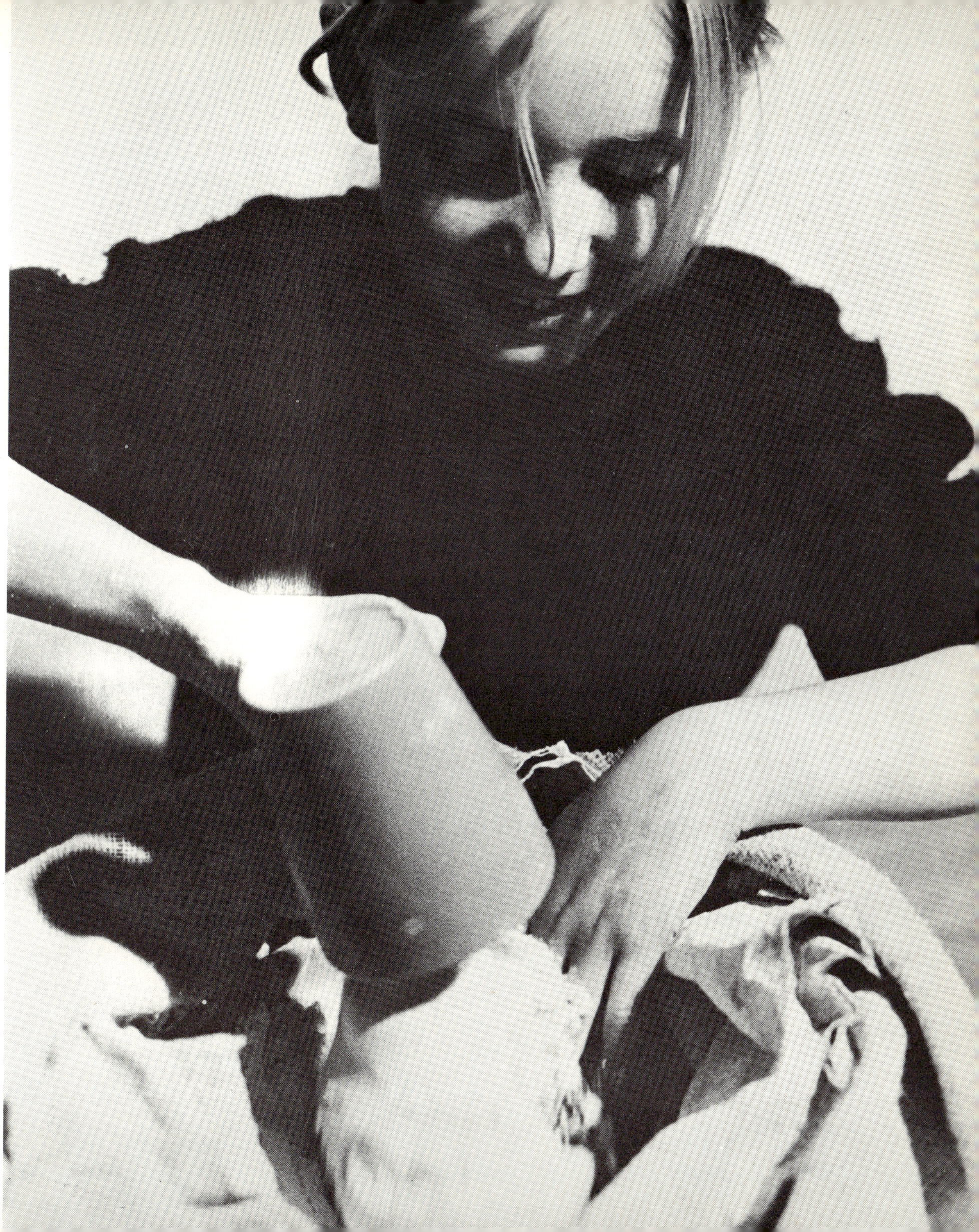

How to Mix Plaster

Put some water into a plastic or rubber bowl. Sprinkle the plaster evenly over the top in small amounts until it does not sink but stays on top of the water.

Then mix it well until it is like heavy cream, being careful not to leave any lumps in it. Plaster must be used quickly because it will harden in a very short while.

When you have used the plaster, let whatever is left in the bowl harden and then crack it out by pushing in the sides of the bowl. *Never pour it down a sink.*

If you sprinkle salt into the plaster and water it will harden faster. If you sprinkle sugar into it the plaster will take longer to harden.

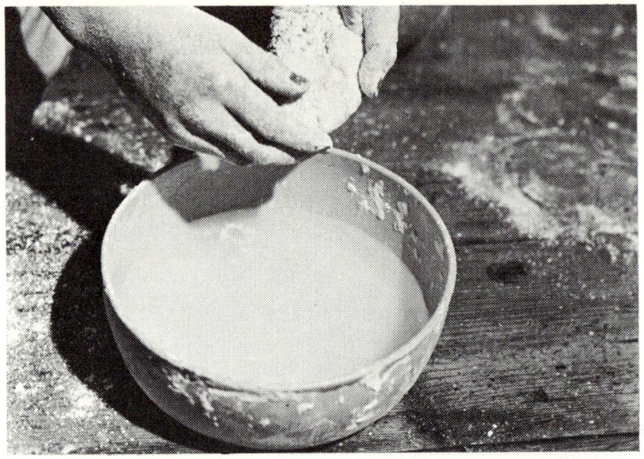

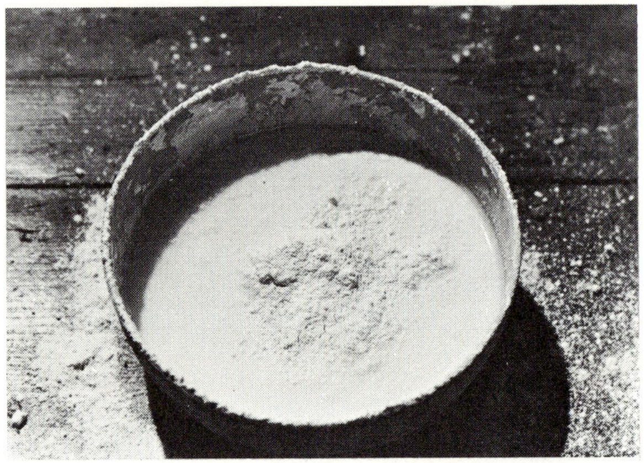

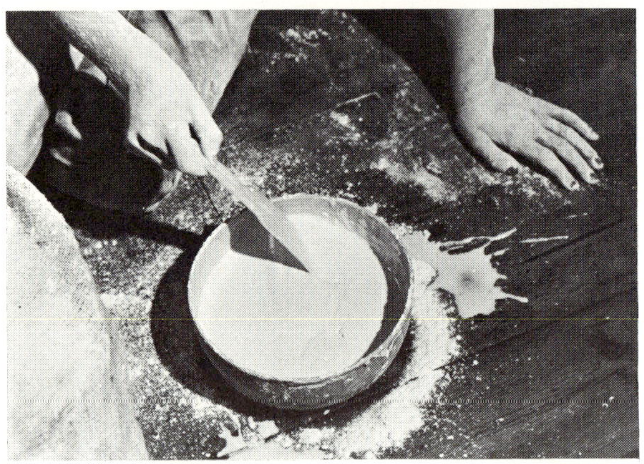

Plaster Casts from Clay

You can make a plaster cast of your clay relief. Here a wall of clay is being built around a relief to hold the plaster. Plaster is being poured onto the relief and spread evenly, at least an inch thick over the clay.

While plaster sets it gets warm and sometimes smokes. Now it is hard. The clay wall has been pulled away and it has been turned over. The clay is gently pulled away from the plaster.

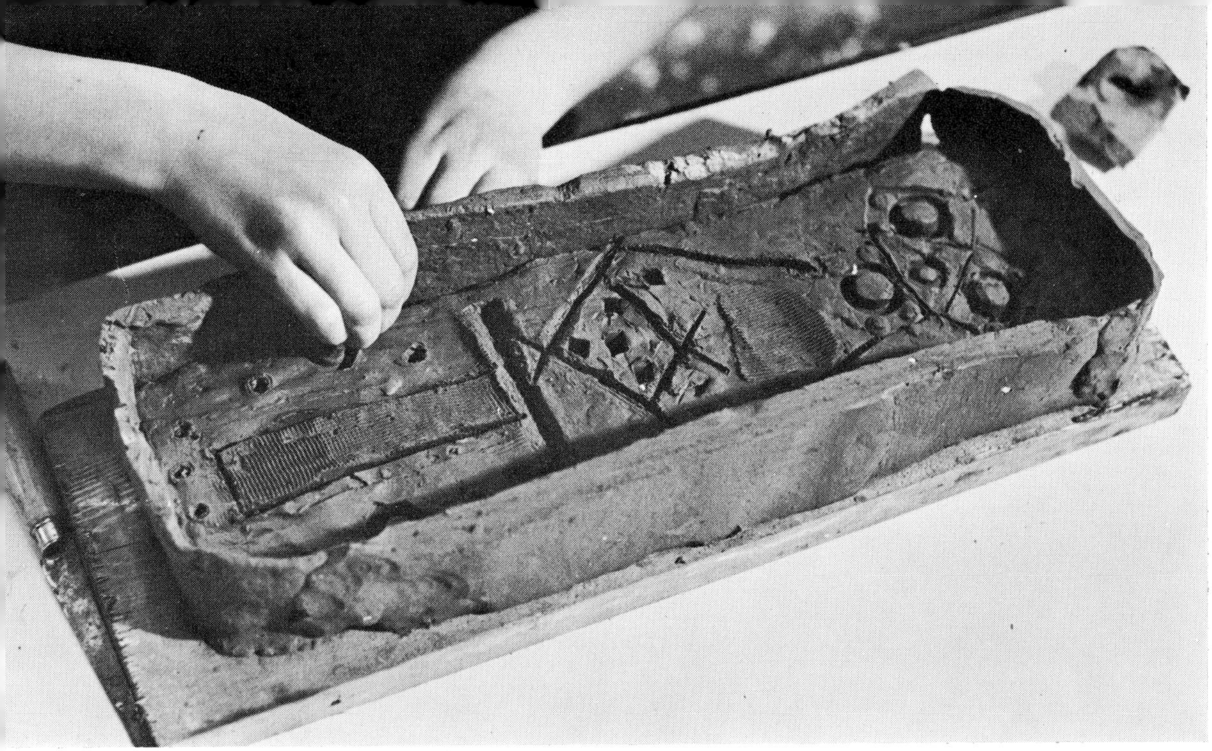
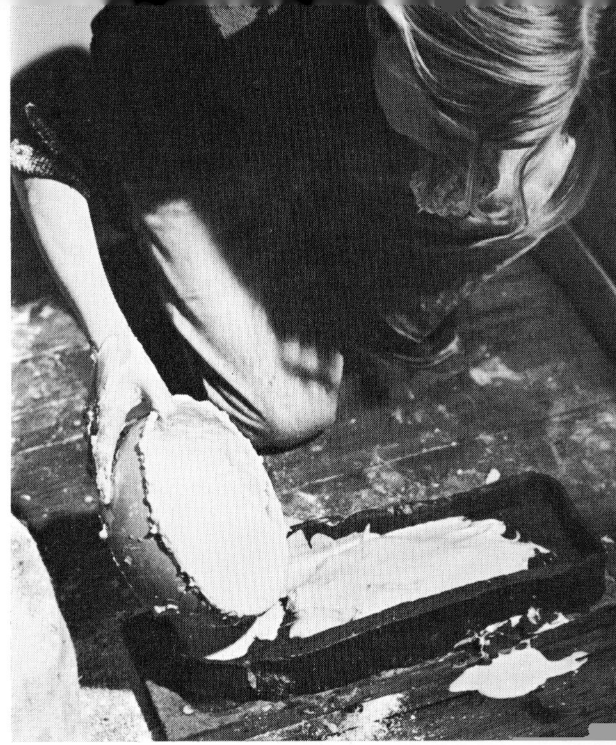
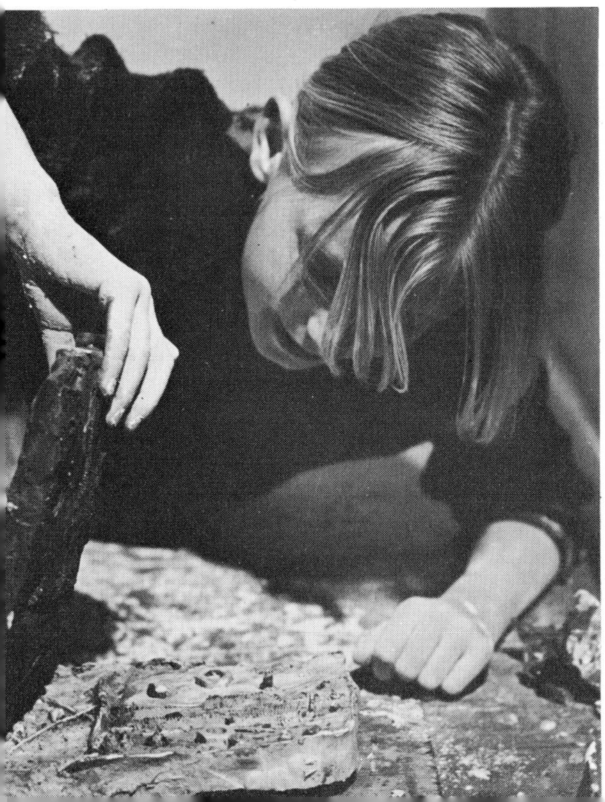
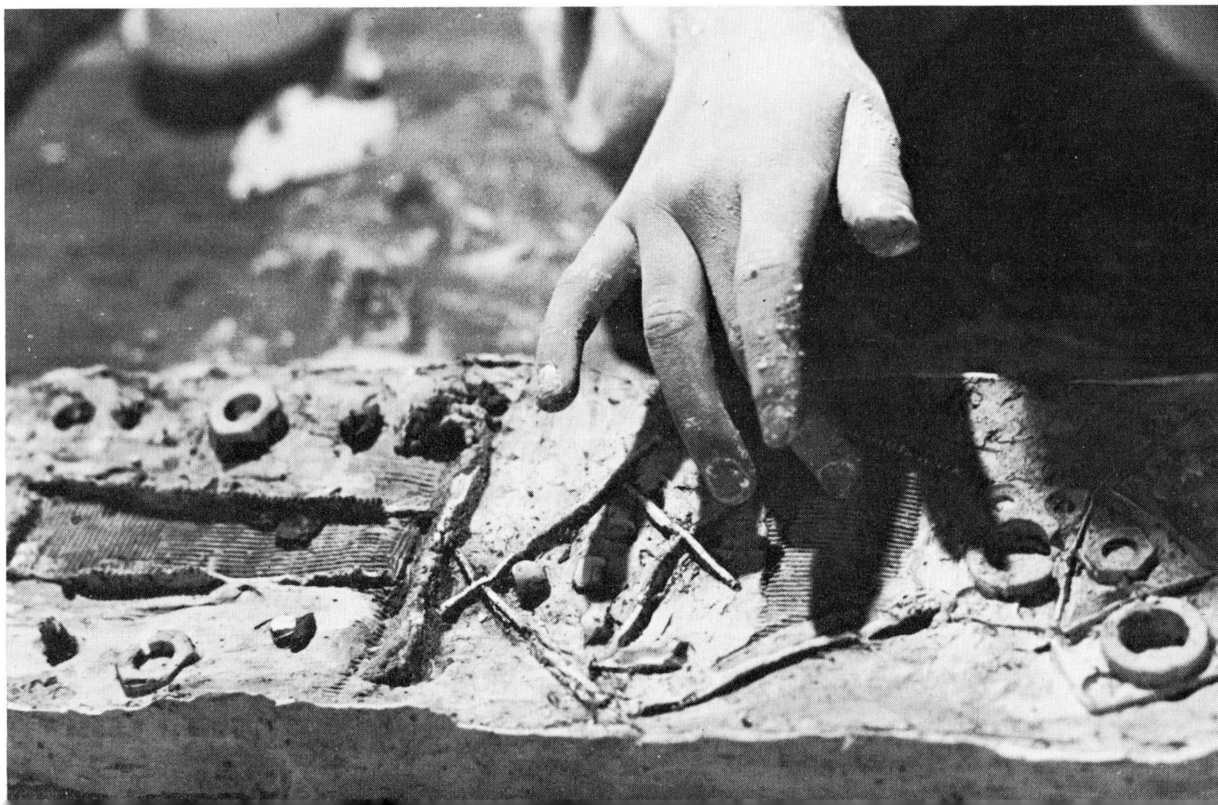

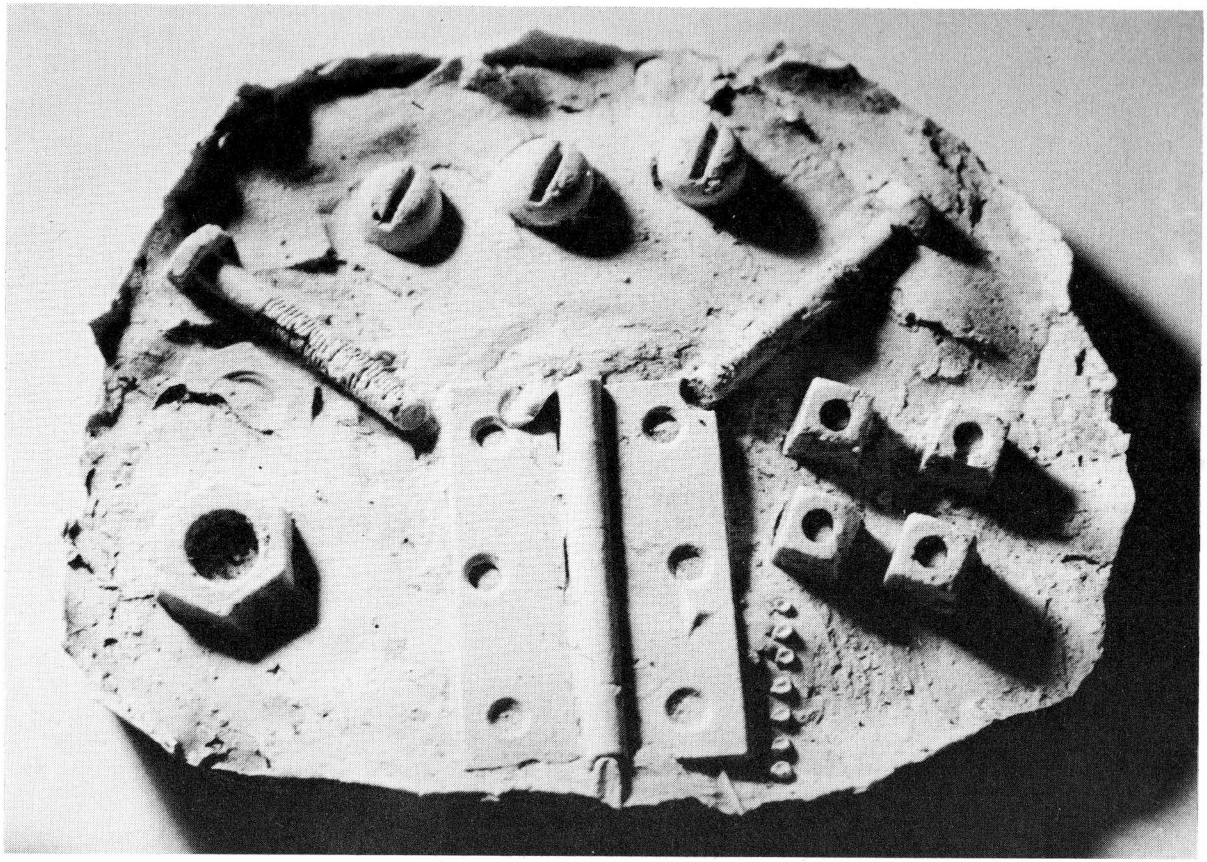

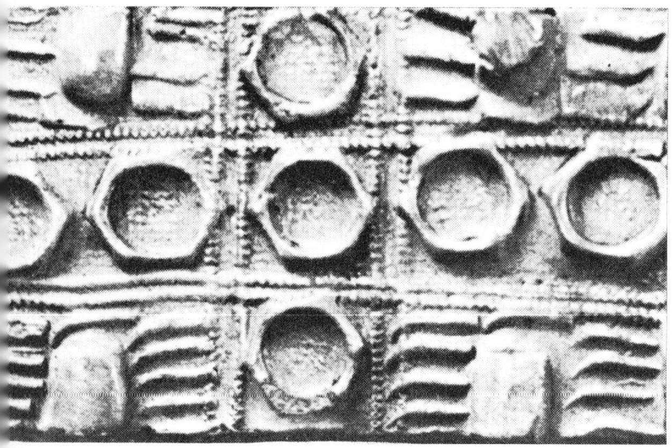

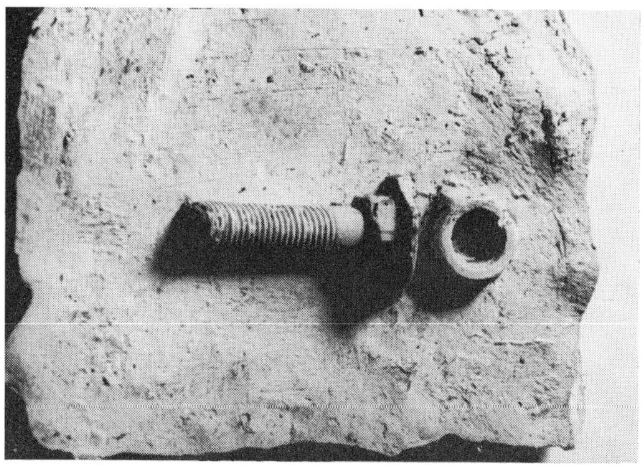

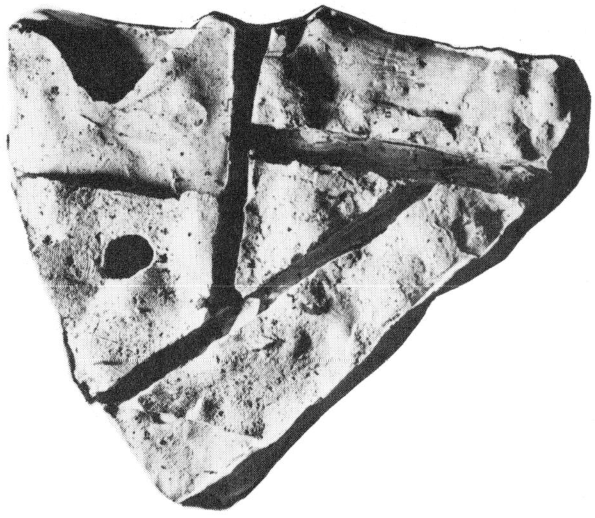

Plaster and Sand Reliefs

If you don't have any clay you can make a plaster cast from sand. Take a cardboard box and half fill it with sand. Make your own design in the sand. Use any object which you think will make a good pattern. Different shapes of wood are being used here.

Mix some plaster and pour at least one inch evenly into the box to cover the sand.

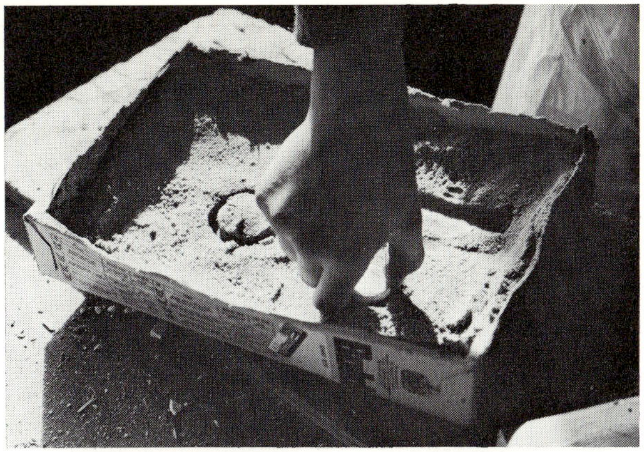

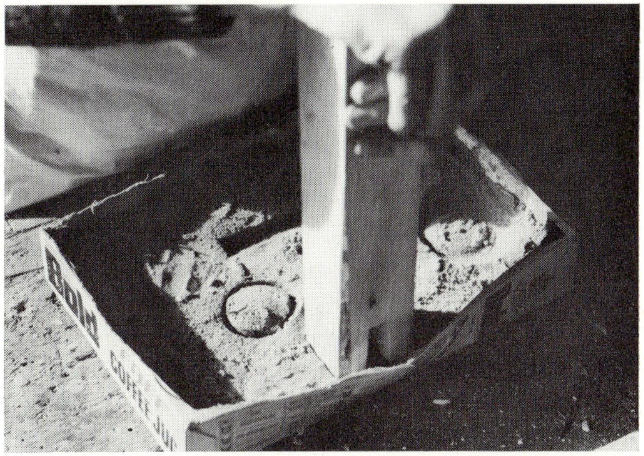

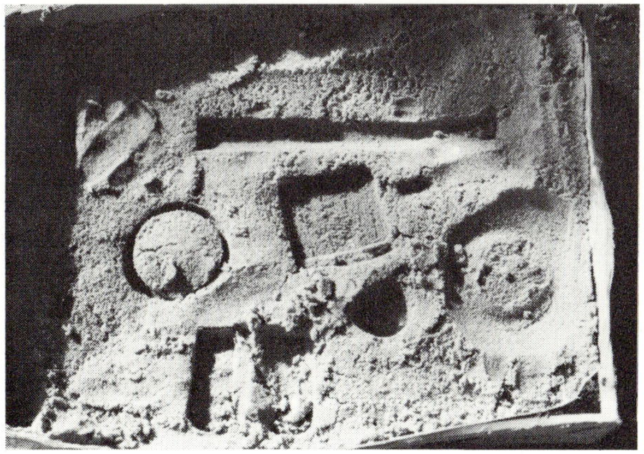

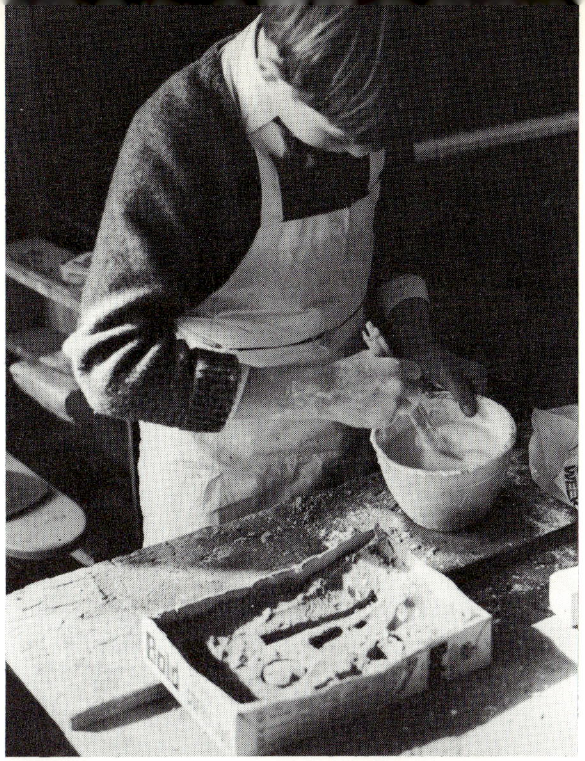

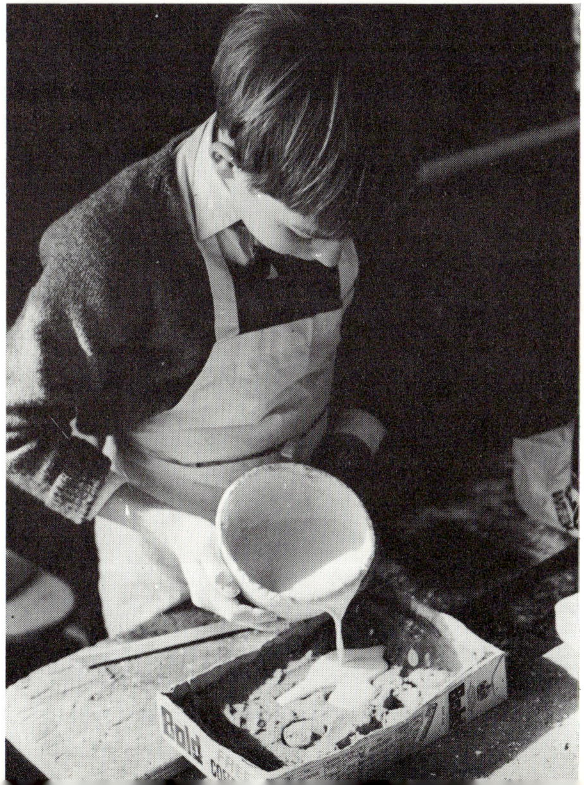

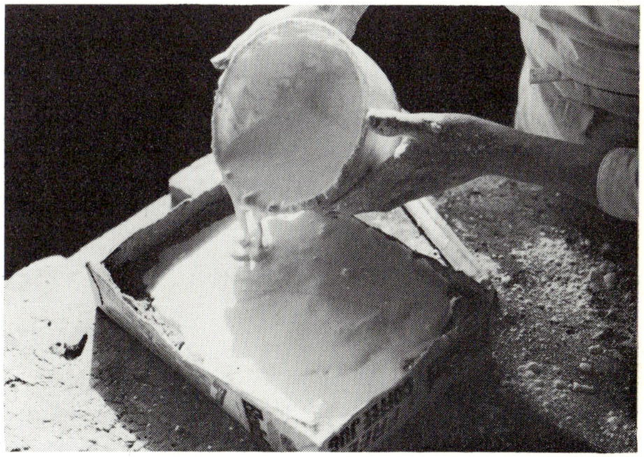

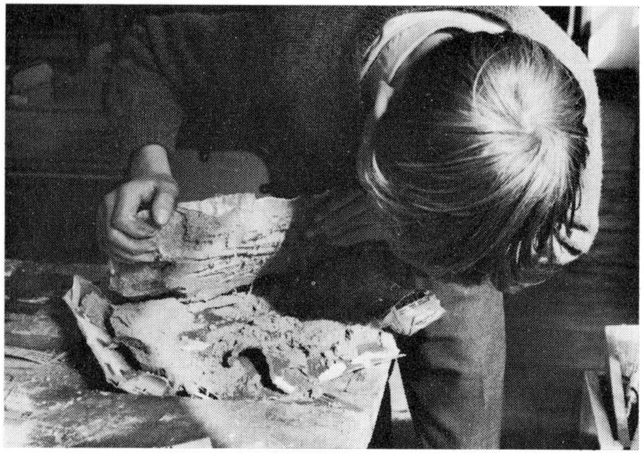

When the plaster is dry, gently tear away the box and pull the plaster away from the sand. Brush the loose sand away from the plaster.

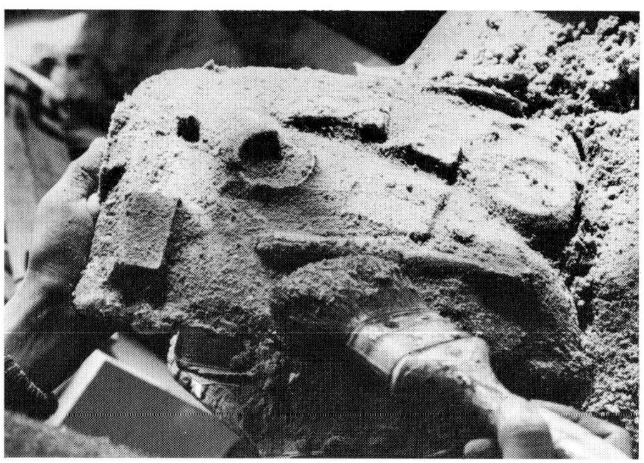

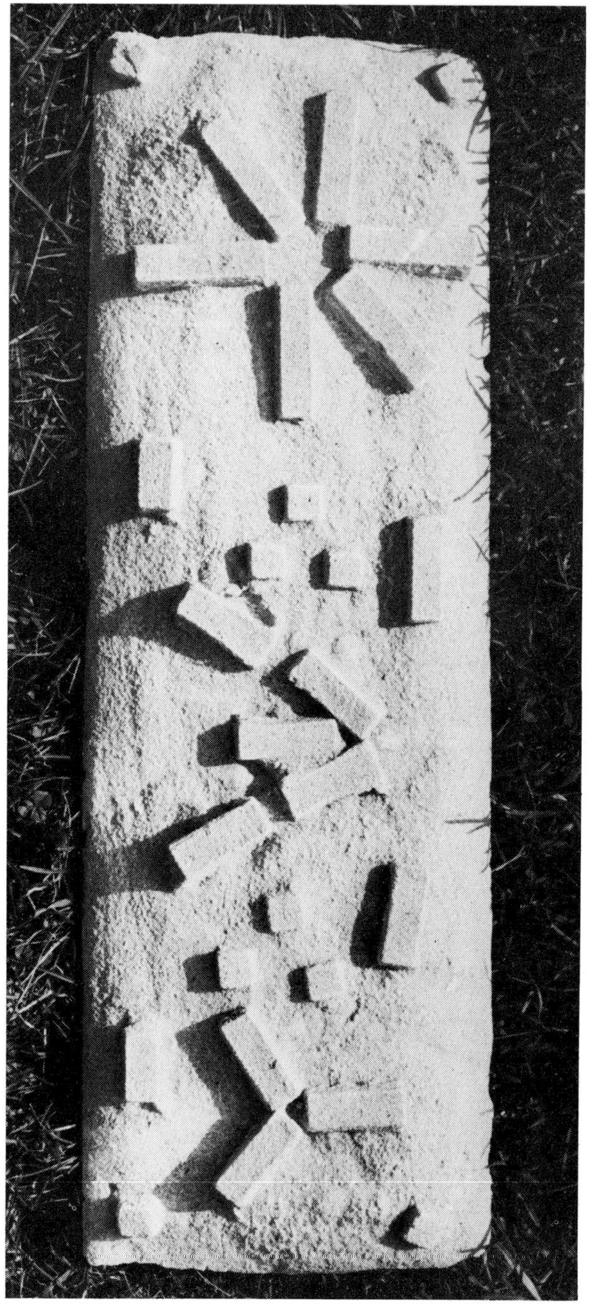

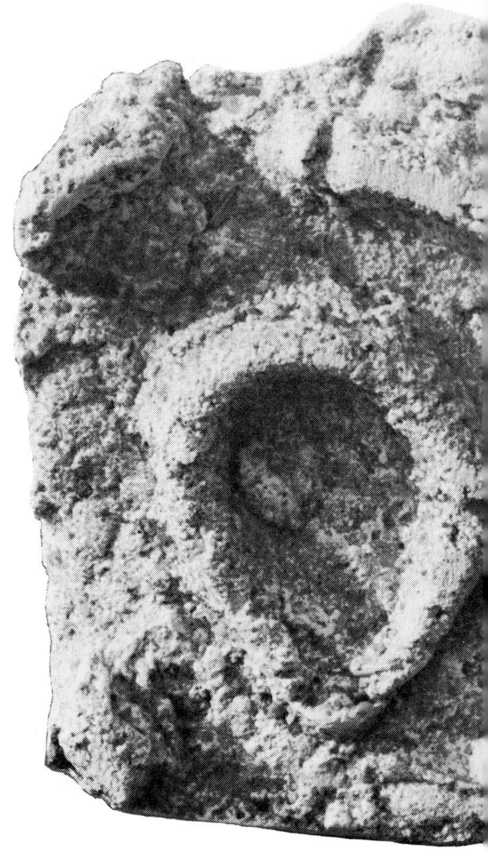

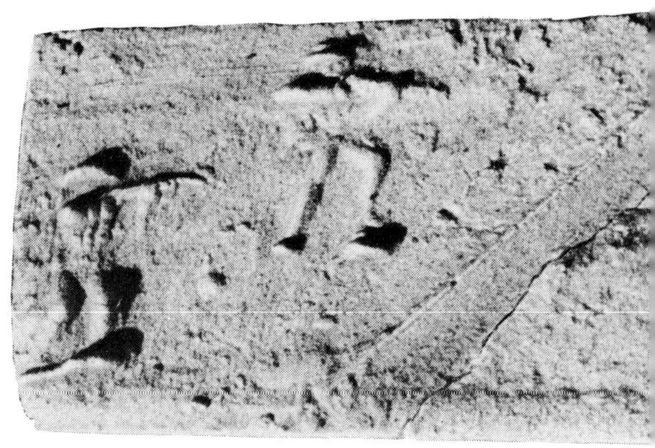

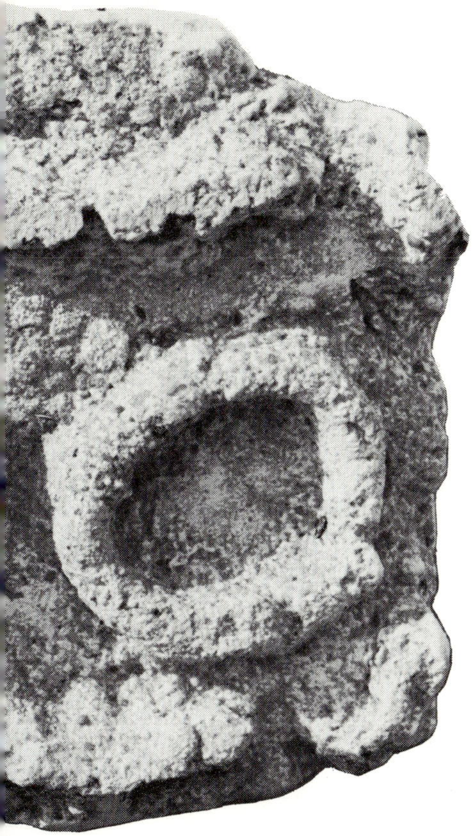

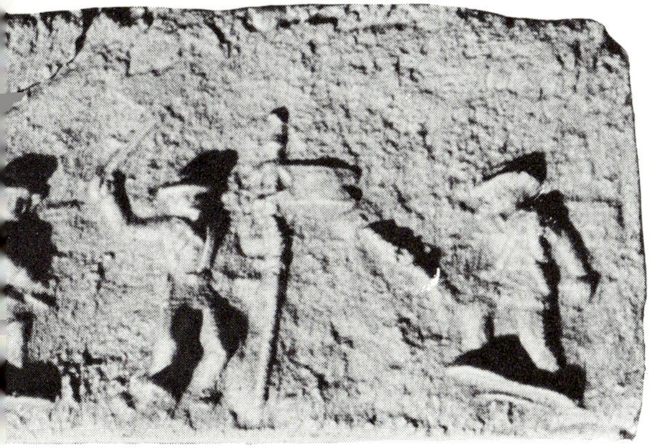

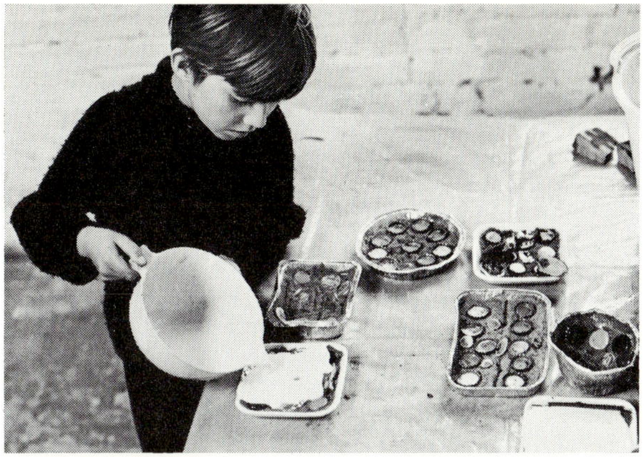

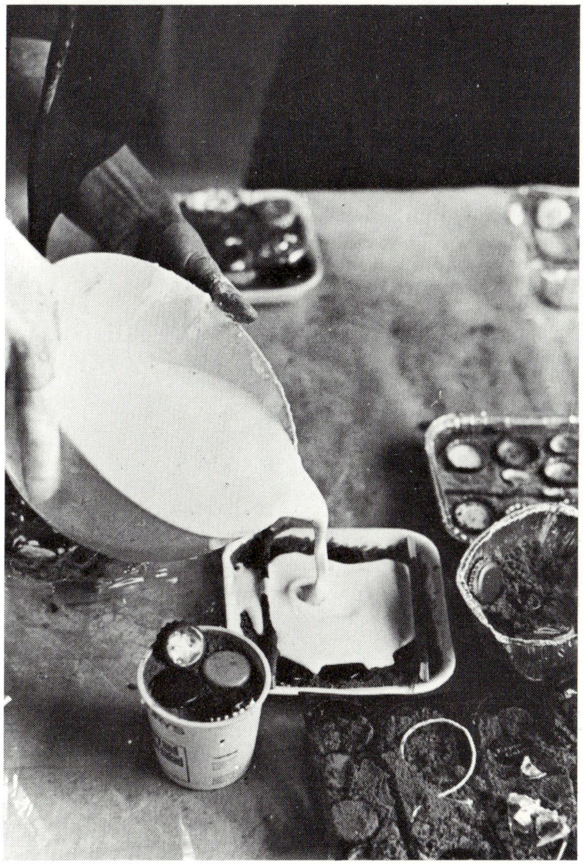

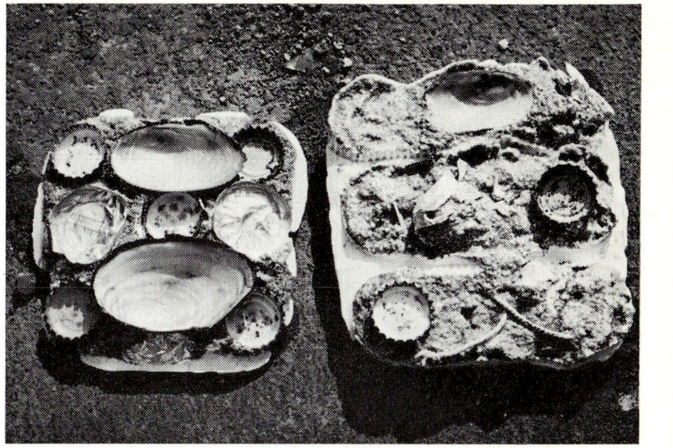

Bottle tops, toy soldiers and other objects were set into the sand to make a design. Plaster is poured onto it in the same way. The objects will stick to the plaster.

You can make all kinds of shapes with plaster and sand like the owl in the centre.

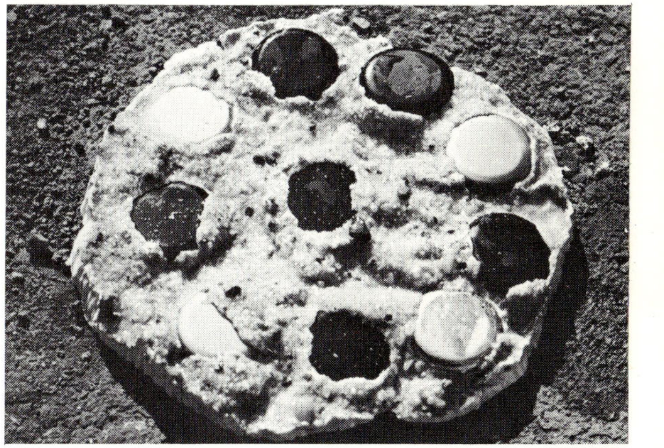

String and Plaster Balloons

You can also use plaster with string and balloons.

Dip string into wet plaster and wrap it around a balloon. Make sure it overlaps in places for strength. When you have finished wrapping burst the balloon. You have a lovely string shape.

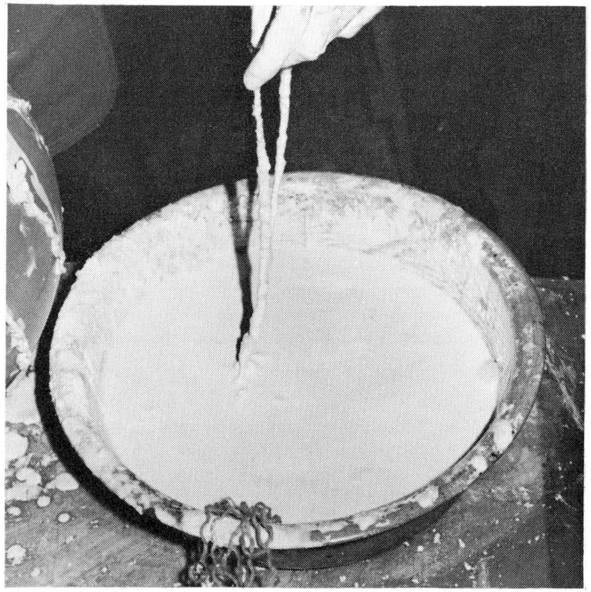

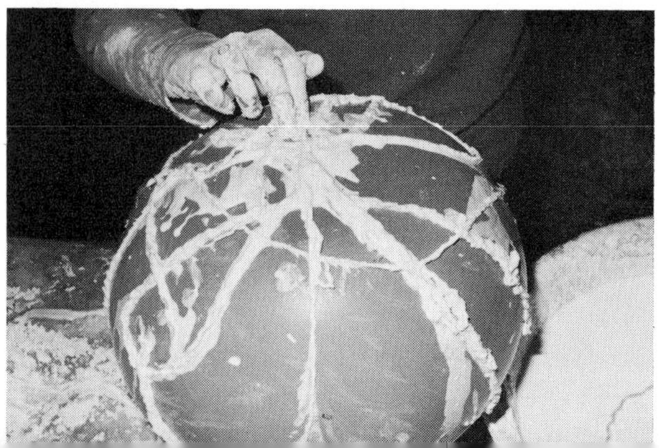

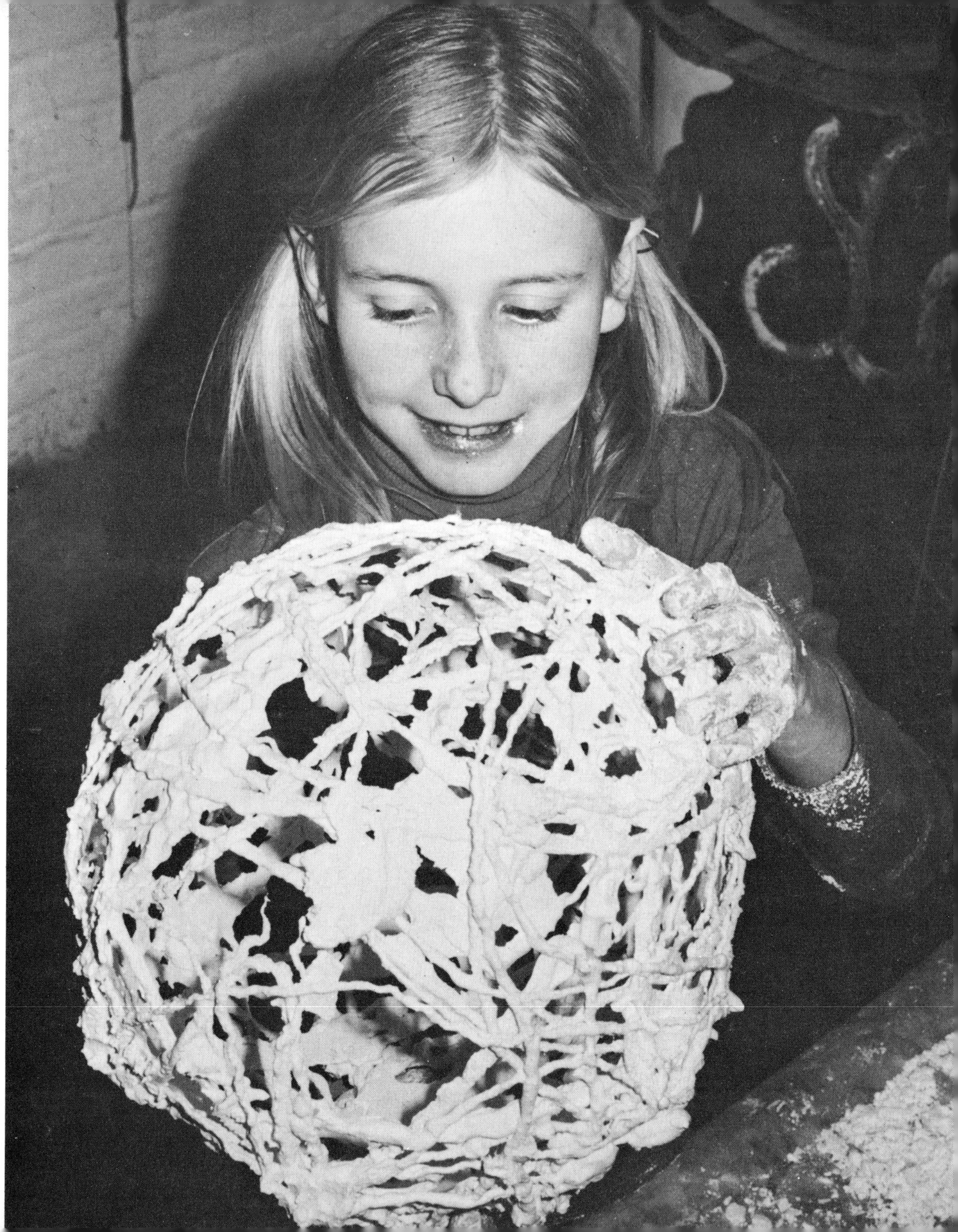

Plastic Bag Shapes

Pour plaster into a plastic bag and squeeze a shape. Hold the plaster very still for a few minutes until it hardens. When it is hard, pull off the plastic bag.

Shapes made in plastic bags. Try and see how many strange shapes you can make in this way.

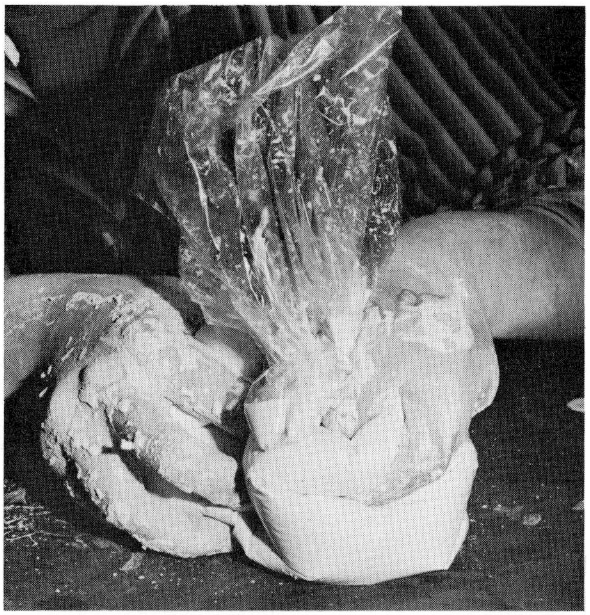

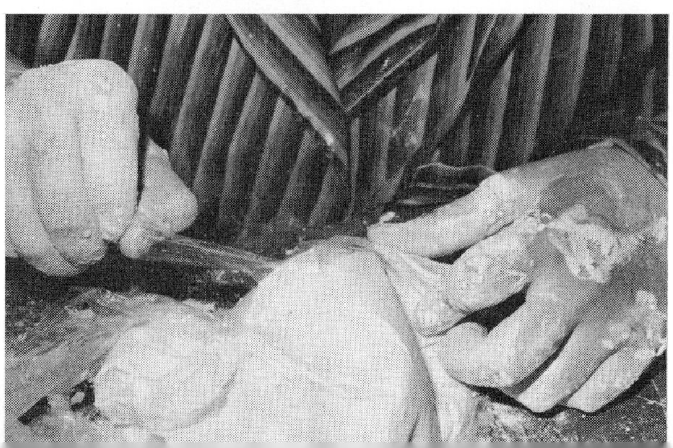

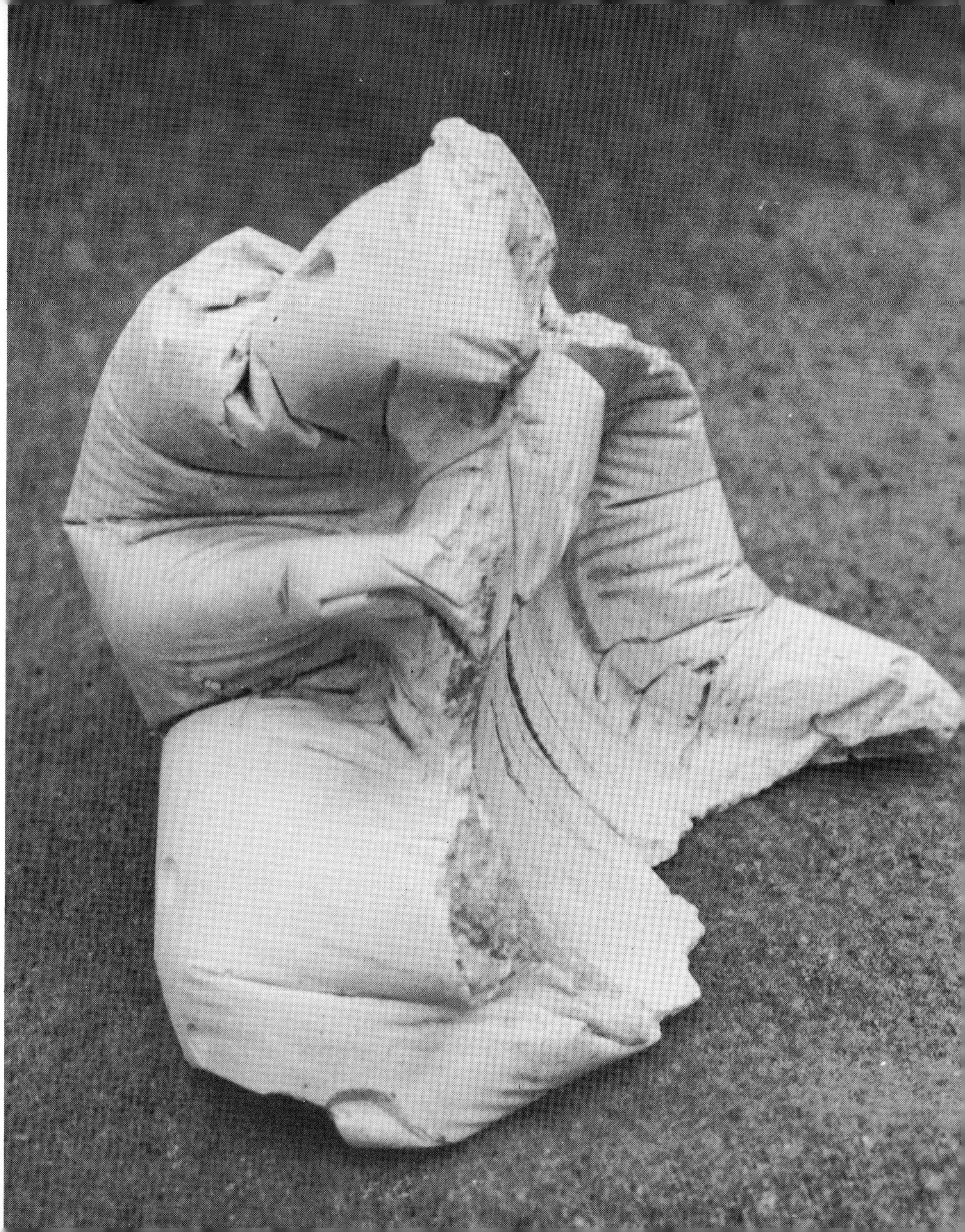

Plaster over Wire

Any wire shape can be covered by dipping string, cloth or newspaper into plaster and winding it around the wire. Fresh layers of plaster are added until it is strong.

This wire is the shape of a foot. A strip of cloth is dipped into plaster and wound around the wire. When one layer is done, plaster is added without rags. Wait until the plaster sets slightly, then it will not drip. The plaster is scraped down with a knife while it is still wet and soft.

Right The finished foot in plaster.

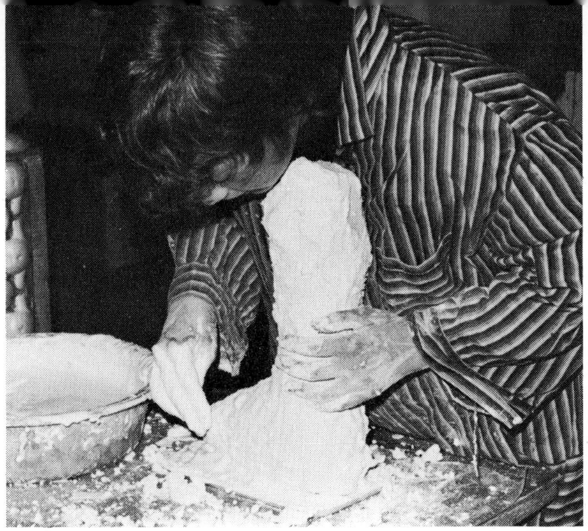

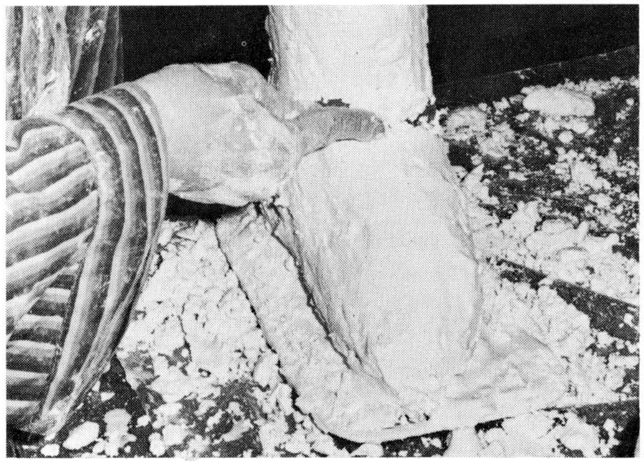

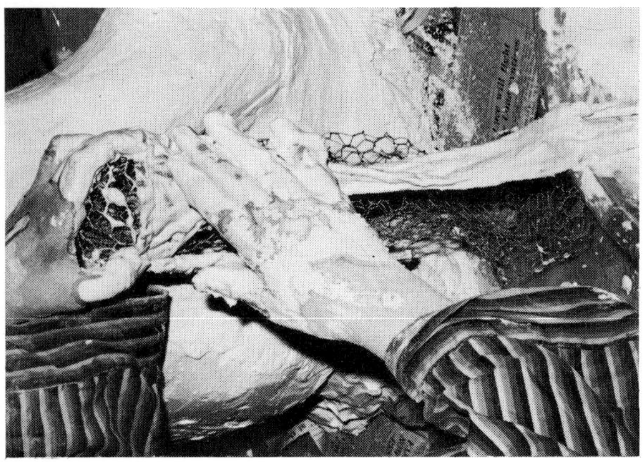

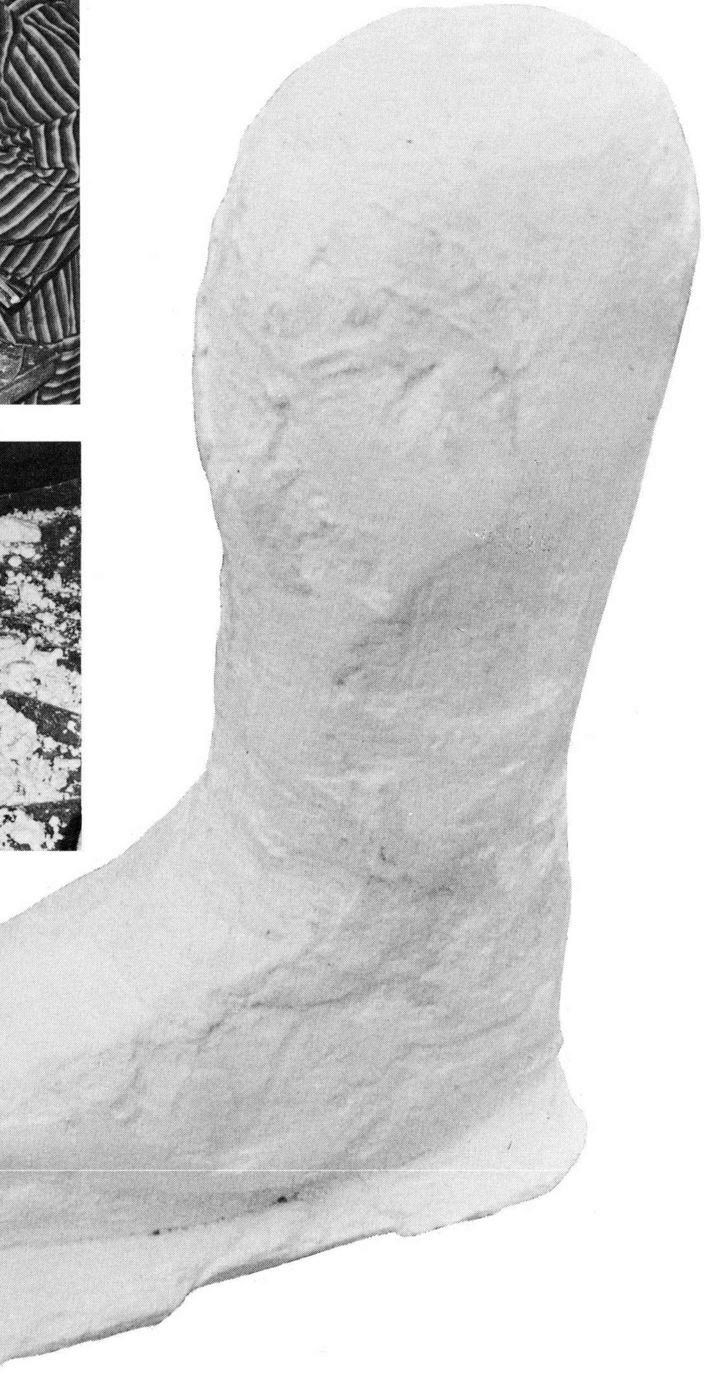

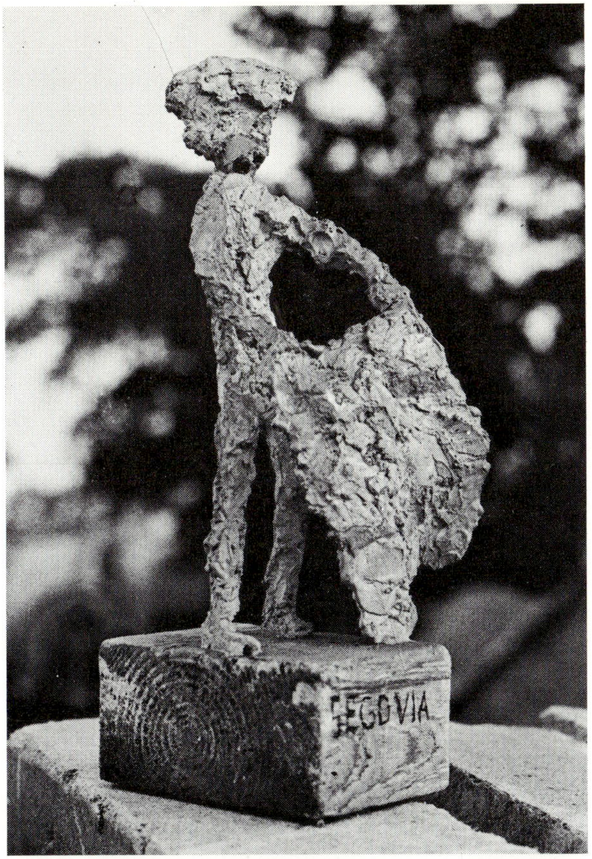

Bottom left The finished plaster can be painted.

Left and right Two plaster men which have been painted.

Below An animal shape in plaster.

Bottom right Two plaster people walking hand in hand.

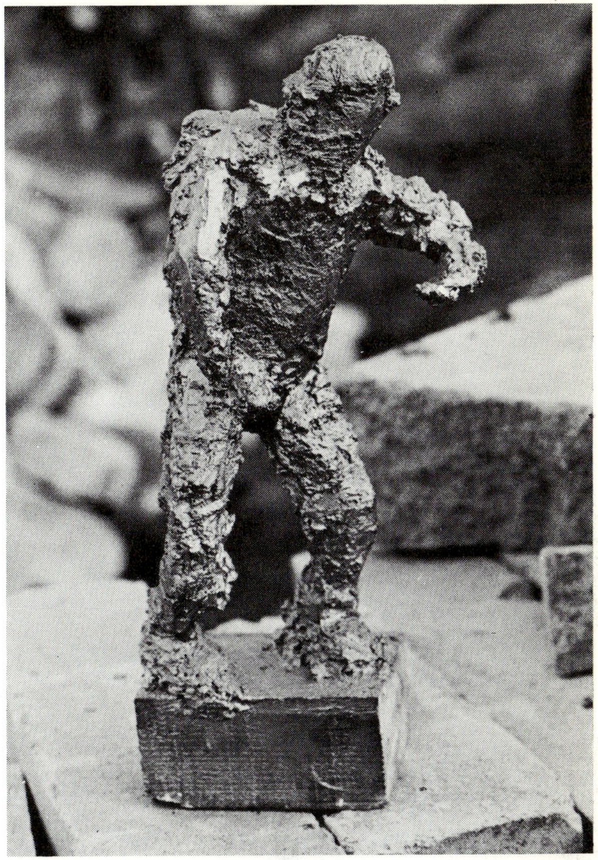

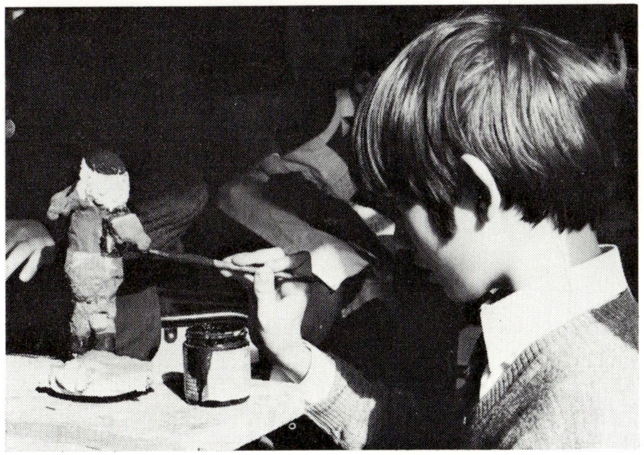

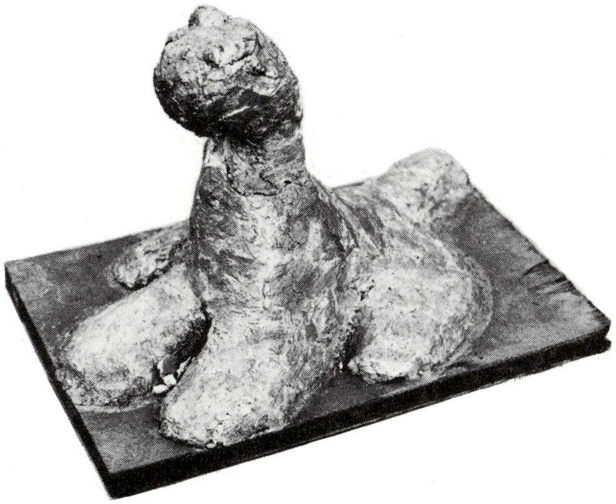

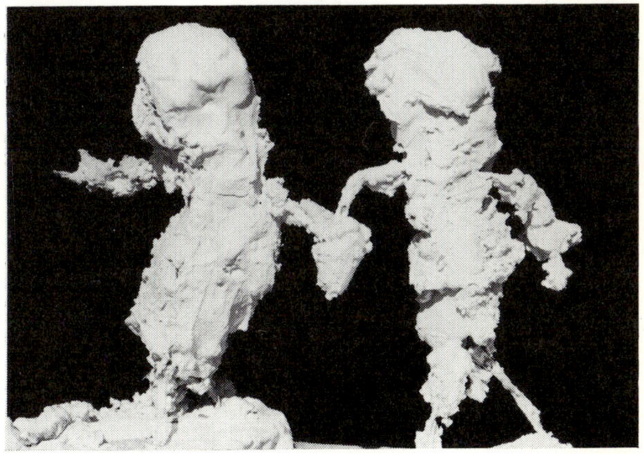

4 CARVING

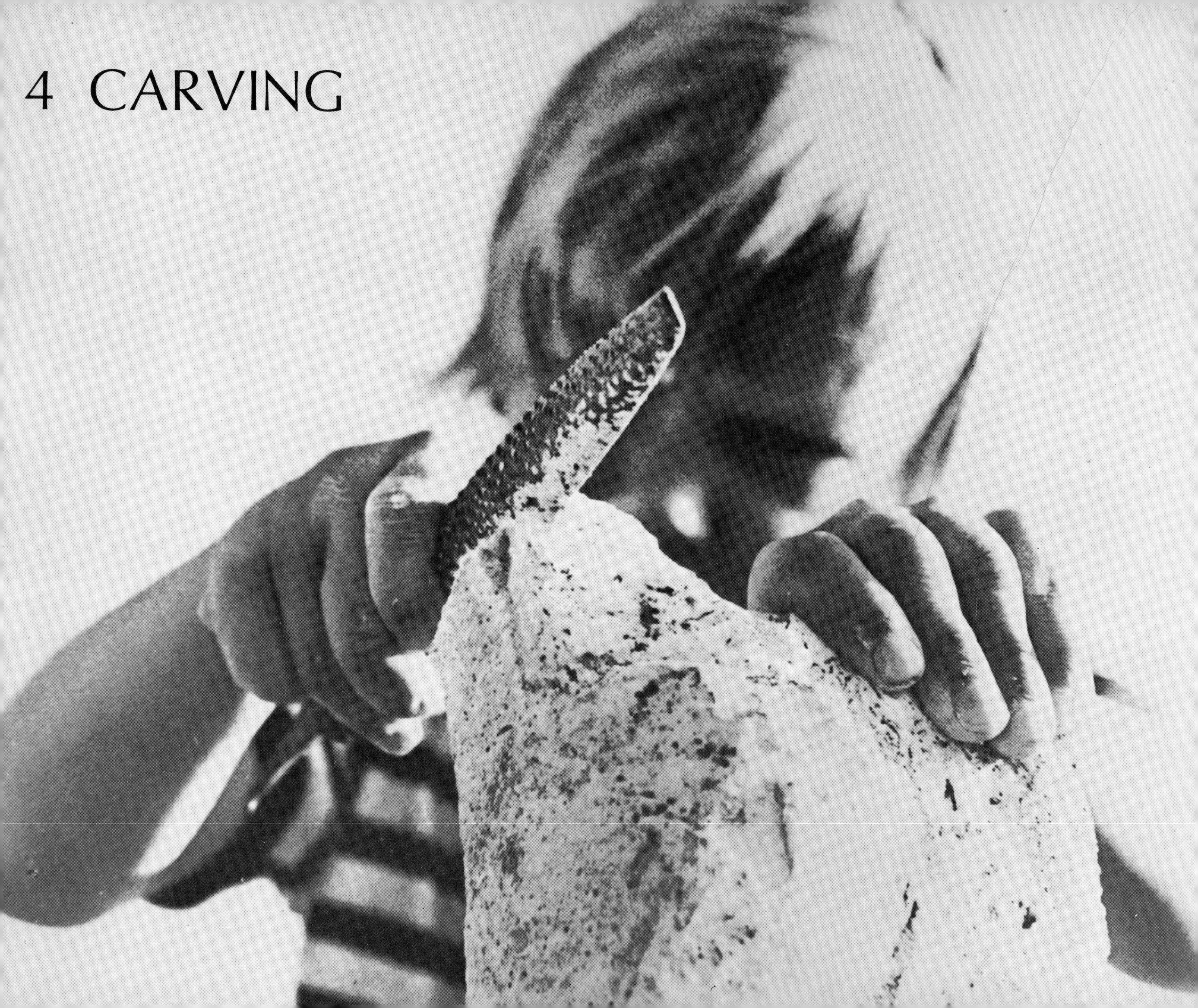

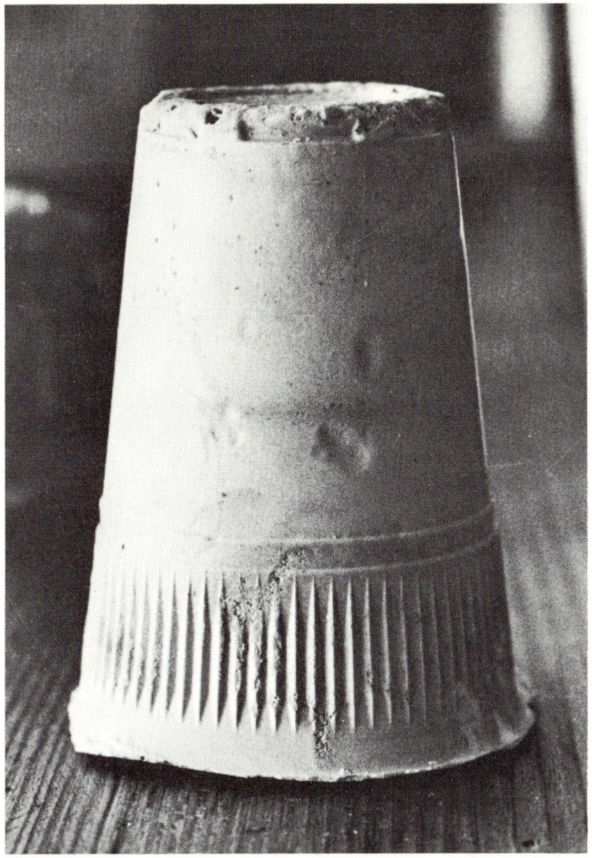

Carving a shape is the opposite of building up a shape.

The picture at the bottom of this page shows some tools which are used for carving.
A block for carving can be made by pouring plaster into a container and letting it set. Cardboard boxes or cups are good containers because they can be torn away when the plaster hardens. Greasing the container with Vaseline will make it easier to pull away.

On the right you can see shapes that have been made in this way.

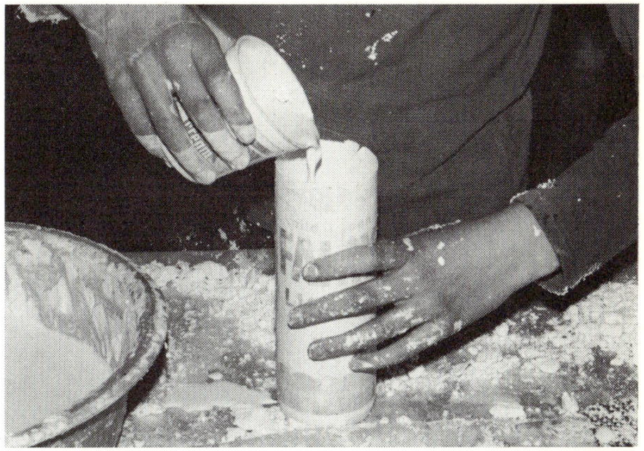

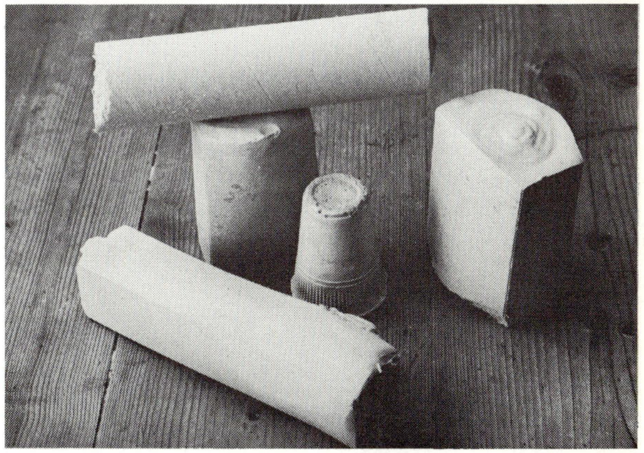

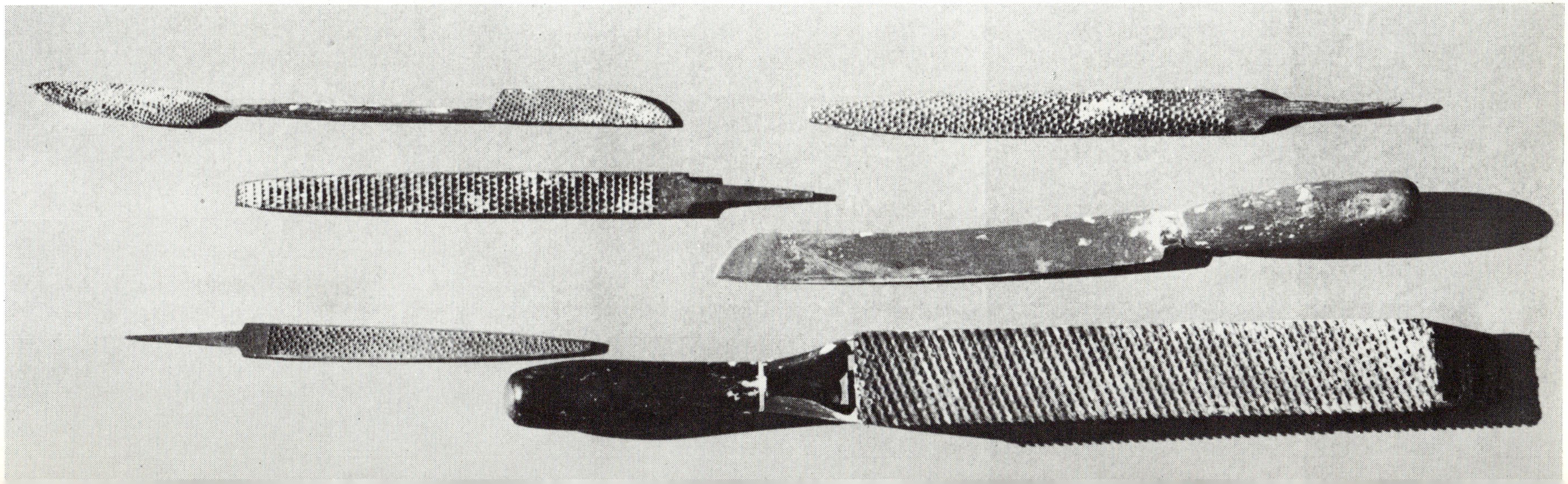

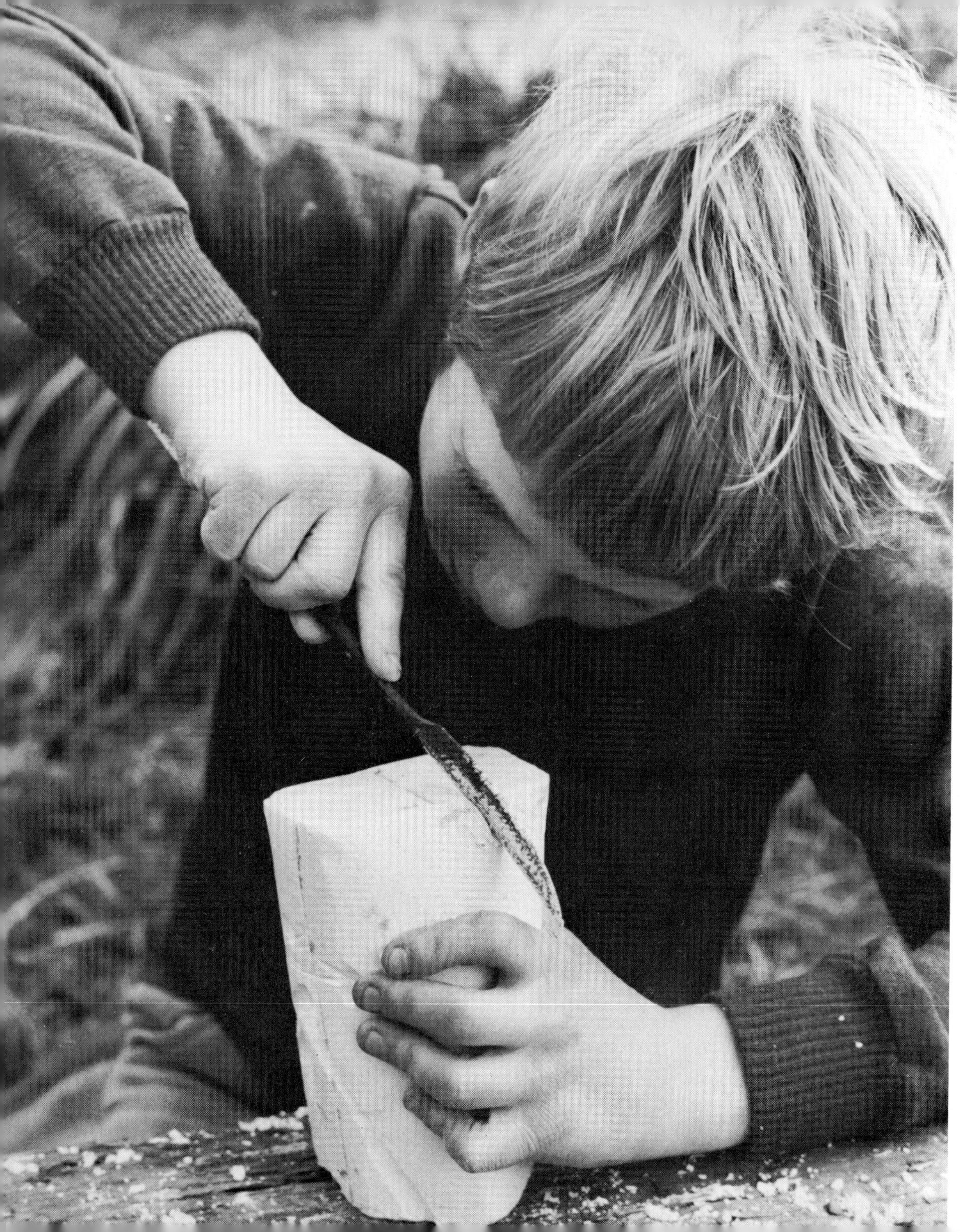

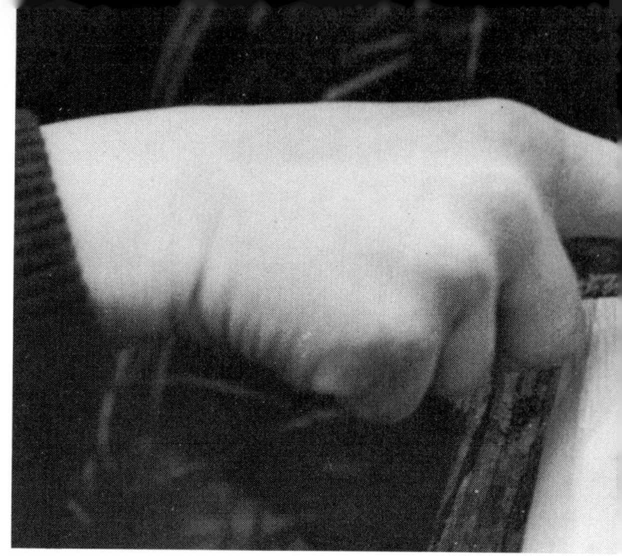

A block of plaster is being carved with a chisel and file. It cannot become too thin anywhere or the plaster will break.

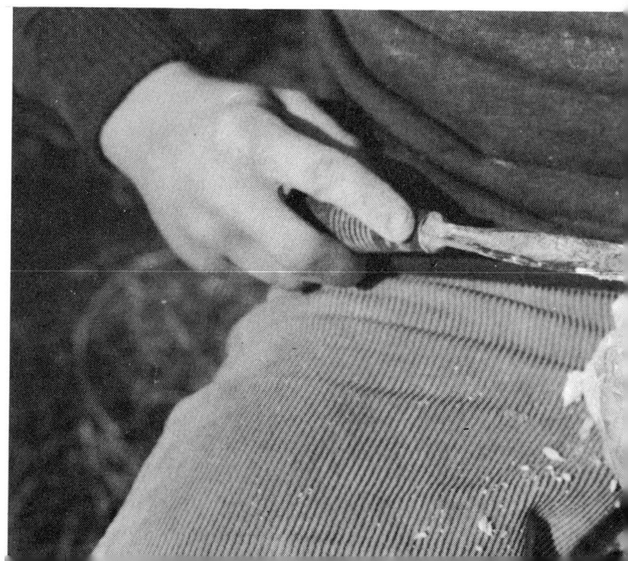

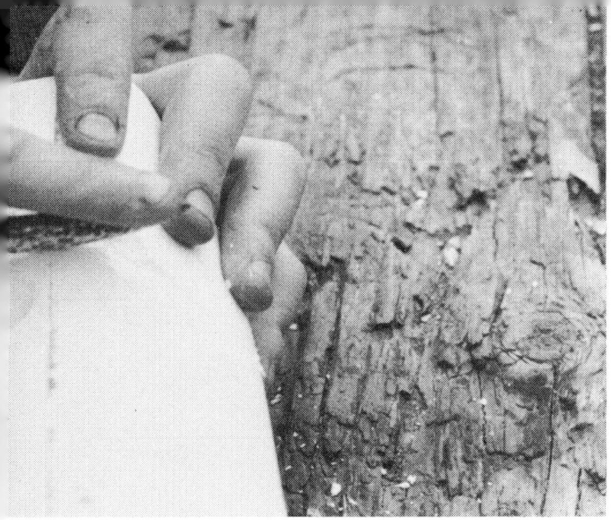

Right The finished carving in plaster.

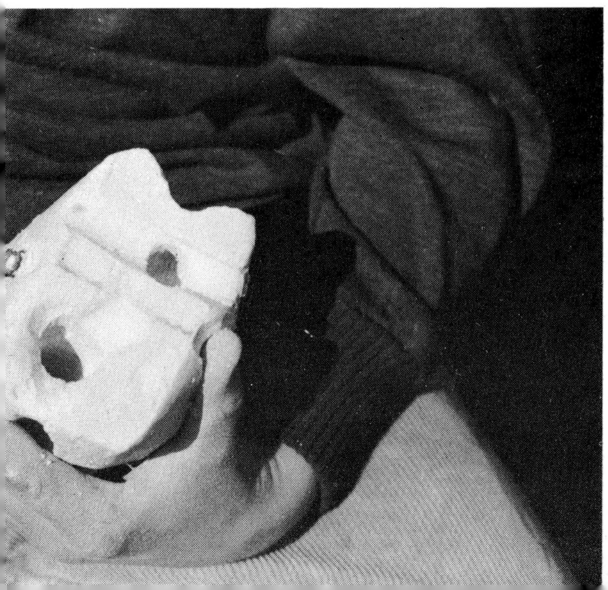

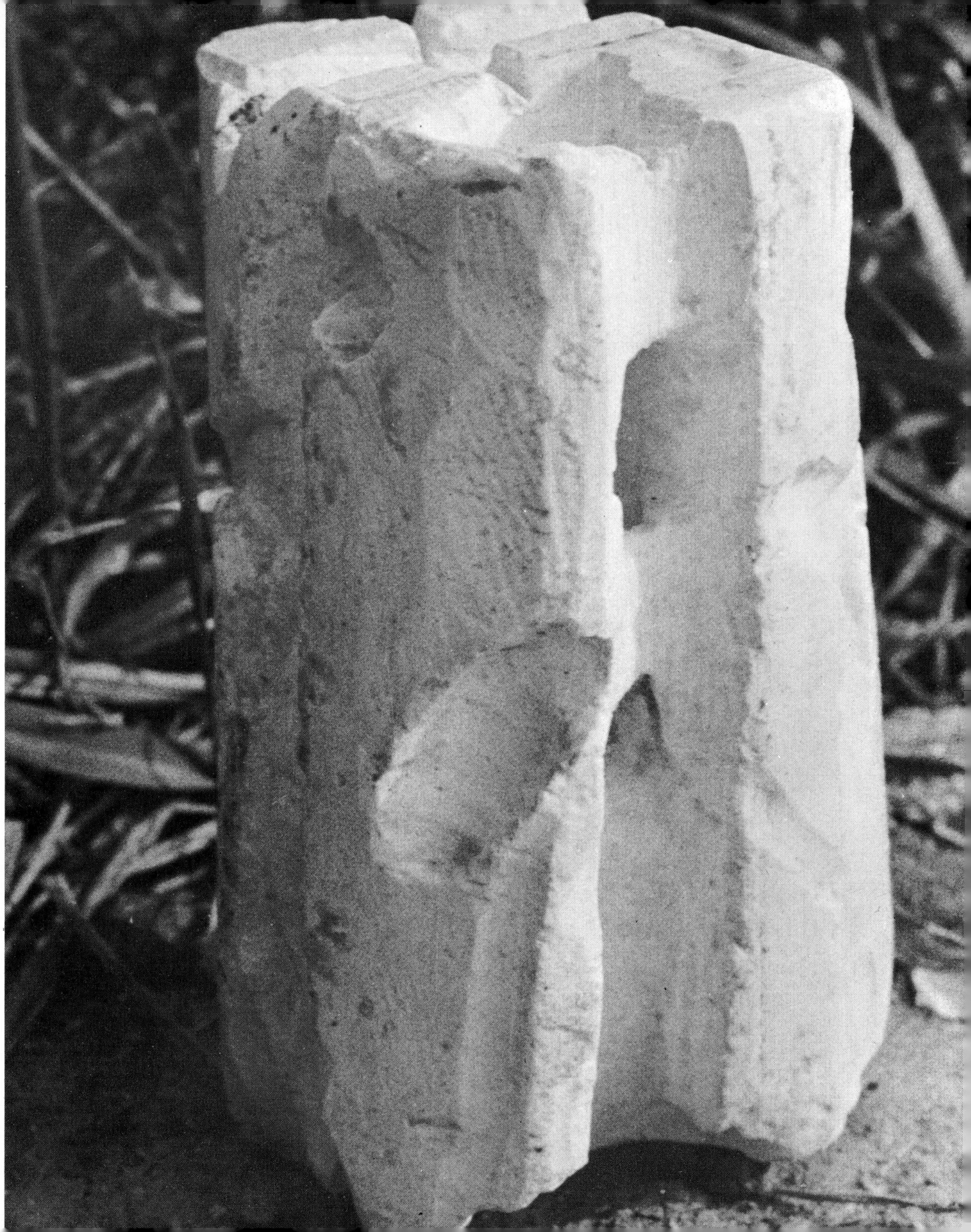

In the centre at the bottom you can see a face that has been carved in plaster and then coloured.

Below and top right Two more plaster carvings.

Breeze blocks (concrete blocks) are also good for carving because they are soft. They can be filed in the same way as plaster.

Below A carving in breeze block.

Right A carving of a foot.

Bottom right A baby, by the author.

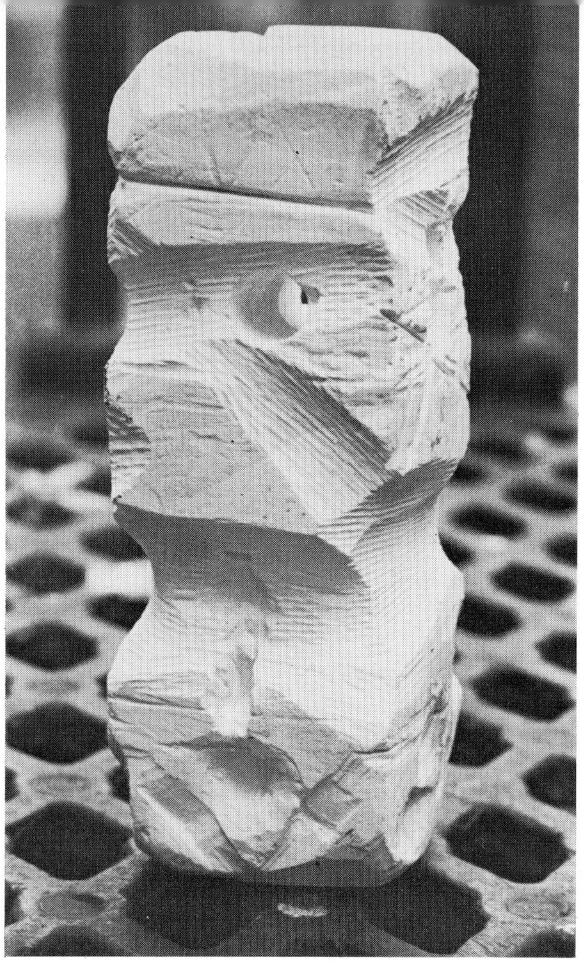

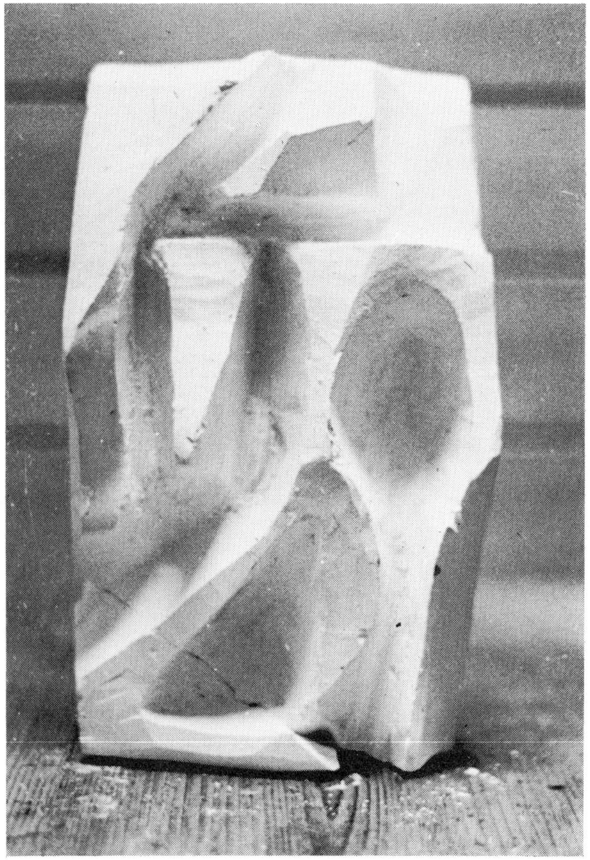

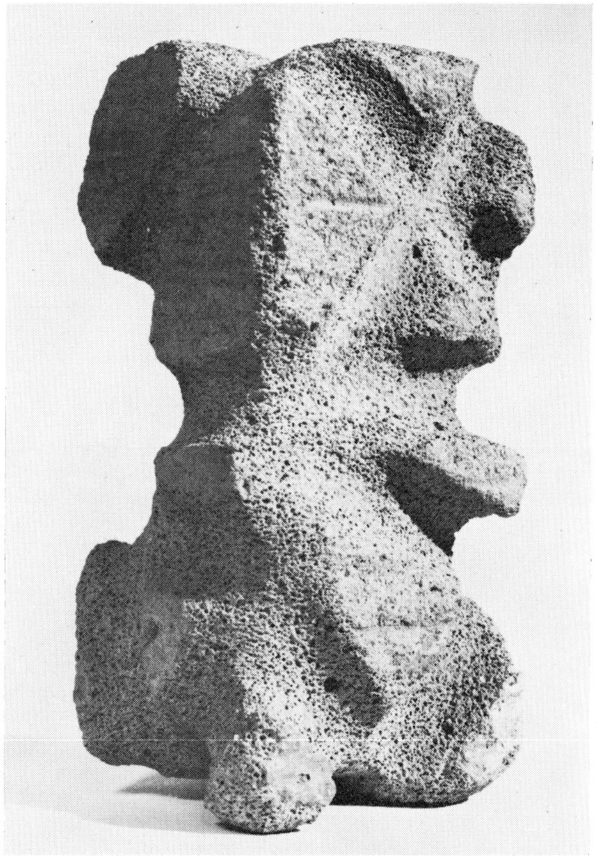

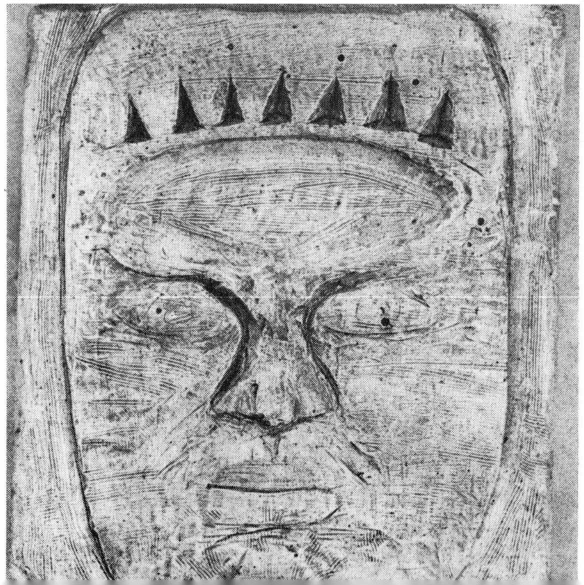

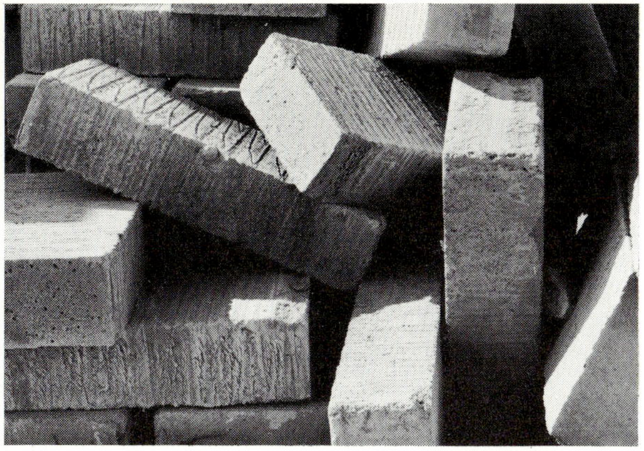
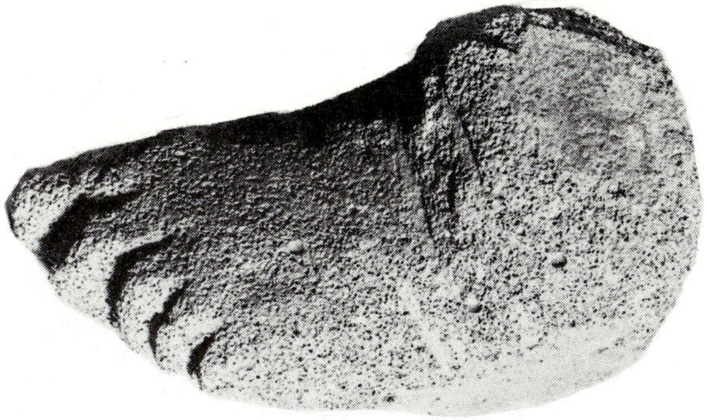
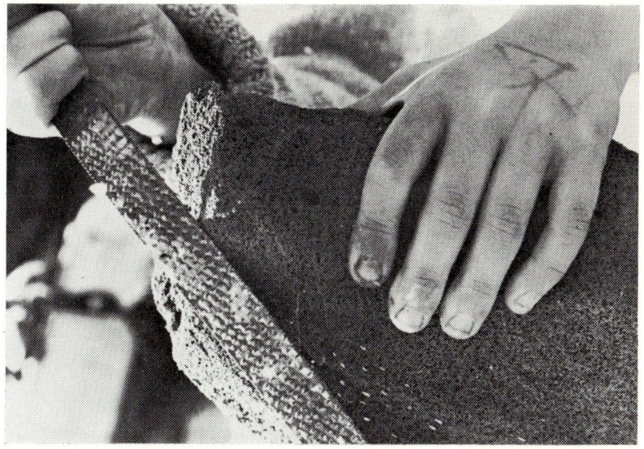
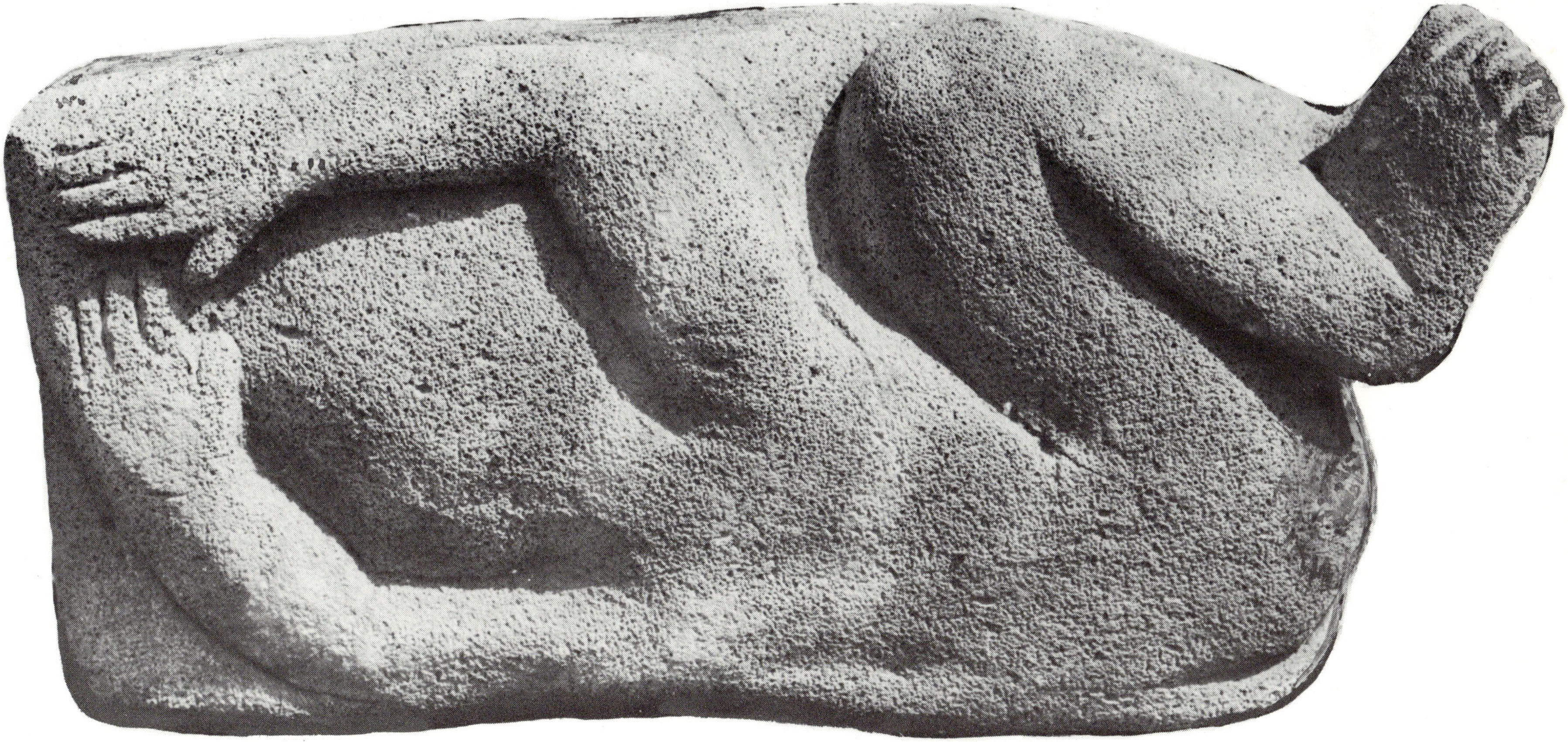

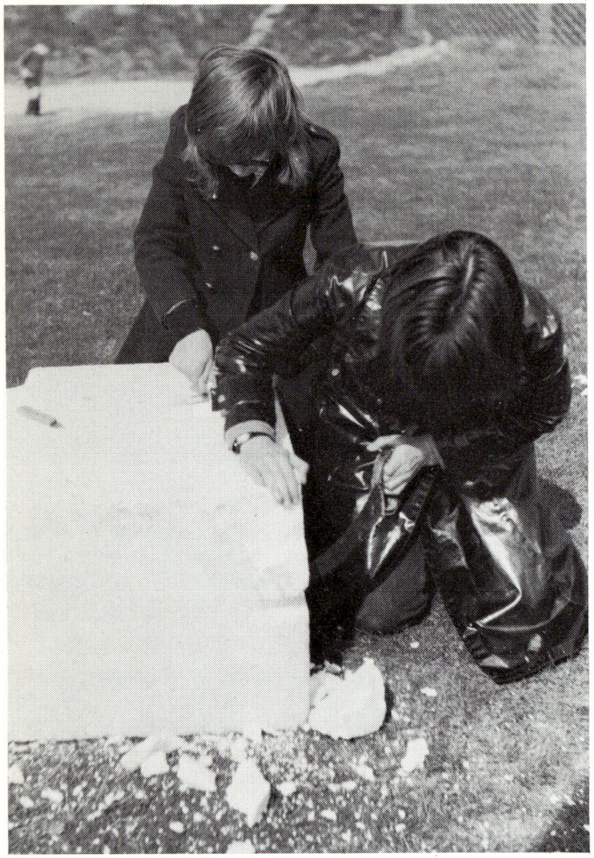
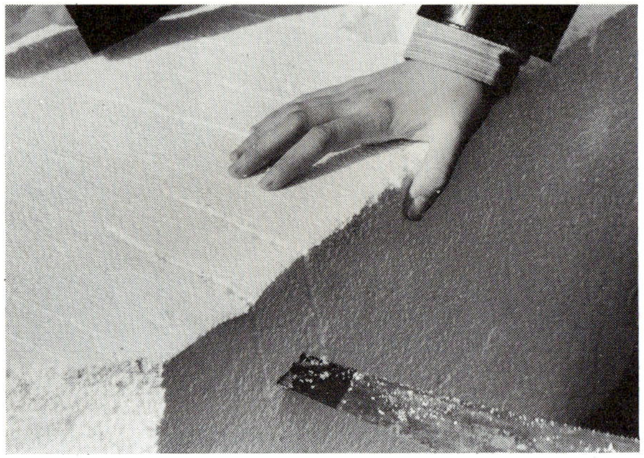
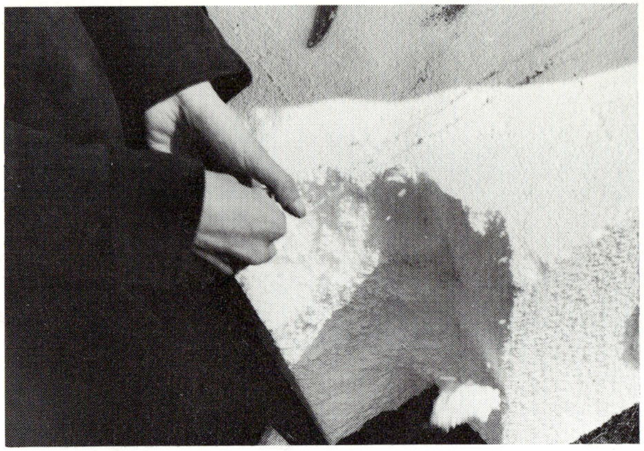

A block of polystyrene is carved with a saw and files.
A piece being sawn out and a corner is taken away.
Holes are being dug into the block.

On the right you can see the finished sculpture piece.

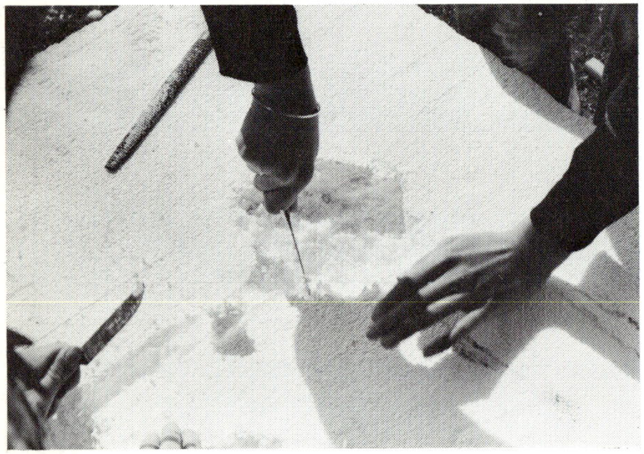
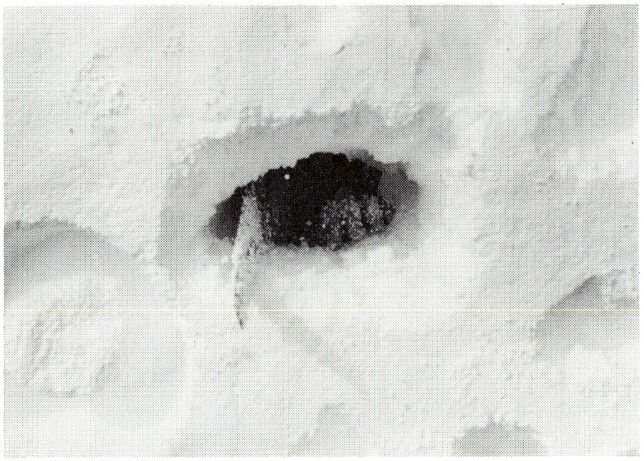
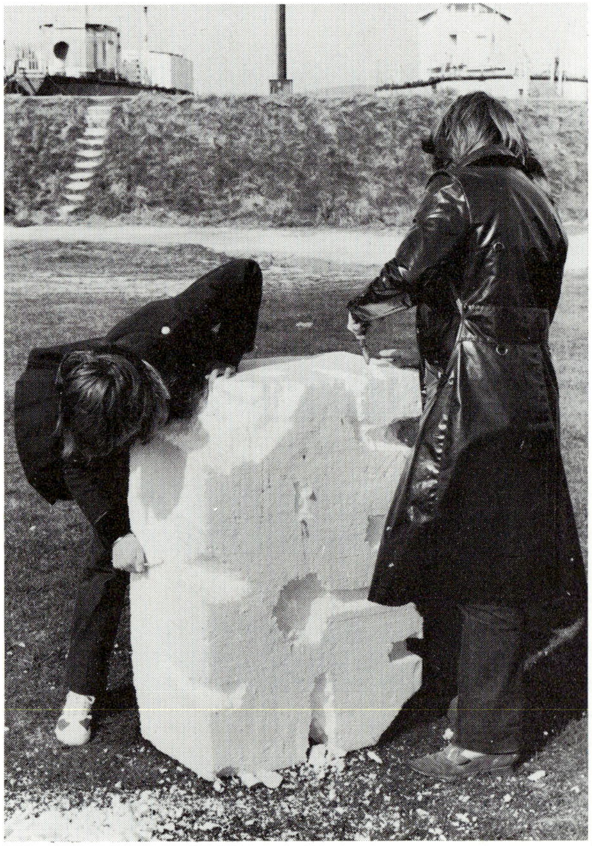

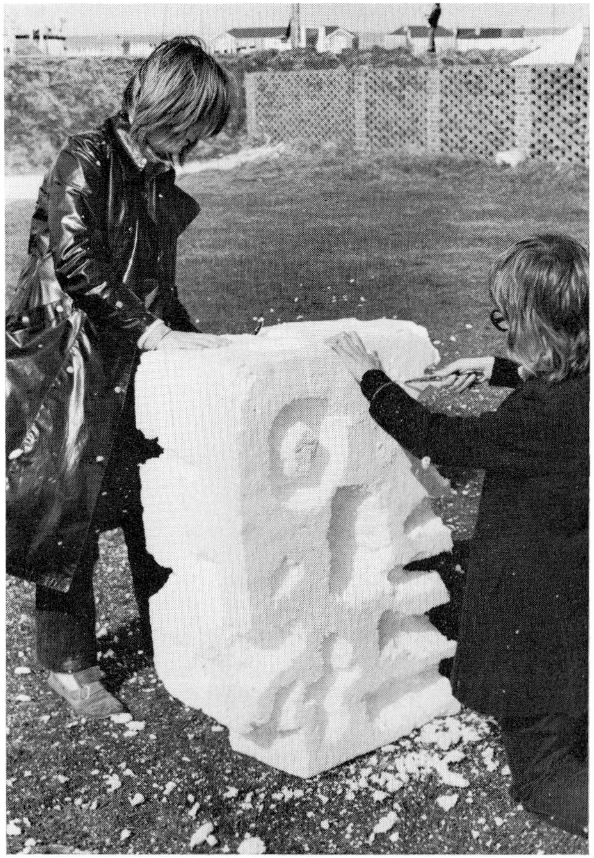

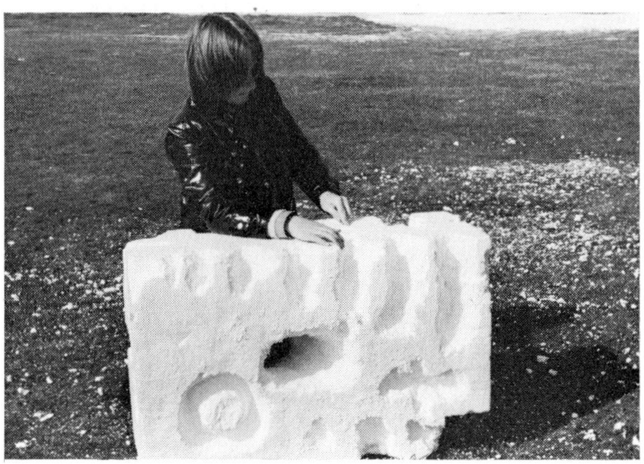

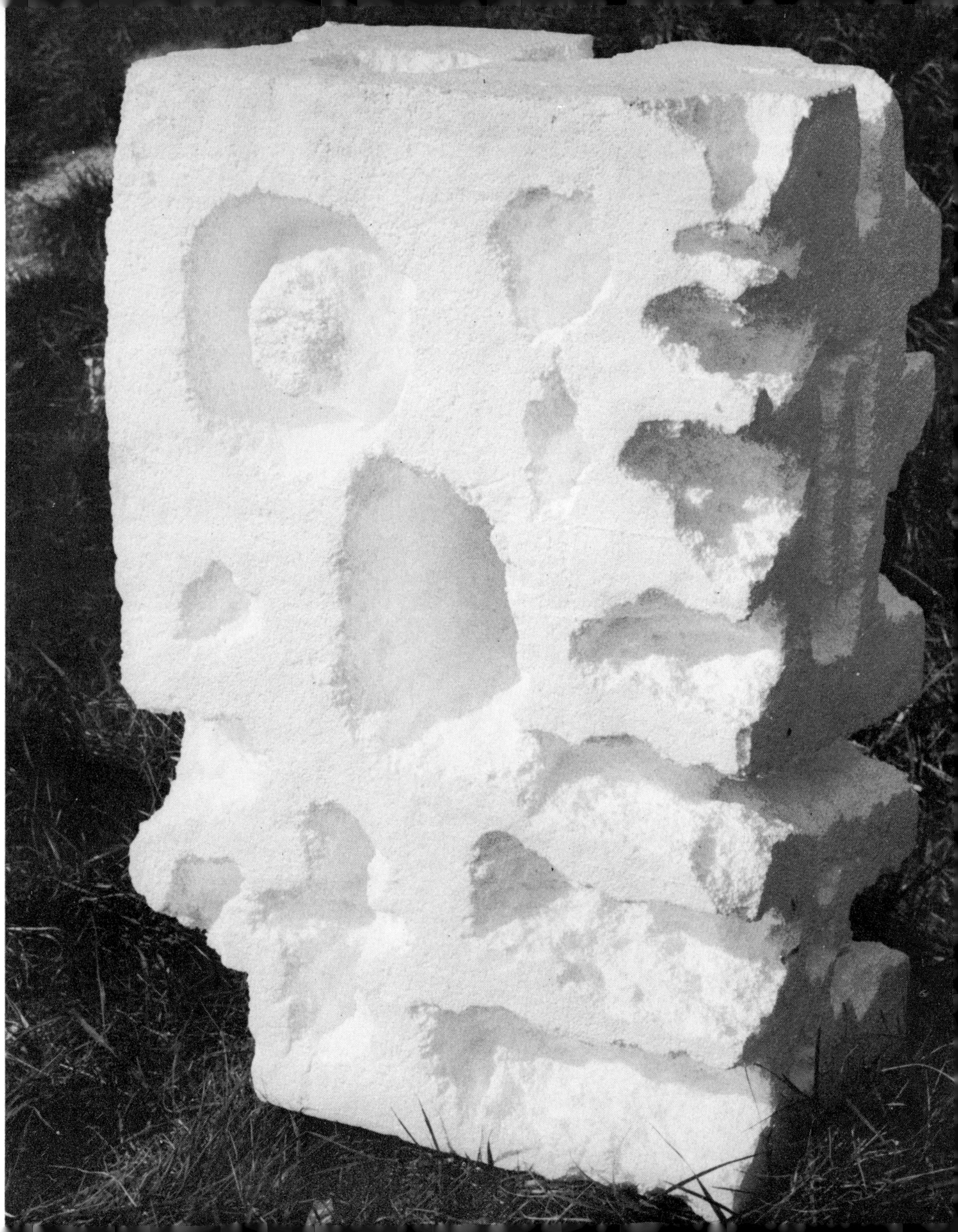

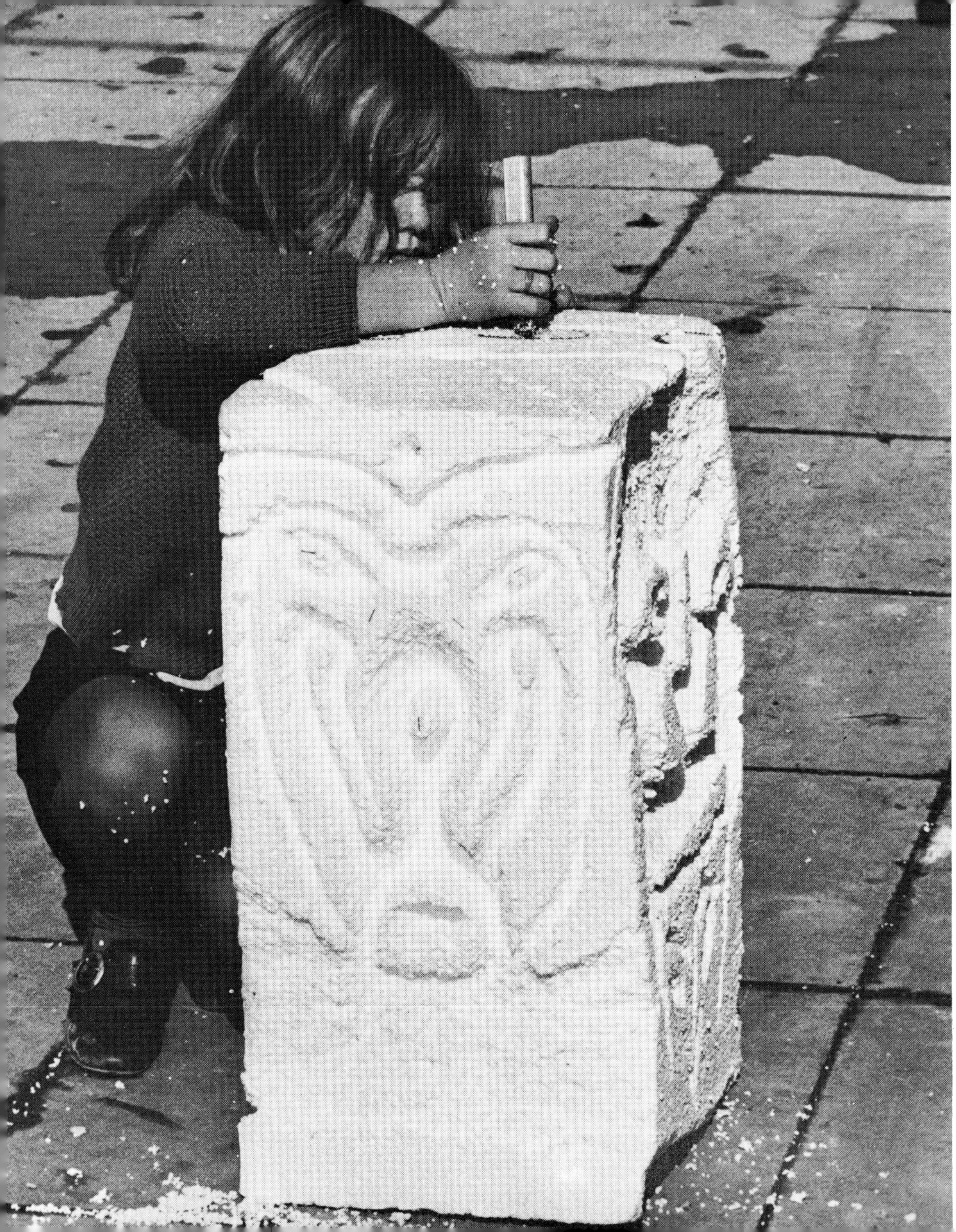

Blocks of polystyrene can be carved with any sharp tool. Knives and files are used here.

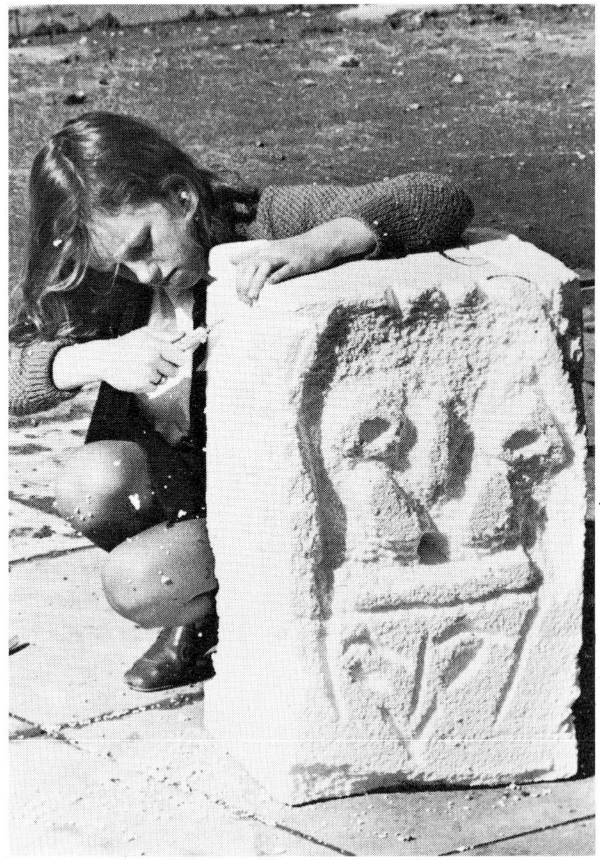

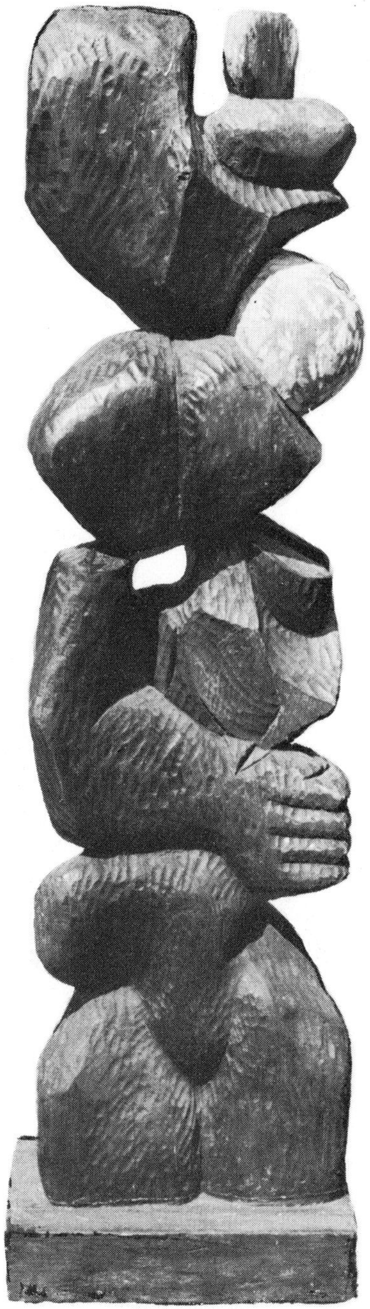

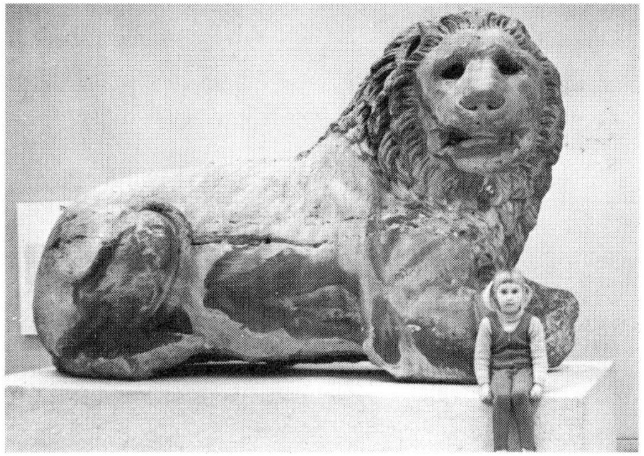

Above A lion carved from a block of marble about 2,000 years ago in Greece.

Below A baboon carved in sandstone in Egypt over 3,000 years ago.

Right Here is a carving of King Amen-Letep III of Egypt. It was carved from granite.

Left A carving in wood by the author.

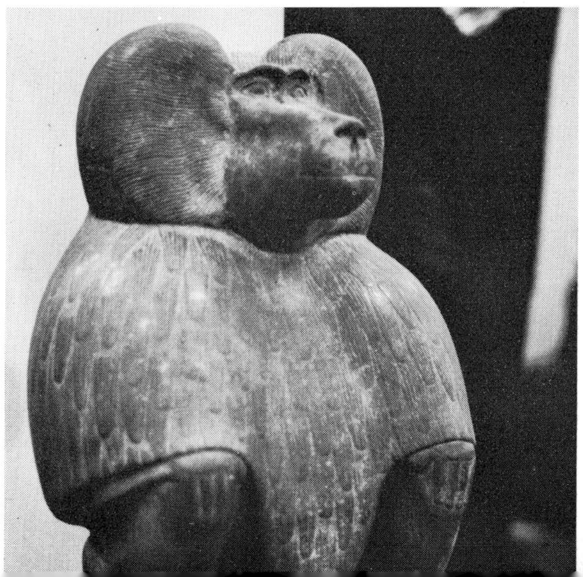

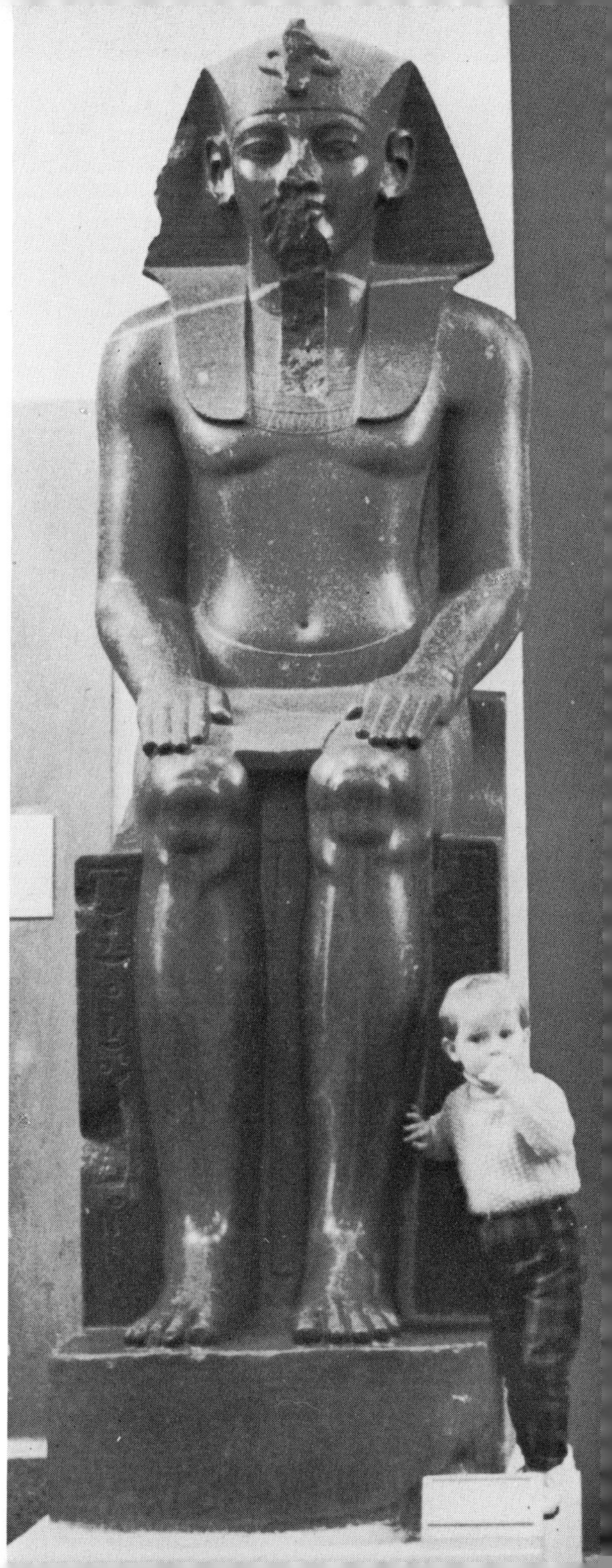

5 SCULPTURE IS EVERYWHERE

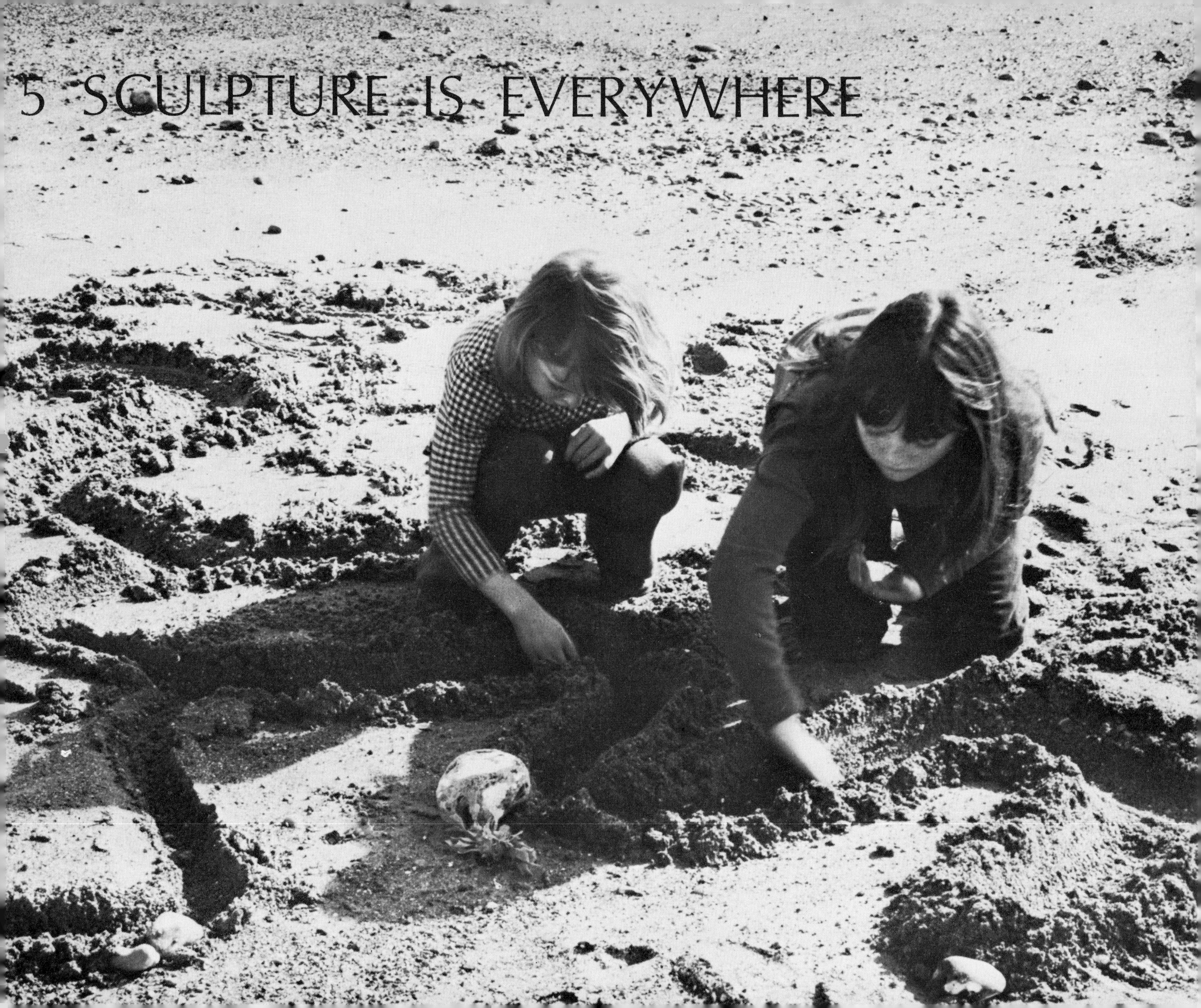

There are many different kinds of material in our world. Some things are soft like

mud
sand
cake
eggs
and ice cream.

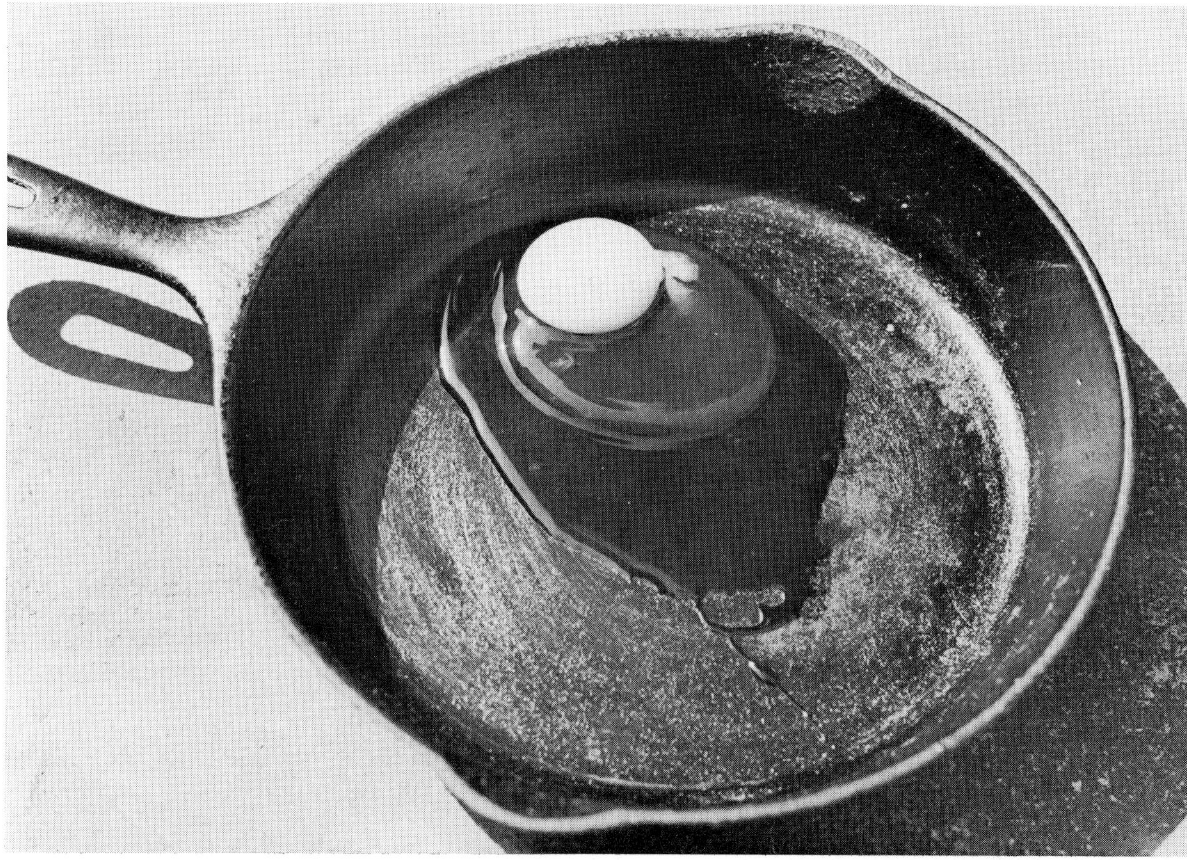

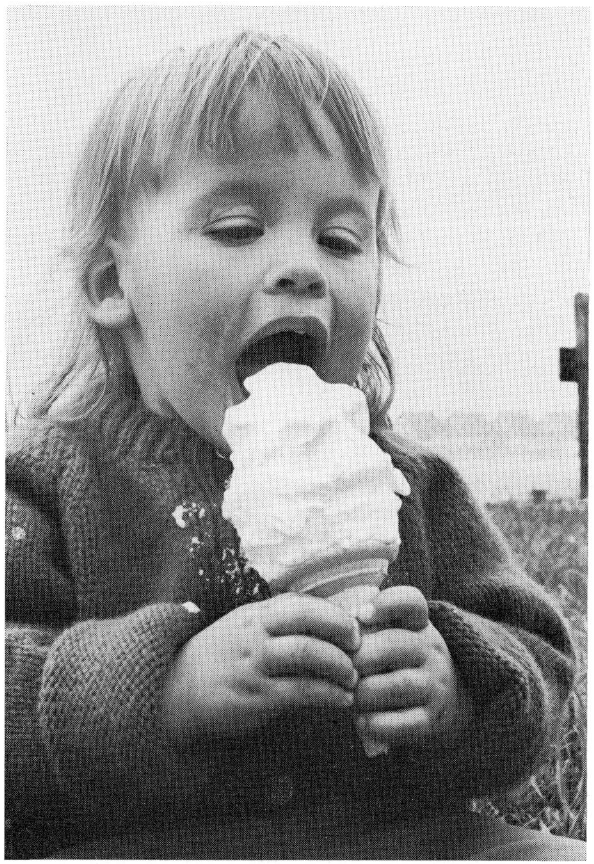

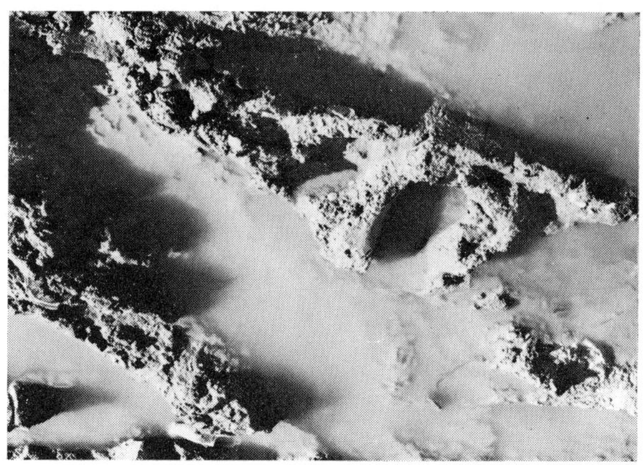

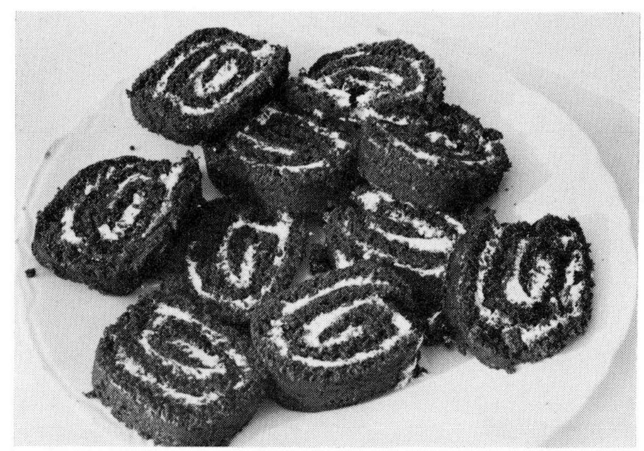

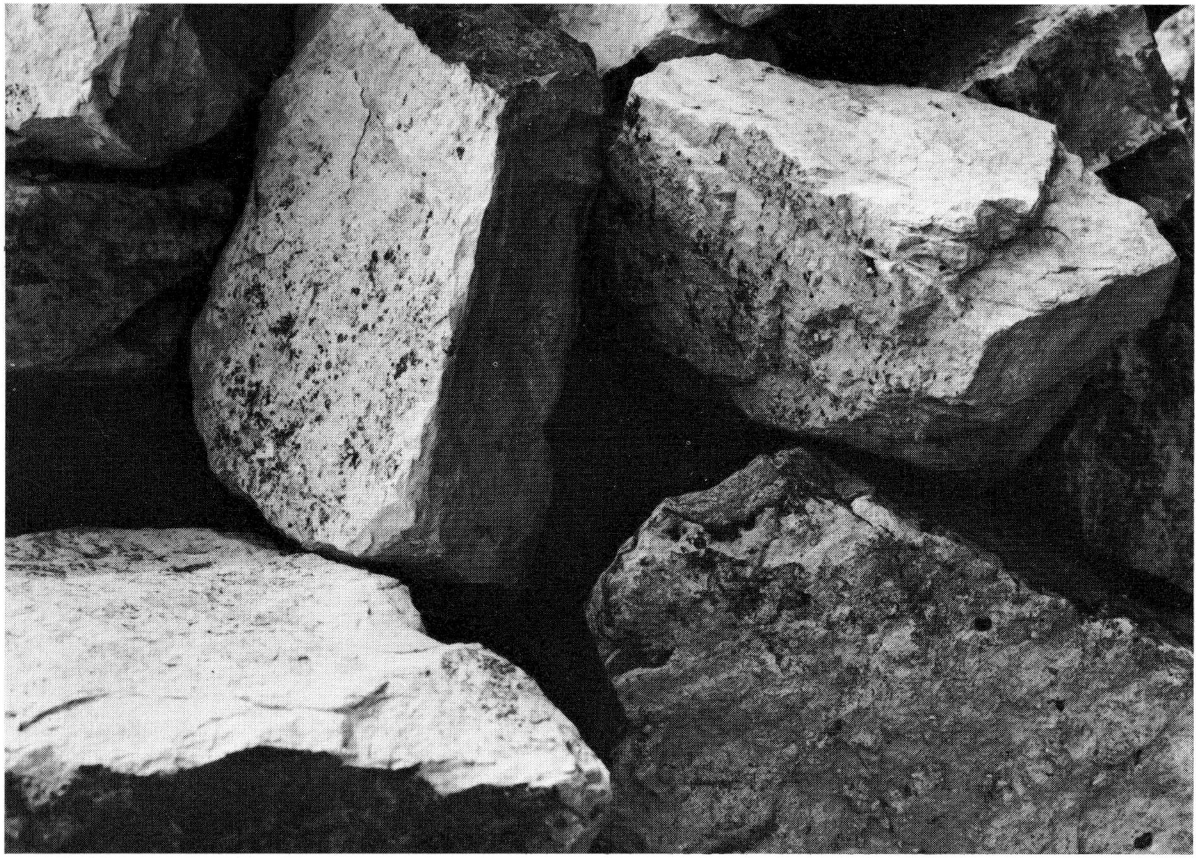

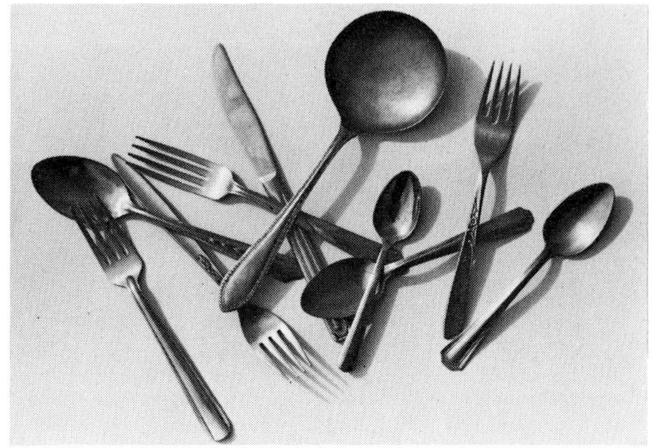

Some things are hard like

stones
bricks
cutlery
wood
and blocks.

We can see all these things, touch them and move them. They all weigh something and they all take up space.

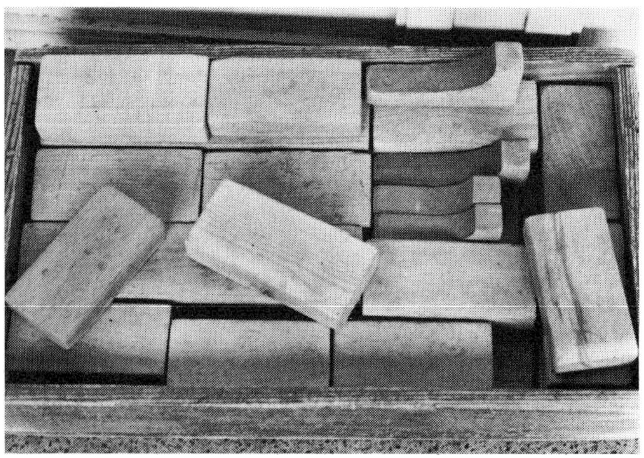

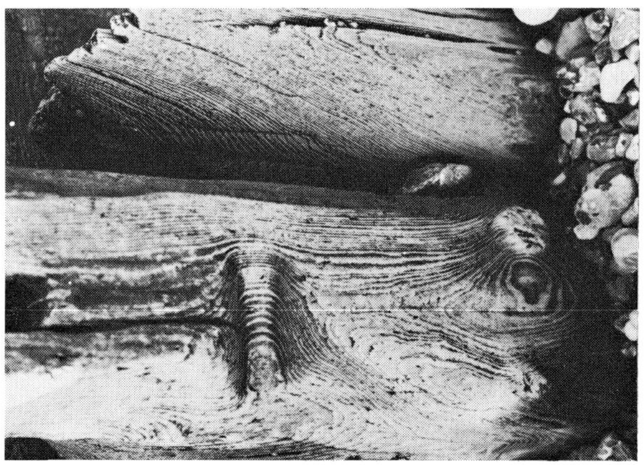

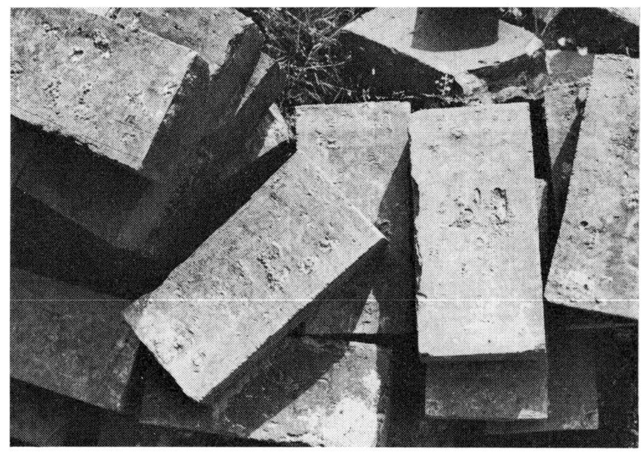

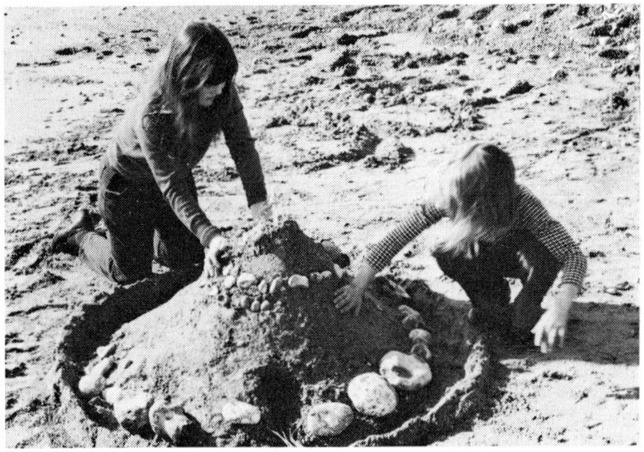

Bottom The girls are building a tower of blocks.

Top These girls are making a castle with sand and pebbles.

Right Father and son are building a snowman.

All these people are handling something they can see, touch and move. They are all making something very much like sculpture.

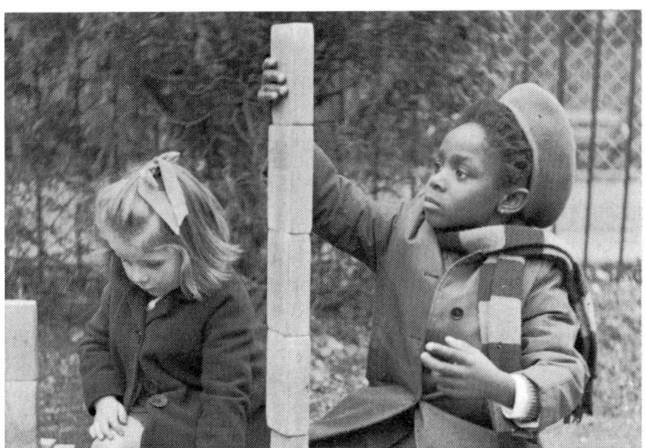

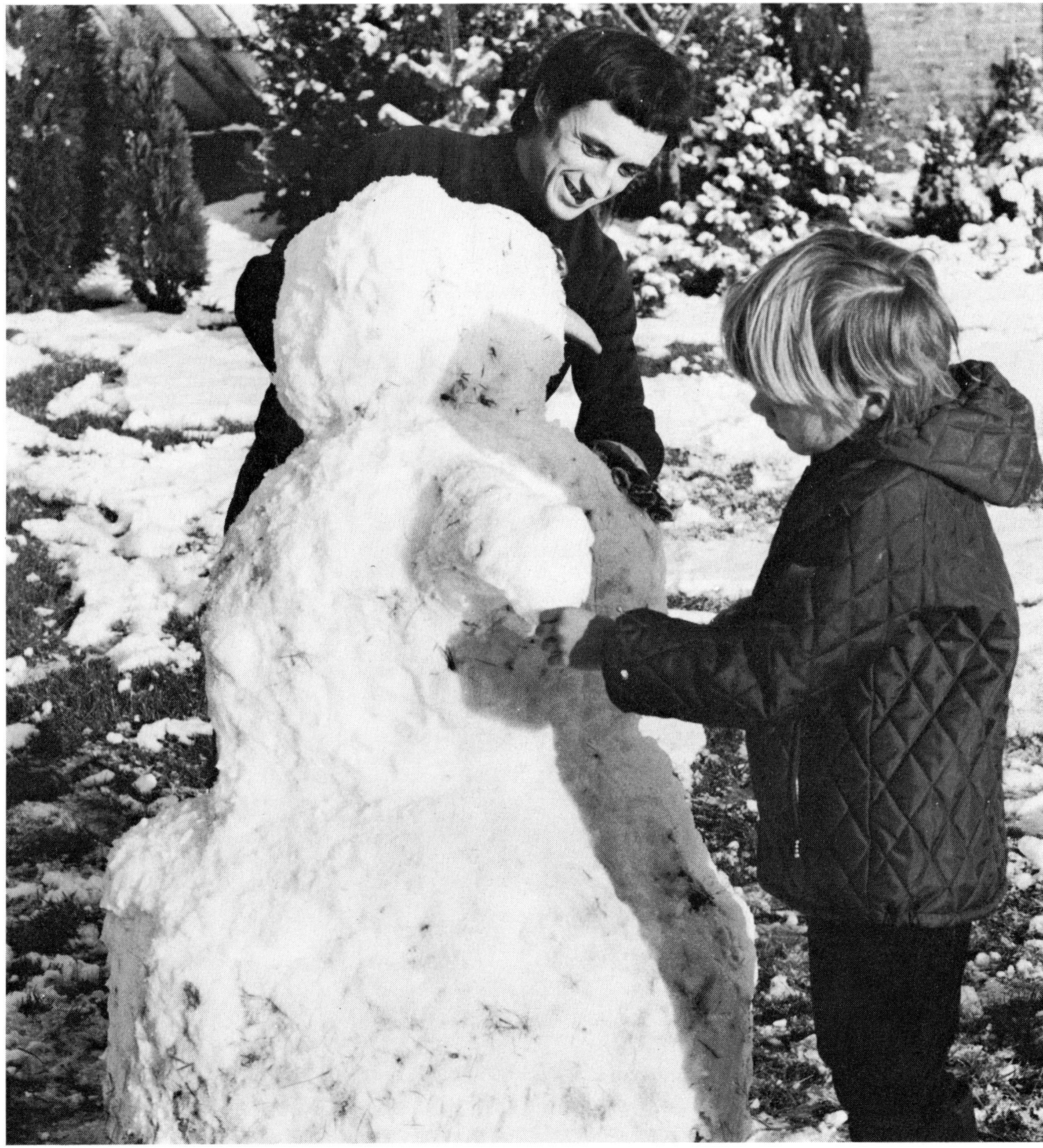

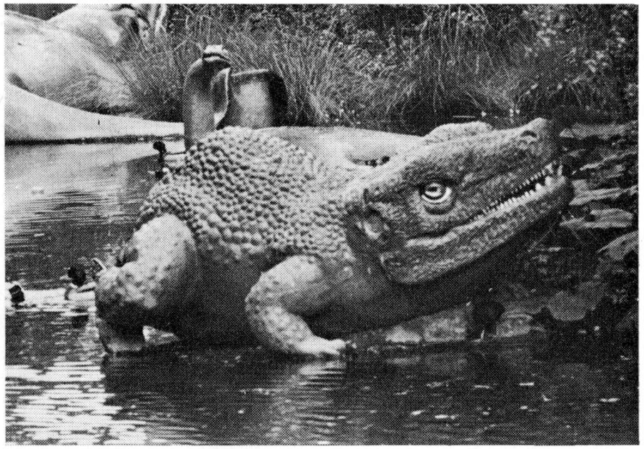

These great monsters were built by Mr. Waterhouse Hawkins in 1853 at Crystal Palace Park in London. When they were almost done, Mr. Hawkins held a dinner for twenty guests as a celebration. The dinner banquet took place inside the half-completed Iguanodon. The monsters are shells of bricks with iron supports and they are faced with stucco.

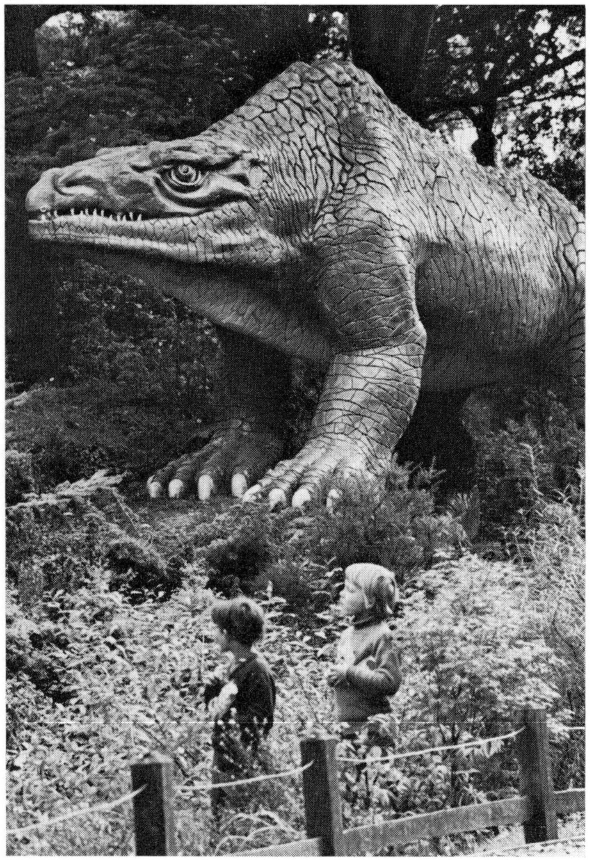

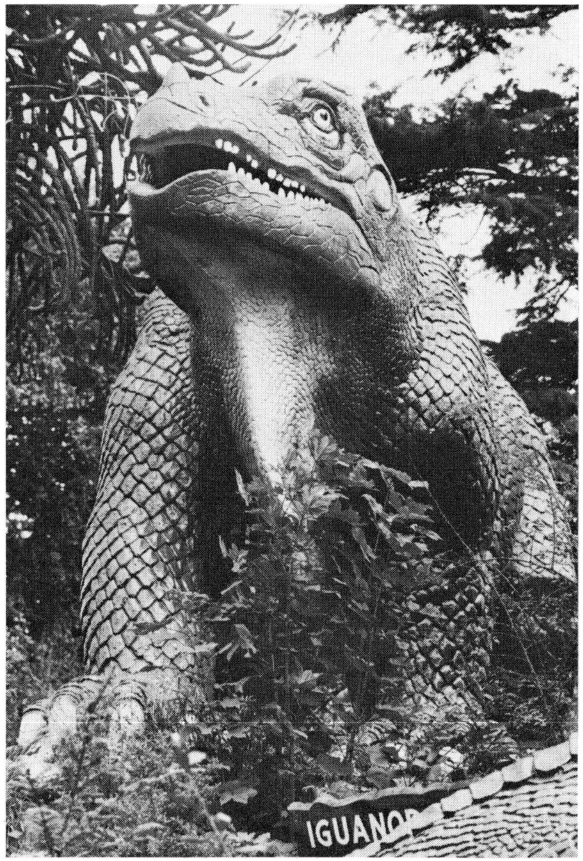

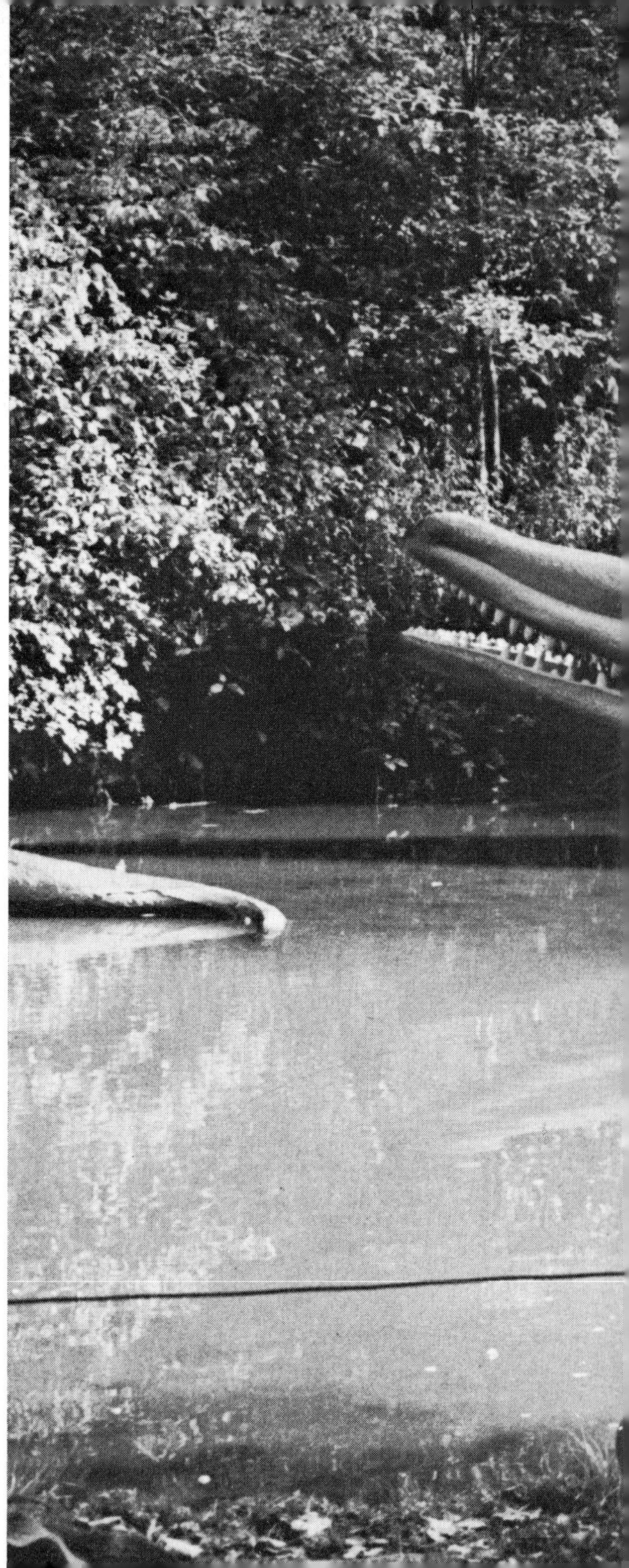

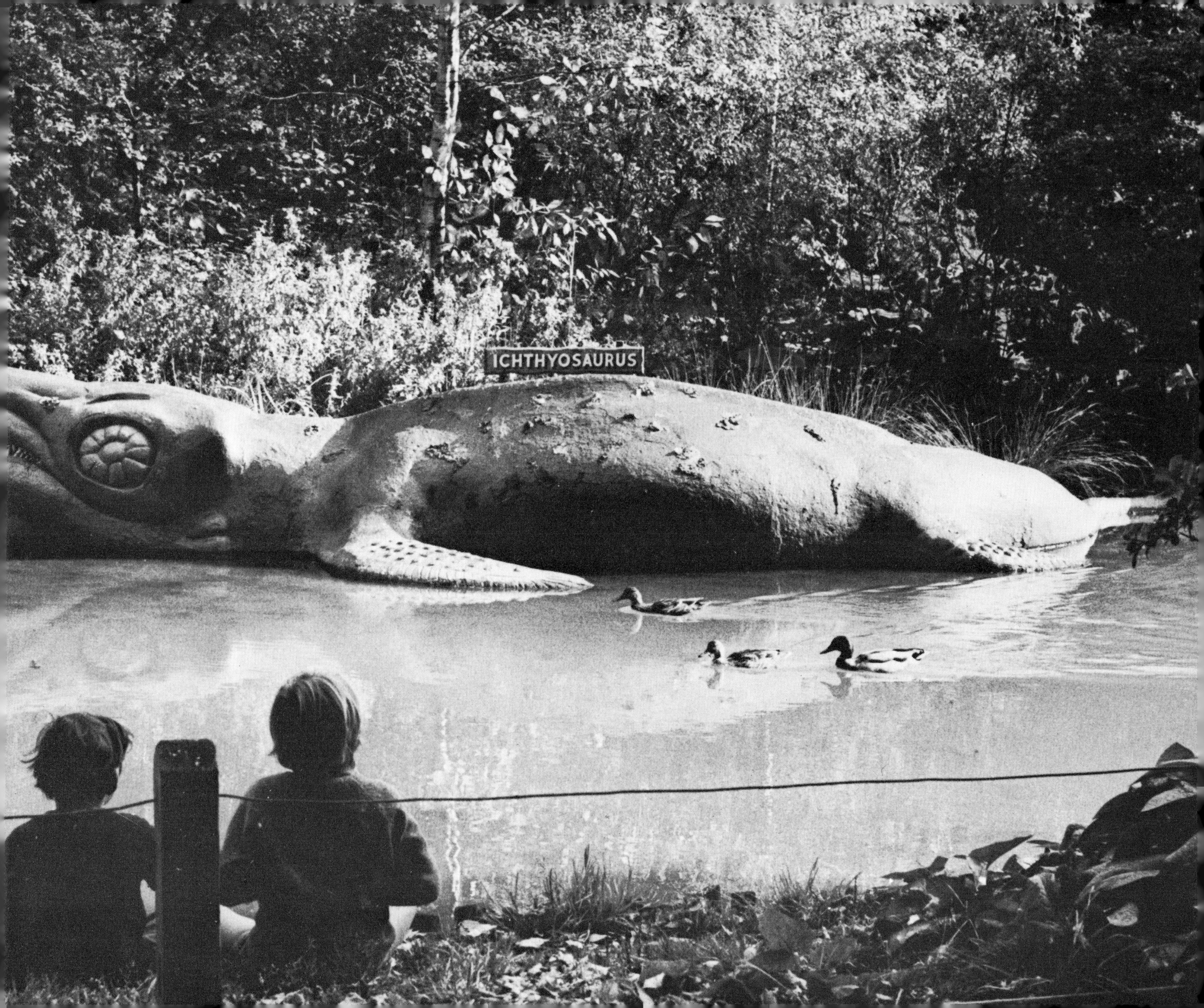
ICHTHYOSAURUS

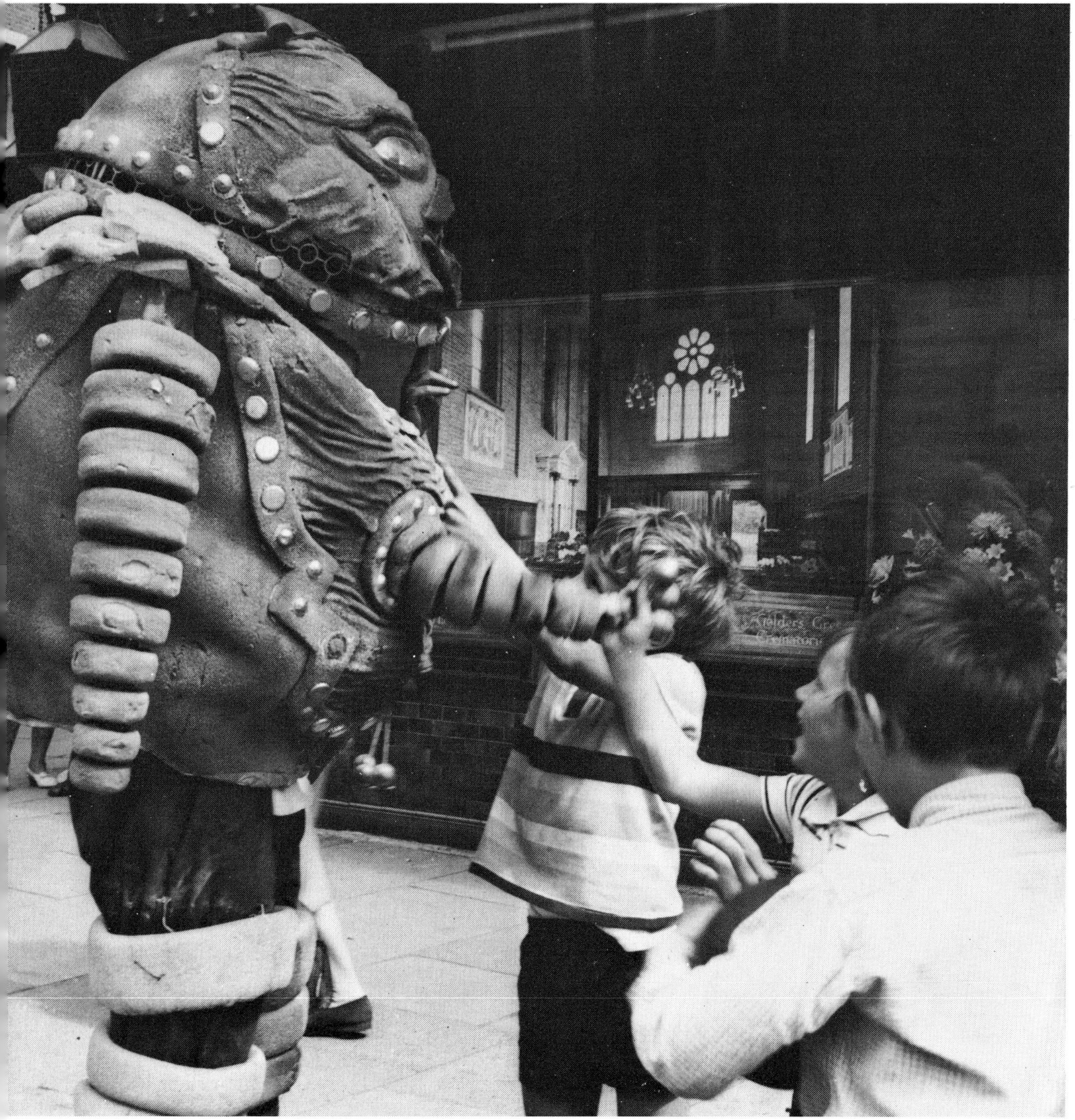

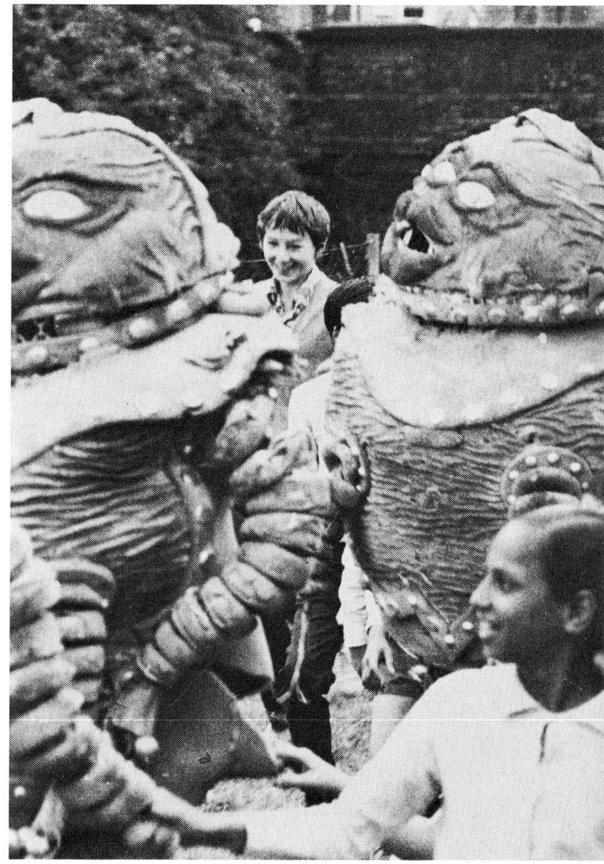

Right These very large sculpture pieces were designed by Alan Holden, seventeen years old. His classmates helped make them in cement. They are at Mayfield College in Sussex, England.

These moonmen come from Inter-Action's Dogg's Troupe, a group of actor-writers who want to make art much more a part of our lives. They are made from foam rubber and walk about and make friends with anyone they meet in the street. Here they are making friends in London.

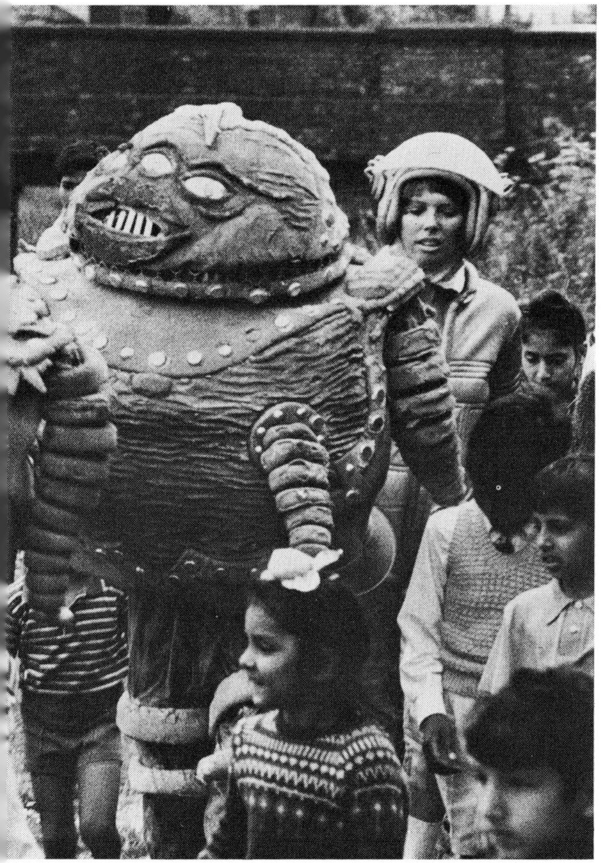

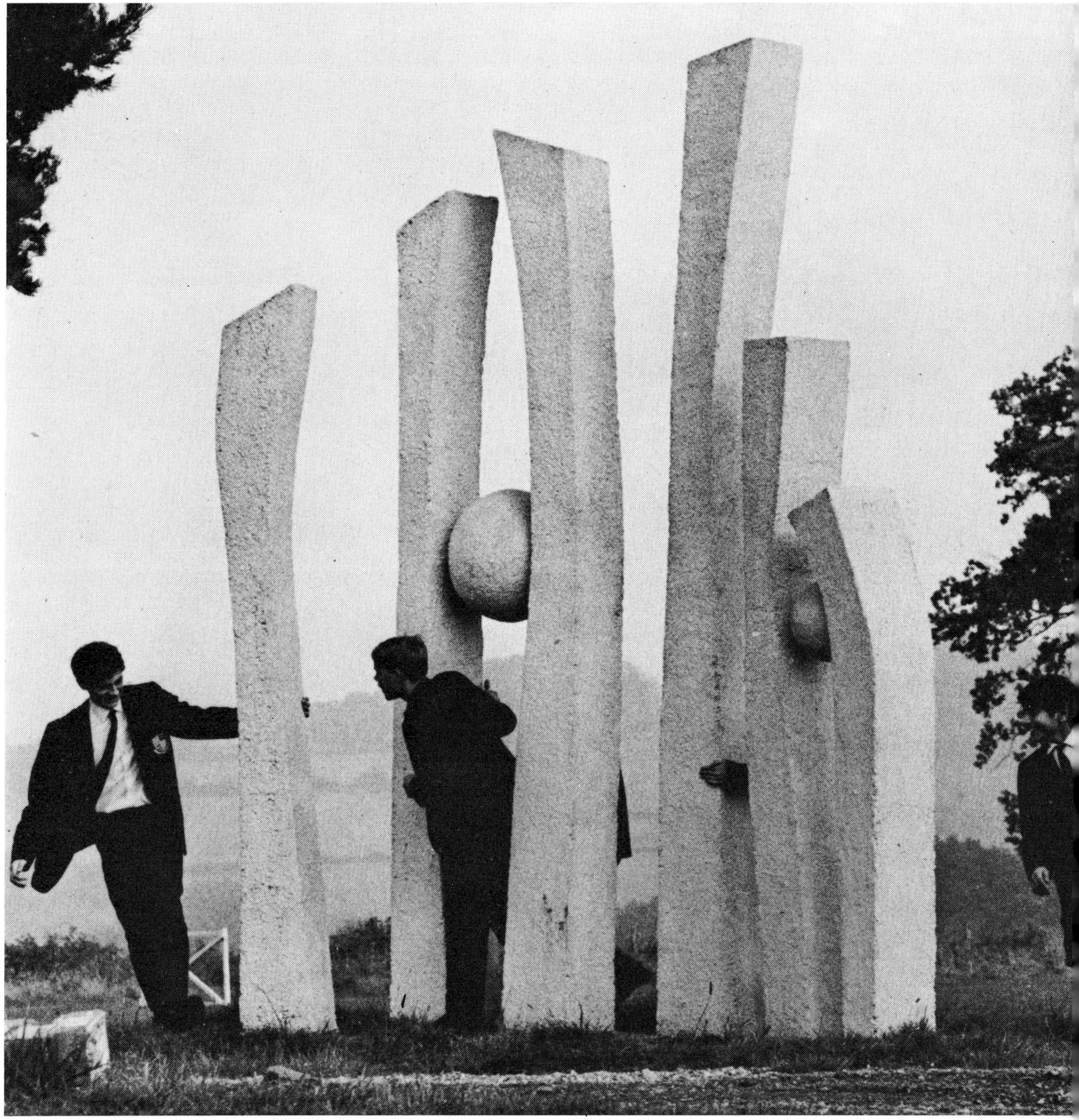

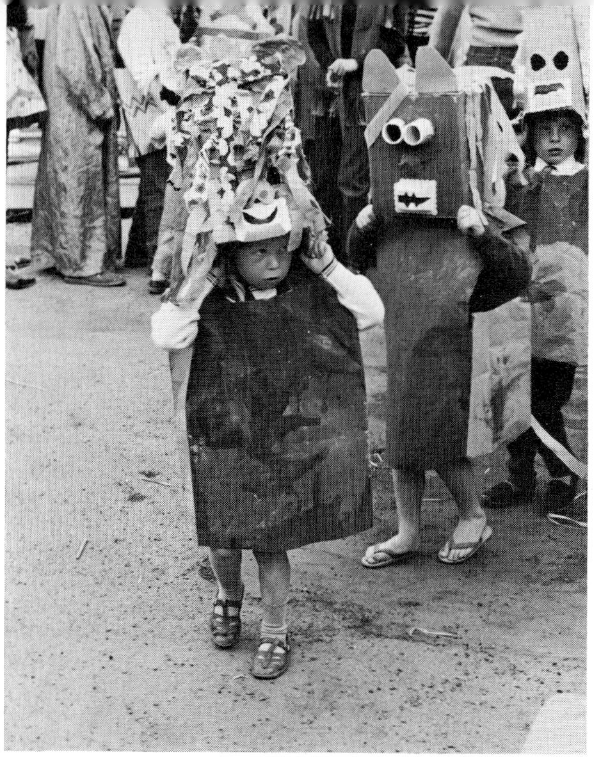

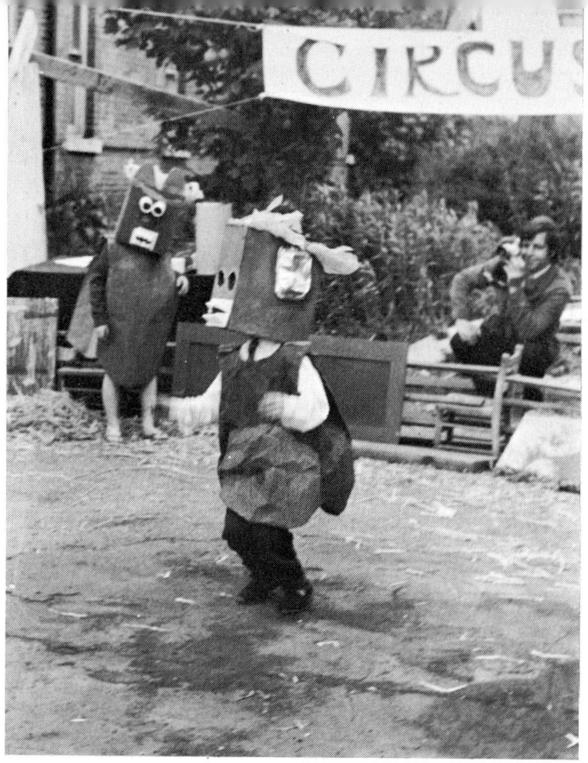

The circus parade—Horace the Happy Horse—the only dancing horse in captivity, and his friends, the gorilla, elephant, lion and ostrich, open the circus. The children made all the animals from junk materials, boxes and big brown paper bags.

A lion and a gorilla.
Two dancing gorillas.
Another paper bag lion.
The Happy Horse and his ringmaster.
'Jump through the hoop' says the clown.

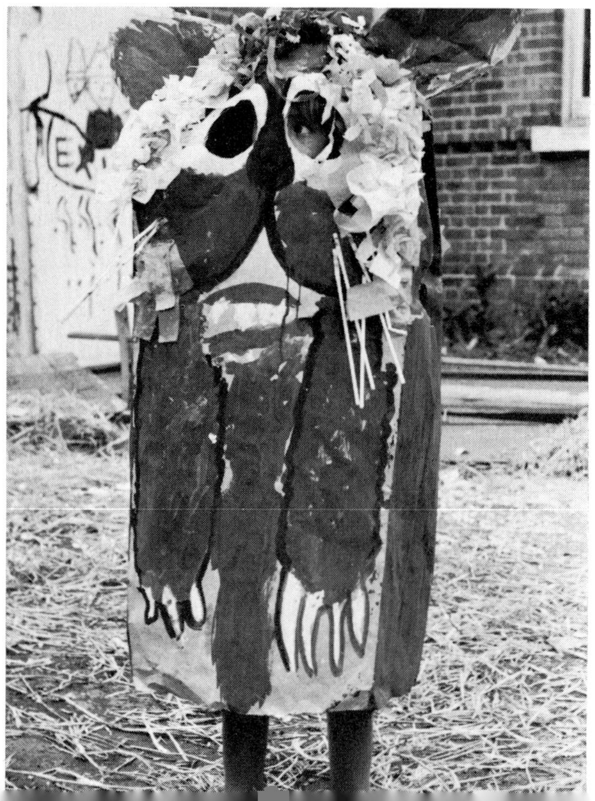

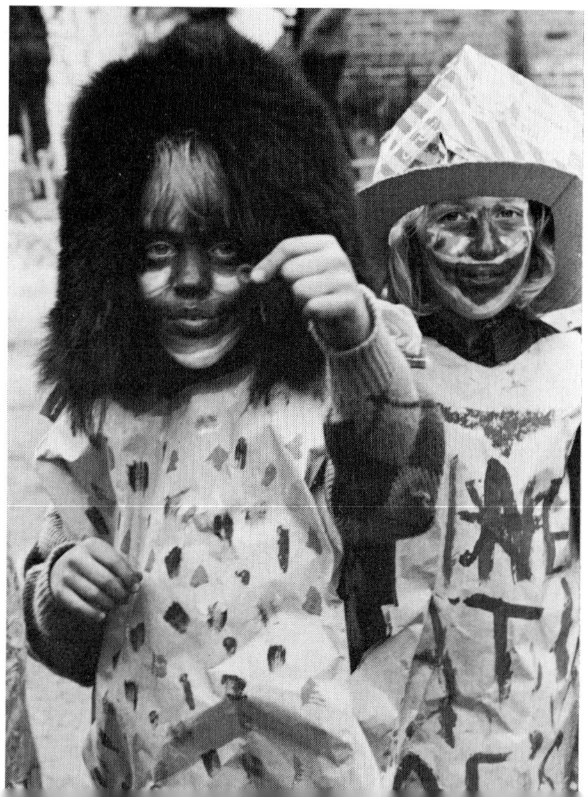

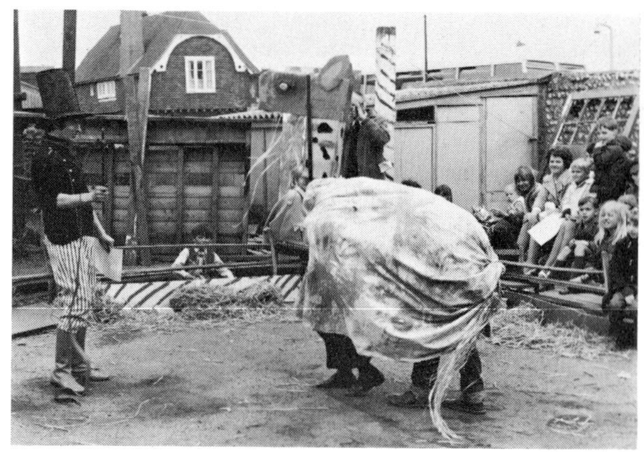

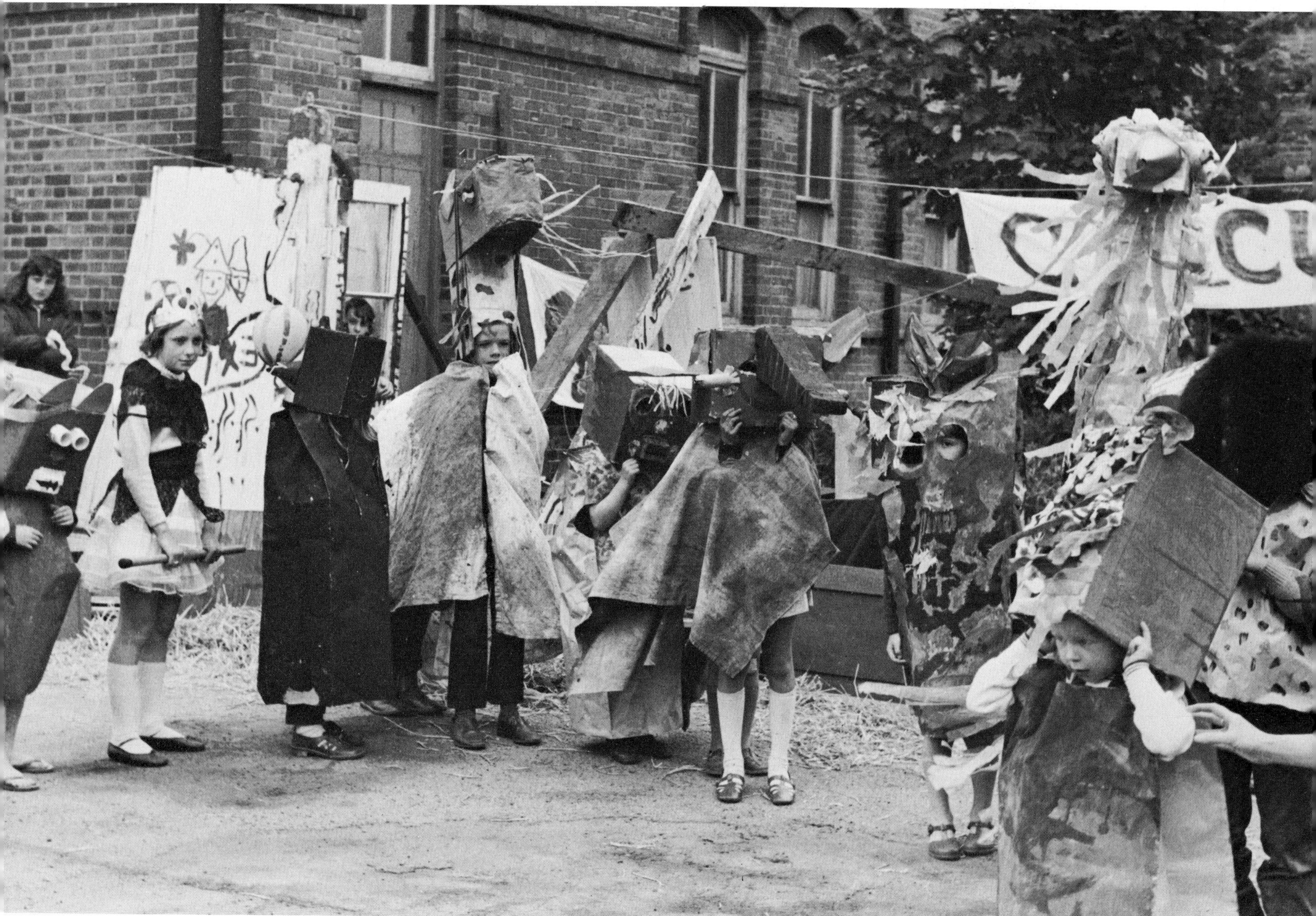

Here is a gorilla carved from stone. He is strong enough to be climbed on. This was one reason why David Wynne carved it for a children's park in London.

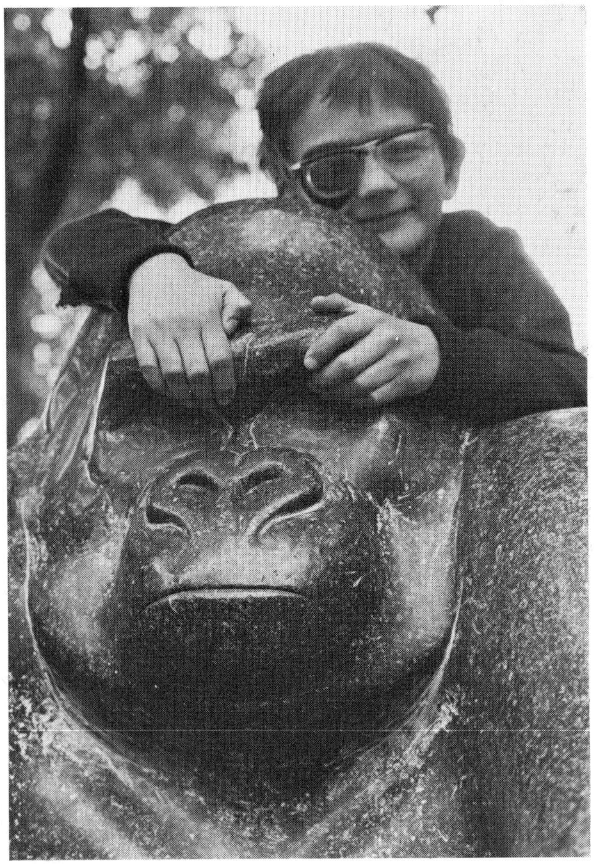

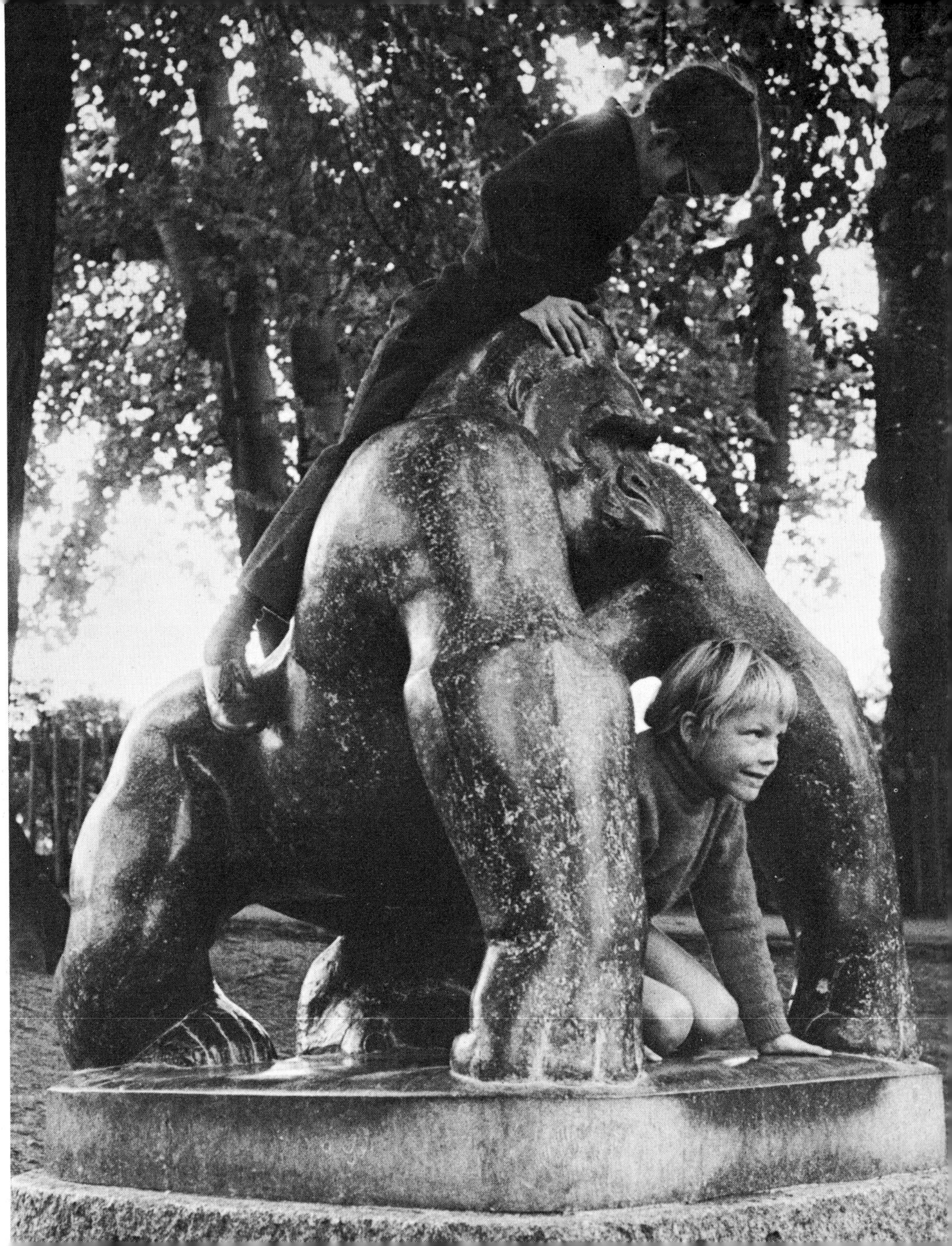

These children are playing with coloured shapes made from very hard plastic. Each shape is different so that they can be used in different ways. The shapes are part of a school playground in England. Stones are set into a playground and a pond is being painted to make a crocodile. The crocodile's head is carved and the stones are the humps of his back. The children use the humps of his back as stepping stones.

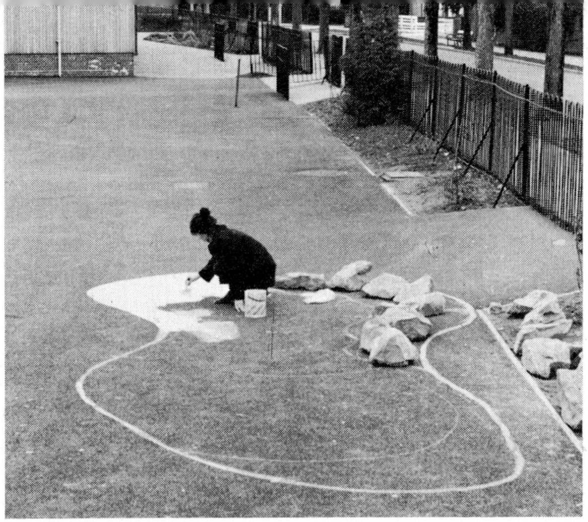

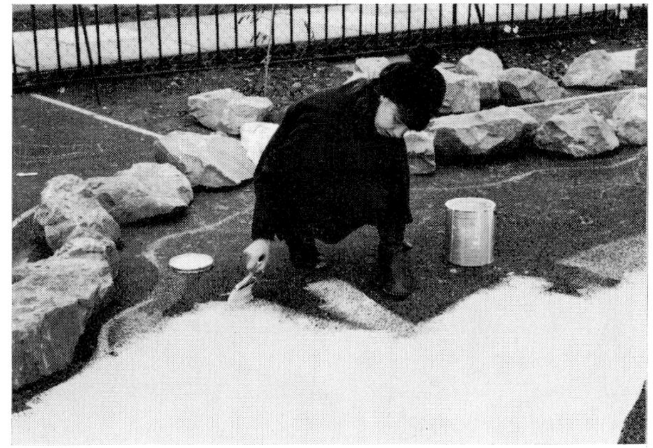

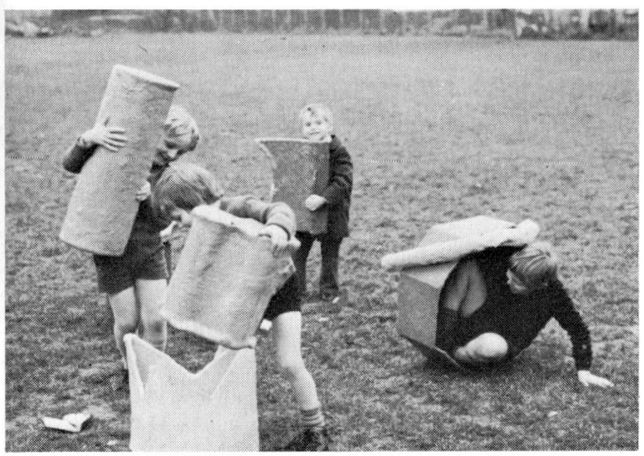

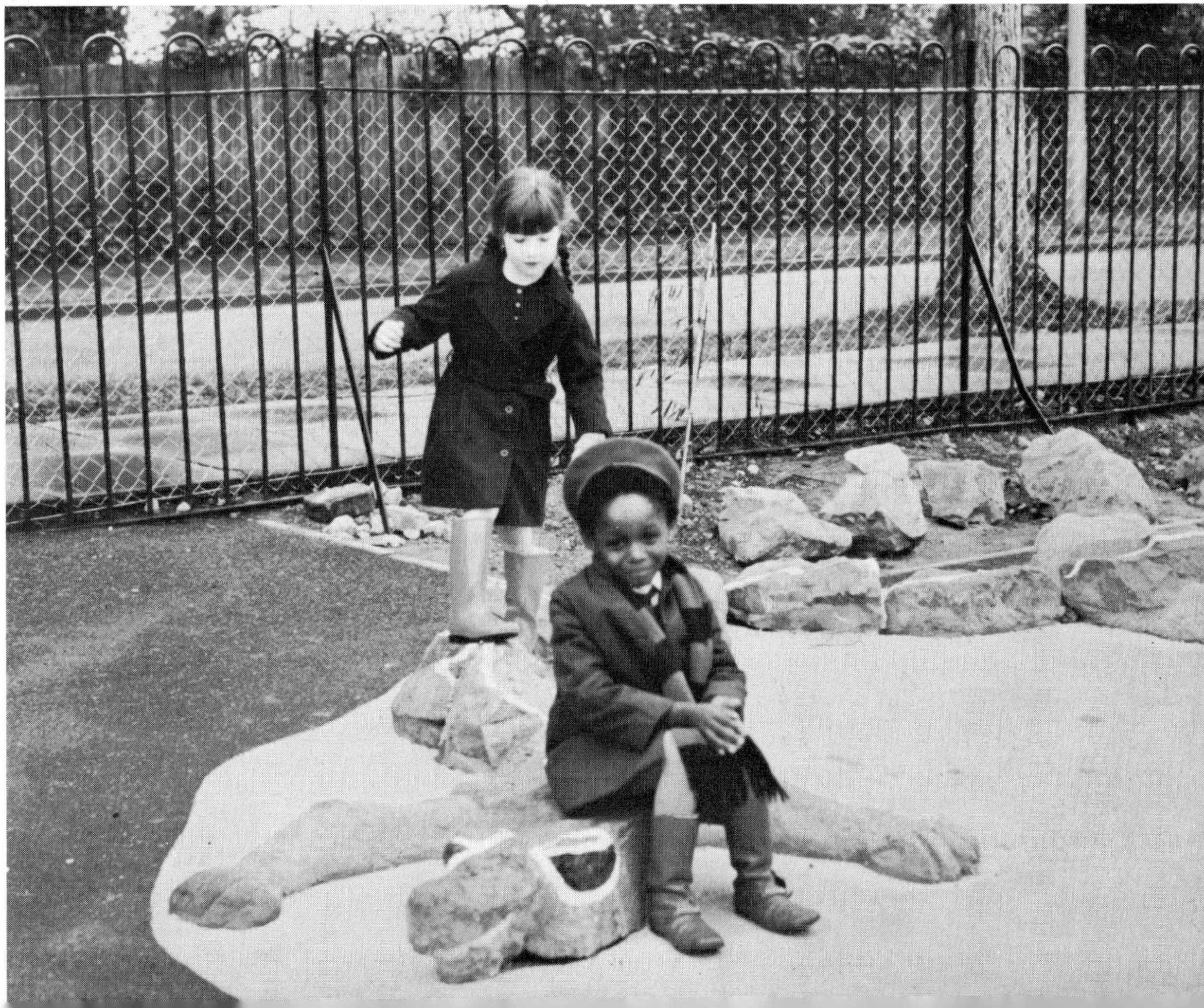

Acknowledgements

With Thanks to Ed Berman, founder-director of Inter-Action, for use of photographs included in the book. Projects were run by members of the Inter-Action co-operative in London. Inter-Action is a charitable trust, established to make the arts more relevant to the community.

Brother Conrad, Mayfield College, Mayfield, Sussex, England

Mrs. Hartman, Pottery Department, Boundstone School, Lancing, Sussex, England, and the children

Mrs. Gwendolyn Todd, Shoreham Pre-School Play Centre, Shoreham-by-Sea, Sussex, England

Margaret Kingdon, the Remedial Unit, Littlehampton, England

Shoreham Youth Workshop, Shoreham-by-Sea, Sussex, England

Jenny Wigzell-Hove, Adult Education, England

Miss Taylor, Headmistress, Victoria Road Infants School, Shoreham-by-Sea, Sussex, England

The Trustees of the British Museum for permission to photograph the sculptures that appear on pages 60, 82, 83 and the cover

and:

Clive
Derek
David
Richard
Carla
Raymond
Julian
Michael
Gideon
Miranda
Linsey
Sian
Simon
Michael
Janet
Sarah

Eva
Anna
Julie
Georgina
Mark
Paul
Jane
Justine
Tiffany
Christopher
Lawrence
Mary
Tracey
and
Blake
and
Genevieve

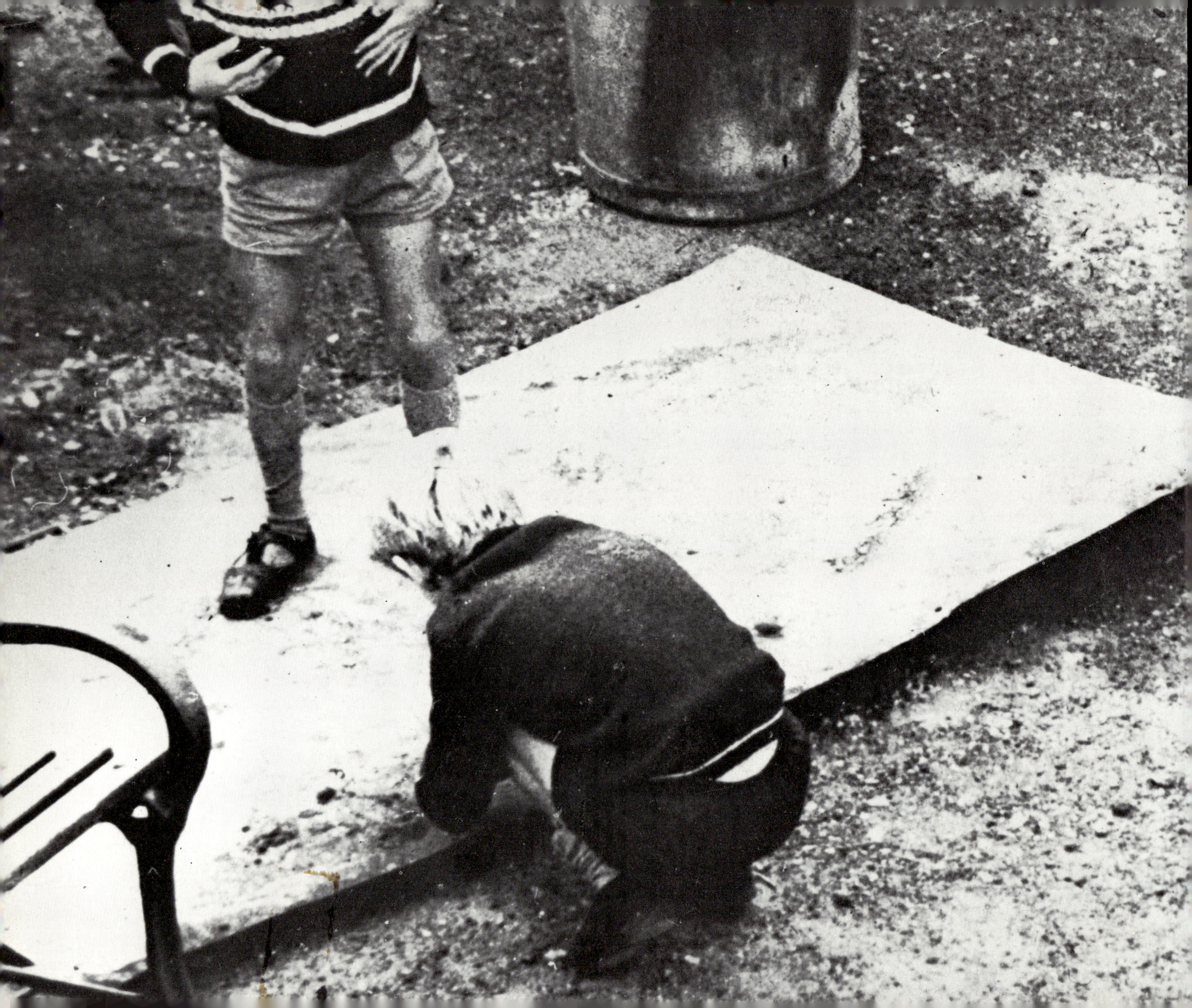